Anyone can make a Million

Morton Shulman

Foreword by
Charles Templeton

McGRAW-HILL
New York Toronto London Sydney

Anyone

can

make

a Million

Contents

FOREWORD

The word for Dr. Morton Shulman is "unlikely." He does unlikely things. He takes unlikely attitudes. And he's about as unlike the common conception of a coroner (his principal occupation) as it is possible to be.

You don't expect a novice in the stock market to devise a system of buying and selling that makes him independently wealthy.

You don't expect an unknown general practitioner, newly appointed to the office of Chief Coroner of Metropolitan Toronto, to transform that normally prosaic office into a political bombshell that dominates the front pages of the newspapers and shakes the government which made the appointment.

You don't expect a coroner to breathe such excitement into his work that it leads a major TV network to the production of a weekly television series.

You don't expect a medical doctor to state in public that members of his profession are sometimes "selfish, incompetent and lacking in dedication."

Nor do you expect a coroner to have exotic tastes, take off for Outer Mongolia for a three-week vacation, chiefly because he hasn't been there, and own a priceless collection of pocket watches.

But that's Morton Shulman.

For reasons that are anything but clear when you first meet him, he is, inevitably, where the action is. As often as not he creates the action.

But it is all done effortlessly, guilelessly. He doesn't seek public attention; he attracts it. He is not deliberately controversial; it is simply that he is essentially unorthodox, and his views—which he never hesitates to state when asked—inevitably raise hackles and flutter dovecotes.

Dr. Shulman at 41 is slight of build, wears his black hair close-cropped, has an almost handsome, youthful face, and wears carefully tailored conservative clothes. He is quiet, almost unobtrusive, until his interest is stirred. Then his face comes alive and he seems to listen with his entire body. With a group of friends he prowls about the room, never still, now sitting, slumped on his backbone, now leaning forward intently, now moving from group to group, now seated cross-legged on the floor. He is swiftly bored and doesn't trouble to hide it. Abstract philosophical talk has no interest for him. It is unlikely he has spent more than five minutes of his lifetime in introspection. When he talks his voice is quiet, gentle. When he laughs the sound would fill a football field.

Those who know him are not surprised he made a swift fortune in the stock market. Nor are they surprised that, having decided to have a go at the market, he approached it in a totally unorthodox way. Any other way wouldn't be Morty.

He approaches every task directly. The best attack is frontal. The pathway to an objective never leads around Robin Hood's barn. If there are problems to solve, get at them and don't waste time in contemplation. Morton Shulman is a "to hell with the torpedoes; full steam ahead" kind of guy. No one would claim he is always right, but only a fool would disregard what he has to say. This book is what he has to say on the stock market.

Charles B. Templeton
Toronto, Canada
May 15, 1966

PREFACE

"I was at the club yesterday, and George McKeown played in our foursome. He's the Chicago manager of Park Reid and Co. Over the nineteenth hole he told me in strictest confidence that Park Reid's earnings are 'way up this year and that they may split the stock. I bought 1,000 shares this morning."

"You know how many good things my Canadian broker has let me in on recently. Well, this morning he phoned with some really hot news! A small mining prospect called Jenny Metals just took over a property connecting with the fabulous Pyramid mine—that's the company that drilled and rose from 25¢ to $20 in six weeks. Jenny Metals is going to begin drilling immediately. I paid 78¢ and it closed at 85¢. I'm selling my I.B.M. tomorrow to buy more Jenny!"

Familiar? Of course. Everyone has heard variations of these two stories. And year after year supposedly intelligent business people similarly lose their heads and throw away their money in search of the easy dollar. After each bitter experience they say, "Next time I'll be smarter," but strangely, they never are.

The interesting thing is that there *is* an easy dollar to be made in our stock markets, but those who make it are almost exclusively promoters and stockbrokers. There is a story of a promoter who, when asked by a close friend what stock to buy, replied with the classic comment, "Buy?! The only way to make money in the market is to print the stuff and sell it!"

He is dead wrong. There are good stocks to buy in the market, but *never, never* on tips.

There are simple ways to make a great deal of money, and some of them don't even involve any investment! Sound unbelievable? It's done every day by a few knowing traders. This book explains the secrets of the market and shows how any speculator can do the same thing.

There are really two stock markets. One is the world of high-grade bonds—of A.T.&T., General Motors, and R.C.A. This is the "Widow and Orphan" market. These securities are purchased for safety, yield, and growth by insurance and trust companies and other institutions, by mutual funds, and by individuals building an estate or seeking a secure income. The other stock market is the one for the speculators. But it is hidden beside and inside the first market, and a person who is speculating often thinks he is investing. The speculative market is the exciting one. It is vibrant and changing and challenging, and it offers to the intelligent and to the nimble unlimited profits and opportunities. Unfortunately, many who challenge it are neither intelligent enough nor nimble enough, and to them it brings heartache and financial loss. This book is an effort to help make the public a little more intelligent and a great deal more nimble. Once the secrets of this speculative market are known, it is immeasurably easier to play its game.

It has always appeared strange that no stockbroker has written a book explaining these relatively simple matters, and the reason apparently is fear of associates' disapproval. For the simple fact is that brokers as a group do not want the public to know. Each individual broker wants *his* clients to make money, for then there are more and higher commissions, but as a group it is to the brokers' advantage if the public continues to buy and trade Park Reid and Jenny Metals. Individuals try to educate their clientele as best they can, but sadly the majority of customer's men do not have a good knowledge of the market themselves; all too often they advise their clients on a basis of limited knowledge and "hot tips." A few leading firms are very thorough in researching individual companies and go to great lengths to educate their customer's men; Merrill Lynch is an outstanding example. Alas, their advice and training is directed largely to the "Widow and Orphan" market and rarely reaches the speculator, who would spurn their advice if offered.

So this book is dedicated to the speculator, that much-maligned creature. After reading it, I hope he will speculate more successfully.

Morton Shulman

Anyone can make a Million

1

FOR WIDOWS AND ORPHANS

This chapter deals with investments suitable for those who cannot afford to take the chance of loss. These include not only the widow and orphan, but also the wage earner with limited savings and the businessman who may need his cash on short notice for opportunities in his own business. The sought-after qualities of investments of this type are various combinations of safety, yield, and growth associated with easy liquidity. There are several subdivisions:

1. government bonds
2. municipal bonds
3. state bonds
4. high-grade corporate bonds and debentures

    5. blue chip stocks
    6. mutual funds

    1. *United States and Canadian Government Bonds* give very good yields, anywhere from 4 to 6%—excellent rates compared with bank interest. There is, of course, no possibility of capital gain, but the factor of safety is the important one in these securities because they are direct obligations of the government.

One would think that government bonds are the ultimate in safety, with absolutely no chance of loss if they are held to maturity. They do, however, fluctuate greatly in value during the years before maturity, the amount of fluctuation increasing with the duration of the bond and the size of fluctuation depending on the general trend of national and worldwide interest rates. As interest rates rise, the market value of outstanding bonds falls. This can be disastrous for the individual with limited means who is forced to sell his government bonds at a time of high interest rates.

Far more serious is the danger of devaluation of the United States dollar. The 1960's have shown a persistent run against the American dollar which the government has fought by many partially effective measures, including restrictions on American tourists and on the flow of U.S. dollars. Unfortunately, the failure of these steps has served to convince economists in the rest of the world that the United States ultimately must devalue, and this in itself produces more of a run against the dollar. When all else will have failed and the government finally faces unpleasant reality (and the moment of truth cannot be far), the price of gold will be raised; this action, in effect, will devalue the dollar. The step is inevitable, and the subsequent rise in the cost of living will cut the true value of government bonds, and of all other fixed-income securities, by very drastic percentages.

While it is true that when the government bonds become due they will unquestionably be paid off dollar for dollar, the sad fact is that the bond owners will pay today's relatively solid money to the government when buying their bonds, but will be given back a devalued dollar as the result of inflation. To make this clearer, let us consider an example. Mrs. Mary Smith has been left an estate of $20,000 by her late husband, and because she feels she can't take the chance of loss, invests all of the inheritance today in U.S. government bonds. When the government is forced to raise the price of gold, other prices will rapidly fall in line, because dollar holders will wish to get rid of this paper money by buying "wealth in the ground" stocks— gold, other metals, oil, coal, and so forth—or physical things like real estate, automobiles, and diamonds. Thus when the government repays poor Mary Smith her $20,000 ten years from now, she will find to her dismay that the money which would buy a Rolls Royce today will probably not buy a Cadillac then, perhaps not even a Buick. In other words the government will have stolen one-half or more of Mrs. Smith's capital, and she will have no hope of recourse.

This is the long-term effect, but the short-term results can be even more disastrous. Because many government bondholders will panic (and justifiably so) when gold is raised in price, millions of dollars worth of long-term bonds will be sold for whatever they will bring, thus driving down the market value and producing an unbearable situation for those forced to sell. Thus a long-term government bond with a face value of $1,000 may bring in only $700 or less if it is necessary that it be sold. When Roosevelt raised the price of gold in 1933, the overnight fall in the value of bonds produced bankruptcy for many individuals and bond firms.

What about outstanding government bonds that have already sunk to a fraction of their issue price? A list of these is published daily in the *Wall Street Journal*.

Bargains they appear to be, but bargains they are not, for it is to be noted that the further off the date of redemption, the greater is the discount. If and when the dollar is devalued,

Government, Agency and Miscellaneous Securities

Monday, March 28, 1966
Over-the-Counter Quotations: Source on request.
Decimals in bid-and-asked prices represent 32nds (101.1
means 101 1-32). a-Plus 1-64. b-Yield to call date. c-Ap-
proximate yield at maturity.

Treasury Bonds

			Bid	Asked	Prev. Bid	Yld.
3¾s,	1966	May	99.28	99.30	99.28a	4.19
3s,	1966	Aug.	99.10	99.12	99.10	4.65
3⅞s,	1966	Nov.	99.5	99.7	99.5	4.65
2½s,	1962-67	June	97.20	97.22	97.19	4.48
3⅝s,	1967	Nov.	98.3	98.5	98.1	4.52
3⅞s,	1968	May	97.30	98.2	97.29	4.84
3⅞s,	1968	Aug.	97.7	97.9	97.9	4.97
3⅞s,	1968	Nov.	97.11	97.13	97.9	4.94
2½s,	1963-68	Dec.	94.24	94.26	94.22	4.56
4s,	1969	Feb.	97.18	97.20	97.17	4.90
2½s,	1964-69	June	93.28	93.30	93.24	4.55
4s,	1969	Oct.	96.31	97.1	96.30	4.93
2½s,	1964-69	Dec.	92.27	92.29	92.25	4.60
2½s,	1965-70	Mar.	92.16	92.20	92.13	4.56
4s,	1970	Feb.	96.21	96.25	96.18	4.92
4s,	1970	Aug.	96.9	96.13	96.7	4.92
2½s,	1966-71	Mar.	90.30	91.2	90.23	4.53
4s,	1971	Aug.	95.21	95.25	95.18	4.90
3⅞s,	1971	Nov.	94.21	94.25	94.16	4.95
4s,	1972	Feb.	95.10	95.14	95.2	4.90
2½s,	1967-72	June	88.22	88.26	88.16	4.59
4s,	1972	Aug.	94.26	94.30	94.21	4.94
2½s,	1967-72	Sept.	88.2	88.6	87.28	4.64
2½s,	1967-72	Dec.	87.25	87.29	87.19	4.62
4s,	1973	Aug.	94.5	94.9	93.31	4.93
4¼s,	1973	Nov.	94.22	94.26	94.17	4.95
4⅛s,	1974	Feb.	94.21	94.25	94.14	4.93
4⅛s,	1974	May	95.22	95.26	95.17	4.88
3⅞s,	1974	Nov.	93.2	93.10	92.30	4.83
4s,	1980	Feb.	93.8	93.16	93.6	4.64
3¼s,	1980	Nov.	88.2	88.10	88.0	4.61
3¼s,	1978-83	June	83.16	83.24	83.14	4.63
3¼s,	1985	May	83.6	83.14	83.4	4.56
4¼s,	1975-85	May	93.20	93.28	93.18	4.74
3½s,	1990	Feb.	83.20	83.28	83.16	4.63
4¼s,	1987-92	Aug.	93.20	93.28	93.16	4.66
4s,	1988-93	Feb.	90.10	90.18	90.16	4.62
4⅛s,	1989-94	May	91.24	92.0	91.18	4.64
3s,	1995	Feb.	79.30	80.6	79.28	4.19
3½s,	1998	Nov.	82.22	82.30	82.16	4.51

these bargain-priced bonds will be dumped just as will be higher-priced ones, and they could easily sell at only fractions of their present bargain prices.

For the above reasons long-term government bonds should be avoided. The one thing they should guarantee, safety, is completely lacking. In fact government bonds represent a rank speculation without giving the advantage a speculation should give—the possibility of capital gain.

Don't buy them.

Government savings bonds come in an entirely different category. By law these may be purchased only in limited quantities by any individual, and they are redeemable at any time at their face value. Savings bonds are comparable to cash in the bank but are preferable to cash in that they receive much higher interest (from 4½% to 5½%). They are a perfectly adequate, safe investment but give no protection against the inflation which has afflicted our economy since 1945. A small proportion of funds in such bonds is a reasonable investment to use in place of a cash reserve.

2. *Municipal Bonds* are direct obligations of the municipality borrowing the money, just as federal bonds are obligations of the federal government. United States municipal bonds have the unique advantage that their income is tax exempt to American citizens, and so they can be issued with a relatively low yield because of their attraction to those in high tax brackets. Canadian municipal bonds are not tax exempt and so give much higher yields, at present around 6% to 6½%. The safety of the capital invested is considerably less than with government bonds, for unfortunately in bad times many a municipality has been unable to repay its bondholders. There is, of course, no possibility of capital gain.

The likelihood of a rise in the price of gold and thus a devaluation of the dollar must be considered in reference to municipal bonds also, and the same painful facts once again apply.

Thus it is obvious that the average investor should not give any consideration to the purchase of such bonds. They give poor yield, no safety of buying power, and no chance of capital gain. Even the individual with a very high income, who buys such bonds in order to cut down his income tax, is making a very serious error; for when the game is over he may very well find that he has gained ten per cent in income and lost fifty per cent in purchasing power.

Don't buy them.

3. *State Bonds* are obligations of the state borrowing the money. The remarks made in reference to government bonds all apply here, with the exception that yields are somewhat higher. Once again there is no protection against inflation, and the potential loss in purchasing power is not offset by any other advantage.

Don't buy them.

4. *Corporate Bonds and Debentures* (exclusive of convertible bonds, which are discussed in Chapter 4) differ from government, state, and municipal bonds in having a higher yield and a somewhat lower safety factor. The vast majority of these bonds and debentures are straight loans from the purchaser to the corporation and present no more protection against inflation than do government bonds. They should not be purchased for the reasons previously outlined. The prices in the list of outstanding corporation bonds reprinted on the next page show how very badly this type of security can behave in times of inflation.

There are, however, a few exceptions, and because of them all corporate bonds should not be overlooked. These happy exceptions come in two groups.

The most common of these is the bond carrying a bonus of either common stock or the option to buy common stock at a fixed price for many years (see Chapter 8 on warrants). Such an arrangement provides a built-in safety factor in that when the dollar is devalued, although the bond itself will lose a part of its purchasing power, the common stock will likely appreciate a similar amount, thus offsetting the loss. This only applies, however, if the corporation is one which can raise its

BONDS

CORPORATION

	Bid	Ask
Abitibi 6¼, 1977	100½	102½
Alta Ga s5¼, 1981	91½	94½
Algoma 5¾, Mar. 1, 1979	94½	..
Algoma Steel 5¼, 1978	91½	94½
Aluminum 4½, 197	90½	93
Bathurst 6, 1984	93½	95½
Bell Phone 5½, 1982	93½	95½
Bell Phone 5,¾ 1982	96	98
Bowater 3,¾ 1980	79½	81½
Brazilian Tr 4¾, 1970	92	95
BA Oil 5⅛, 1977	90½	93½
BC Tel 5 , Nov. 1, 83	89½	92½
Canada Cement 5¼, 1976	91½	94½
C Breweries, 5, 1983	88½	90½
C BAlm 5,¾ 1980	95½	98½
C Chemica 17, 1980	99½	102½
CIL 5¾. 1977	95½	98½
CPR 3½, Oct. 1, 1966	98	100
CPR 5, 1983	87½	90½
CW NGas 5⅜, 1983	90½	93½
Consumers Gas , 1978	88½	91½
Dominion Stores, 5½, 1976	94½	97½
Dominion Tar 5¼, 1978	91½	94½
Dryden Paper 4¾, 1974	89½	92½
Eaton Accept. 5¾, 1981	94	96
Eaton Realty 5, 1978	89½	91½
Eddy, E. B. 4, 1974	84½	..
GMAC 6¼, 1977	98½	101½
GL Paper 5, 1976	91	93½
GL Power 4¼, 1975	86½	89½
Gr WGas 5½, Dec. 1, 80	92½	95½
HB Oil Gas 4. May 1, 75	83½	86½
Husky Oil 6, Nov. 2, 84	95½	98½
Imperial Oil 3, 1969	91½	93½
IAC 5½, 1978	88½	92½
Inland NGas 6¼, 1983	98	100
John Labatt 5½, Jan. 2, 1979	93	97
Jockey Club, 6, 1980	98	100
Lakeland NGas 6, 1982	96	98
Loblaw 5¾, 1981	94½	97½
MacMillan B. 5⅜, 1978	91½	94½
NO NGas 5¾, 1982	93½	96½
NW Utilities 5⅜, 1983	90½	93½
Quebec NGas 5¾, 1985	90½	93½
Regent Refining 4¼, 1975	86½	90½
Rio Algom 5¾, April 1, 1983	91½	94½
Security Cap. 6¾, 1978	94½	..
St. Lawrence 5, 1978	89½	92½
Shawinigan 5¾. 1981	94	96½
Shell Oil 4¼, 1976	86½	89
Shell Oil 5⅞, 1977	97½	100½
Simpsons 5¾, 1981	93½	96½
Toronto Star 5½, 1978	93½	96
T Canara 5.85, 1987	93½	96½
Braders F. 5¾, 1981	84½	87½
Union Gas 5¾, 1981	95½	98
Wcoast Tr 5½, 1988 A	90½	93½
Weston G. 5¼, 1982	90½	92½

prices and profit margin when inflation strikes—in other words, to companies selling "things". It particularly does not apply to utilities, who often must receive permission from various government bodies before they can raise their rates.

Thus, certain corporation bonds may be purchased today that give a good yield, a fair degree of safety, plus a bonus of stock or stock options that promise the likelihood of capital gains. There are many such issues, and so there is usually little difficulty in making such purchases. An excellent example of this type of issue was the 6½% five-year debenture issued by the Traders Finance Corporation in 1965. The yield was good, the safety factor excellent, for this company is one of Canada's largest and most conservative in its field, and yet each $1,000 bond carried a bonus of twenty-five seven-year options (warrants) to purchase stock in the company. A delightful result of such a purchase was that a capital gain could be guaranteed! This could be accomplished through the immediate sale of the bonus stock or stock options. In the case of the Traders Finance bonds, the stock options could be sold immediately for $2.50 each or $62.50 in total per $1,000 bond. The bondholder would still get back his $1,000 plus interest in five years and would have had an immediate 6¼% capital gain!

A less common type of corporate bond whose purchase is recommended is one in which interest and principal are payable in more than one currency at the holder's option. Thus, if the United States were to devalue its dollar, the bondholder would be protected because he could take his capital back in another currency. (In actuality U.S. dollars would be received but in an increased amount, depending on the extent of devaluation.) An outstanding example of such an issue was one made in the United States by the American Petrofina Company. This debenture gave a yield of 5½%, and both interest and principal were payable in six different currencies. Because of the fluctuations which have already occurred among these currencies, the debenture in the few years since issue at $1,000 may now be sold for $1,200. This type of security represents the best of many worlds—safety, yield, and capital gain—and should be purchased whenever available, provided that the issuing company is sound.

Because this type of bond is in great demand, there is usually an immediate profit to be made following its purchase. An example was the debenture of the Institute Ricostrz Industries guaranteed by the Italian government and issued in June, 1964, in several countries. This issue, incidentally, illustrates free riding, which is the purchase of securities without putting up any money (see Chapter 9). The contract below shows the purchase of ten such bonds on June 26, 1964. No money was paid, but the selling broker was instructed to deliver the bonds to another broker against payment; that is, payment would only be made when physical delivery of the bonds was effected. Because of the slowness in delivery of all new issues and particu-

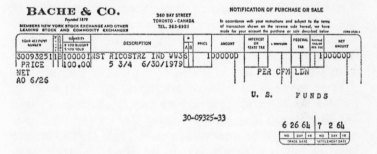

larly those from Europe, actual delivery was not made until September 30, 1964. By this time the bonds had moved up considerably in value.

In this very strange transaction a profit of $820 was made without a cent being put up!

Thus among corporate bonds there are many good opportunities for both widow and orphan, but they must be chosen carefully. The three questions to ask are:

a. Is the company sound?

b. Is the yield satisfactory?

c. Does the bond carry a "kicker"; that is, does it carry a bonus, or is it multipay?

If the answer to all three questions is yes, *buy them.*

5. *Blue Chip Stocks* represent a share in the ownership of the leading companies in North America. These companies are called "Blue Chip" because they have been in business half a century or more and have paid dividends consecutively for many years.

These stocks are a relatively safe investment with excellent possibilities of growth and capital gain. Unfortunately, they also have an excellent chance of going down drastically in any recession because of the tremendous rise such stocks have enjoyed in our past twenty-year market boom. Another disadvantage is the very low yield blue chips now give. In fact, earnings and dividends have not come close to keeping pace with the increase in price of these stocks, and many of them now pay dividends considerably smaller than bank interest. The time to buy such stocks undoubtedly will come again, but they do not represent good value today and should be passed over by the average small investor.

6. *Mutual Funds* are in many ways the ideal investment for the investor seeking safety, yield, and growth, but whose time

is fully employed outside of the market and who thus cannot closely watch his investments. A mutual fund takes the money of its shareholders and invests it in many dozens of different securities, thus spreading the risk far wider than any individual could possibly do. There are hundreds of mutual funds, and each of them gives a different emphasis to its investments. Some funds specialize in safety with a high proportion of their funds in bonds; others primarily seek high yields and put most of their money in high dividend stocks and debentures; and some sacrifice both safety and yield in order to purchase only the stocks of companies which are likely to increase in price through growth of the firm. There are, of course, various gradations of the three types of mutual fund, with the vast majority using a combination of the three methods.

Over the past twenty years, performance of mutual funds has varied almost as widely as that of individual stocks, but many of them have given a truly incredible performance. I purchased shares in one fund, the Investment Company of America, nine years ago. Since that time I have received annual dividends averaging between 10% and 15%, most of which were non-taxable because they were capital gains. (If I were a U.S. citizen, I would have to pay taxes at a low preferential rate on capital gains.) In addition to this my shares, which were then worth $7.57, now have grown to a value of $13.61 each. In 1965, for example, I received a dividend of $1.14 per share, of which only 27¢ was classified as income and the balance was a capital gain. During that year the company's net asset value increased by 24% while the Dow Jones went up only 11%. This was not just a lucky year, for in 1964 the net asset value went up by 14% and in 1963 by 20%. Even more significant, in the first quarter of 1966, while the market was falling, the Investment Company of America's asset value rose by another 4.2%. Below is a chart from I.C.A.'s annual report, showing the results of a $10,000 investment in the company's stock thirty years ago.

The success of any individual mutual fund depends on the financial acumen with which its managers are endowed. In choosing which one to buy, there is a very simple yardstick—past performance. A prospective investor must decide whether he wishes to place his money in a fund specializing in one of the three factors of safety, growth, or yield, or intends to take a blend of the three. Except for an individual in very unusual circumstances, the wisest choice is usually the latter one.

One way *not* to decide which mutual fund to buy is through advice of your stockbroker. Every mutual fund does a great deal of buying and selling of securities through one or more brokers. In return these brokers are expected to advise those clients purchasing mutual funds to buy only into the fund providing the stock business. Under these circumstances impartiality is impossible. Better to seek advice from your banker.

Mutual funds are divided in one other way, and this is where most investors go wrong. There are open-end funds and closed-end funds. An open-end fund is one in which there is no limit to the amount of stock that will be issued by the fund; in fact, they will issue just as much as they can sell. Their stock is sold to the public at its net breakup value plus a commission or loading charge which covers the salesman's and broker's commissions. The great advantage of this type of fund is that the stock can be redeemed, that is, sold back to the fund at any time at its breakup value with no commission charged. Most investors who buy mutual funds buy open-end funds.

The closed-end fund is not so common; it is a fund that has a fixed amount of stock which cannot be increased ad infinitum like the open-end fund. Its stocks, except when originally issued, can be purchased like any other stock only from a shareholder who wishes to sell. The fund itself will not redeem its stock from its shareholders. The interesting feature of closed-end funds is that invariably they sell at a discount from their net asset value of anywhere from 20% to 45%! This is one of the few cases where a stock purchaser can be sure of getting a

ILLUSTRATION
OF AN
ASSUMED
INVESTMENT

*Three Different
Results from
the Same
Initial Investment*

Investors in The Investment Company of America have found, in the past that the Fund provided sufficient flexibility to permit the accomplishment of different objectives, or at least the accomplishment of objectives . which differed in emphasis. Summaries of different results achieved from the same initial investment are shown at right. The results under the second assumption are shown in detail in the chart on Pages 14-16.

1

Results with
Income Dividends
and Capital Gain-
Distributions
Taken in Cash

Cost of Original Investment, January 1, 1934	$ 10,000
(4,219 shares)	
Value of Investment on December 31, 1965	$ 57,426
Total Dividends from Investment Income in Cash	$ 26,350
Total Distributions from Capital Gains in Cash	$ 46,962
Number of Shares Owned December 31, 1965	4,219

2

Results with
Income Dividends
Taken in Cash and
Capital Gain
Distributions Taken
in Shares

Cost of Original Investment, January 1, 1934		$ 10,000
(4,219 shares)		
Ending Value of Shares Originally Acquired	$ 57,426	
Ending Value of 13,033 Shares Acquired as Capital Gain Distributions	177,374	
Total Value of Investment on December 31, 1965		$234,800
Total Dividends from Investment Income in Cash		$ 58,664
Number of Shares Owned December 31, 1965		17,252

3

Results with
All Income
Dividends and
Capital Gain
Distributions Taken
in Shares

Cost of Original Investment, January 1, 1934		$ 10,000
(4,219 shares)		
Cost of Shares Acquired with Income Dividends without sales charge		117,220
Total Cost of Investment		$127,220
Ending Value of Shares Originally Acquired	$ 57,426	
Ending Value of 14,553 Shares Acquired with Income Dividends	199,066	
Ending Value of 25,848 Shares Acquired as Capital Gain Distributions	351,792	
Total Value of Investment on December 31, 1965		$607,299
Number of Shares Owned December 31, 1965		44,620

bargain, for he is really buying dollar bills for between 60¢ and 80¢.

The reason that closed-end funds sell at a discount is that theoretically if a fund were to sell a large block of one stock, they would depress the market and so would receive less than the current price for their block. Like so many other market fallacies, this is completely untrue. In actuality many brokers specialize in handling large blocks, and if the company stock is sound, there is no difficulty in selling such blocks at market prices and sometimes even at premiums above the market.

Typical examples of closed-end funds are Tricontinental in New York and Power Corporation in Canada.

Both of these companies are strong, well-diversified funds which can be purchased at considerable discounts from their true value. At the time of writing, Power Corporation had a breakup value of $18.60 but could be purchased for $11.50. Tricontinental had a breakup value of $31.00 but could be purchased for $24.00.

Thus, some mutual funds represent the best possible investment for the individual who cannot afford to take large risks but *is* prepared to take a small risk.

The three questions to ask before making such a purchase are:

  a. Is the fund closed-end and selling at a large discount from its asset value?
  b. Are the individual stocks held in the fund in leading firms in their particular industries?
  c. Is the fund's past record a good one?
If the answer to all three is yes, *buy it.*

In summary, there are six types of investments normally available in the "widow and orphan" market. Because of the long upgoing (bull) market associated with the weakening of the U.S. dollar, four of these are not suitable for the investor who cannot afford large risks. This investor should choose his investments among the mutual funds and the special corporate debentures described earlier.

There is one other investment in this class that is highly suitable—the convertible bond. But because this bond is such an important investment method, it will be discussed in a separate chapter.

2

THE PENNY STOCK MARKET

Consolidated Dominion went from 20¢ to $50.
Quantro went from 3¢ to $20.
Triangle went from 10¢ to $19.
The dream of every stock-market gambler is to buy just such a vision—to invest $1,000 and see it turn into $500,000. Because of these dreams, thousands of men have become millionaires—not by buying penny stocks, but by selling them. It is now standard promoter practice to pay a few hundred or a few thousand dollars to buy a property within a short distance of a producing mine or a "hot" prospect and then to issue up to a million dollars worth of stock at anywhere from 30¢ to a dollar to the gullible public. Of every million dollars worth of stock

issued, far less than half will be used for actual exploration of
the property, and in some cases none of the money is so used.
A portion of the cash will go into the treasury of the company,
a large amount will go to the telephone and telegraph companies to pay for the long-distance calls to the suckers, and the
vast majority will go to make new millionaires of the promoters.

The myth of the fortunes made from the penny stock that
finds a rich ore body and goes to $20 or $30 has been carefully
fostered by a mining industry which depends on the promotion
type of financing for its vigour. Unfortunately, it is a complete
myth. *There is not a single member of the public living in
North America today who has made a sizable sum of money by
investing in the penny mining market.*

The Irish sweepstakes persuade millions of North Americans
to make a donation to Irish hospitals by giving back a portion
of the "take" and by making a few of their benefactors rich
beyond their dreams. The penny mining market has never
made a member of the public rich, and yet through extremely
clever publicity has persuaded the supposedly intelligent professional classes of North America to continue to annually do-
nate millions to this very uncharitable group. How do they so
successfully perpetrate this same fraud year after year?

The routine is as formalized as a ballet. The promoter either
forms a new company or purchases control of an existing company listed on a Canadian stock exchange. A typical example
was Fax Mines,* a company with a listing on a Canadian stock
exchange trading at 5¢. The company had no assets and had
sold its total capitalization of 5 million shares. A well-known
Canadian promoter, Edward Collins, purchased one million
shares of the company's stock for $70,000 from the original or-
ganizer of the company. This gave him effective control of the

---

* Fax Mines, Jenny Mines, Jerrett Motors, Canadian Jefferson Securities,
Edward Collins, George Crawford, Fred Gora, Henry Severn, Heather Investment Services, and Strang Advisory Services, are fictitious names used
in this and the following chapter to illustrate an often-repeated situation.
Any resemblance to living persons or firms is purely coincidental.

company, as the remaining four million shares were widely distributed, with no individual holding more than ten thousand shares. A promoter never attempts to move a stock when in this situation, because the other shareholders may begin to sell their stock to him. Instead, Collins called a special meeting of the shareholders, which because of the company's inactivity was attended only by himself and his associates. At this meeting he called in all of the company's stock and changed the company's name to get rid of the old tired Fax Mines image. The shareholders were given one share in the new company for every 10 shares they had held previously. The new company, Jenny Mines, had an authorized capital of five million shares, but there were now only 500,000 outstanding, of which 100,-000 were held by Collins.

At this time there was a very active uranium boom in Canada. Several companies near Elliot Lake had discovered ore bodies and were going into production to supply ore to the United States. Collins arranged for his brother-in-law, George Crawford, to purchase a piece of bush land ten miles from Elliot Lake and 25 miles from the proven mines. Crawford paid $250 to the prospector who staked the property and promptly sold the land to Jenny Mines for $50,000.

Jenny Mines had no money, however, so Collins underwrote (purchased) 200,000 shares of stock from the treasury of the company at 25¢ a share so as to supply the $50,000. The company then announced that in return for this underwriting they had granted Collins one-year options to purchase another 1,500,000 shares at prices ranging from 30¢ to $1.00.

At this point Crawford returned the $50,000 to his brother-in-law. These men now had reached the point where, by laying out $250, they had received 200,000 shares of company stock plus options on an additional 1.5 million.

Next, Collins paid $3,000 to an employee of a large trust company who had access to the files listing the shareholders of several large mines for whom the trust company acted as transfer agent. For his $3,000 he received 12,000 names and addresses of individuals who were then holders of successful mining stocks. The "trust" company employee didn't have to copy out all these names, for his firm had every name on a mailing plate, and the employee merely ran all the plates through the machine, thus producing a master list in one hour of overtime. (Another promoter did not wish to spend the $3,000 and rented a third-floor office on Bay Street from which he entered a trust company's office at midnight while the janitor was kept busy with a bottle of whisky. No one at the trust company ever suspected, although the promoter grumbled that he always left the plates much neater than he had found them.)

The 12,000 investors now began to receive a well-printed, glossy "information bulletin" sent out by Collins' brokerage house, which he grandly called "Canadian Jefferson Securities". The weekly bulletin expansively and optimistically described the uranium boom then going on in Canada and pointed out some of the extraordinary price changes that had occurred; stock of some companies had literally quadrupled or better in days. The third bulletin described in loving detail the romantic story of Gunnar Mines, a legitimate company which had jumped in a few days from $2.50 to $13. Along with this bulletin was a stamped postcard. The receiver was invited to sign and return it in order to receive, with no obligation, full information on a new exciting prospect near the successful mines described earlier. This company was "about to begin drilling", which could very likely send its price from its then 39¢ to over $10.

Promoters consider a 3% return from a promotional mailing to be satisfactory, and Collins expected to get back 350 to 400 postcards. To his amazed delight, he received 1,600 signed postcards, probably due to the front-page publicity given the Canadian uranium strike and the atomic bomb.

Within a few days these 1,600 individuals, practically all of whom were in the United States, received a long-distance call from Toronto which went like this: "This is your Canadian broker calling. My name is Fred Gora, and I want to tell you about what will probably be the greatest opportunity in your lifetime—to get in on the ground floor of a great Canadian mine before the sharks up here know about it. The name is Jenny Mines, and she probably has such a big uranium ore body that you can stick Gunnar and Consolidated Denison in one corner of it and you wouldn't even see them. The price is only 39¢, and although I'd like to offer you more, the president of our firm will only allow me to sell 1,000 shares to new customers. The idea is, we'll make you money on this one and then try to do more business at some future date. You want to check with your banker? Well, of course, go right ahead, but I have only been allotted 25,000 shares to sell to new clients, and you represent my last thousand. I have over 300 more people I haven't phoned yet, and my last call was to a banker in New York City; he wanted 20,000 shares, and I could only give him one. Jenny is listed on the stock exchange, you know, and we're only distributing stock at this low price because they insist on a wider distribution before it moves over $1.00. Okay, I'll send out a contract to you tonight. Please put a cheque in the mail for $390. You don't even have to pay the regular stock exchange commission."

As a result of these 1,600 calls, 400,000 shares were sold, and payment was received for 350,000. Collins now needed more stock for his "clients" and so exercised his options on Jenny Mines at 30¢. Ten days later the 400 original phone purchasers received a second call: "This is Fred Gora phoning from Canada, bringing good news about Jenny Mines. The outlook for the company has improved so much that Jefferson Securities have put another $100,000 in their treasury. The stock has been very active on the stock exchange and has now moved up to an all-time high of 65¢. Some very good news is going to be released tomorrow. I am not allowed to reveal it yet, but I can tell you this, that it will put the price of the stock much, *much* higher. Because you are now a regular client, the president has given me permission to sell you a small amount of stock at to-day's price; this is only because you showed faith in us before, when Jenny was 39¢. We have very little available, and only to our regular clients, but I have managed to squeeze out a maximum of 3,000 shares for you—and frankly the president said to try to talk you down to half of that, but I want to make this money for you so that we will do a lot of business in the future. So just put your cheque in the mail for $1,950, and you can skip the commission. Jenny Mines is going to make all of us very rich men."

In the meanwhile, Eddy Collins had really put $100,000 in the treasury of Jenny Mines in order to exercise his stock option, but he had no intention of leaving it there. Jenny Mines now hired "Crawford and Company" to do a magnetometric survey of the property for the sum of $85,000, two-thirds of which was immediately passed back to Collins under the table. Strangely enough, this was the good news that Fred Gora had predicted, and the company now made a public announcement that the survey was under way and would be followed by diamond drilling.

The stock continued to move higher on the stock exchange, reaching $1.00 three weeks later. By this time Collins had twelve salesmen working the phones, busily selling Jenny Mines all over North America. He exercised further options, paying Jenny Mines $250,000 for further blocks of stock at higher prices. Needless to say, most of this money quickly found its way back to Collins via the drilling company that Jenny Mines hired.

This drama was rapidly reaching its climax, and a crescendo of stock selling occurred. Announcement of the imminent drilling was made to the *Northern Miner*, advertisements were placed in the mining and daily press with a map showing the proximity of Jenny Mines to successful mines, and a tremendously high-pressure phone campaign was conducted to sell Jenny Mines at $1.00. "Jenny closed at $1.10 today. We are letting you have it at 10¢ under the market." Unfortunately, the clients did not understand the unintentional pun in that sentence.

Friday, January 28, 1963, Jenny closed at $1.20 on the stock exchange. Saturday morning Eddy Collins paid off his salesmen. They received an average of $9,000 each for the ten weeks' work. Fred Gora, his best salesman, had earned $21,000. They smiled and shook hands, and the salesmen went to look for another similar promotion.

Fred Gora boarded a plane for Vancouver with his $21,000 in $100 bills in a breast pocket. He soon fell asleep in his aisle seat, and the thick packet of bills fell into the aisle. The stewardess could not believe her eyes and hurried forward to give the money to the pilot. His first thought was of dope pushing, and he radioed ahead to ask the Royal Canadian Mounted Police to meet the plane at Calgary. Some minutes later Gora awoke, and feeling the absence of his money pack, became volubly upset until the stewardess calmed him and returned the money.

When the plane landed in Calgary, the R.C.M.P. quickly whisked Gora into a private office and began a polite but insistent cross-examination as to the source of the money. Gora swears that when he refused to talk, the police corporal blurted out, "Mr. Gora, we are aware that one of your acquaintances has been smuggling hog bristles from Communist China into the United States via Canada. This is a very serious offence. We insist on knowing if your money is from this source."

The amazed swindler burst out laughing and replied, "Hog bristles! Are you kidding? This is my pay for selling moose pasture to American investors!" The constable apologized and escorted Fred Gora back to his airplane.

On Monday, January 31, Jenny Mines opened with no bid-offered at $1.00. The first trade was at 60¢, and within twenty minutes the stock sold down to 14¢, where it remained for several days while short traders (professionals who had sold stock they didn't own in the expectation of just such a collapse) bought back the stock they had sold over $1.00. Jenny then gradually declined to 3¢, and it has traded in a 3¢ to 6¢ range since that time.

Collins made a gross profit of 2½ million dollars, out of which he had to pay just under $400,000 to his various associates. He decided for reasons of health to close Jefferson Securities on February 1, then moved to Nice, where he rented the large villa that he still occupies today. Strangely he did not dissipate his illgotten wealth in the vice traps of Nice but, being a hard working individual, opened a new business. This was an advisory service, giving market advice to European investors who were interested in North American securities—but more about this type of swindle in another chapter.

Unbelievable as this story sounds, it has been repeated hundreds of times in the past decade, and some individuals have fallen for the same fable many times. Doctors are the prime suckers, for they have excess cash with no business to put it in; they are too rushed to properly investigate any stock; and they are trusting by nature. There is probably not a doctor in all of North America who has not been stuck at least once by Eddy Collins or others of his ilk. Dentists and lawyers are a close second, but chartered accountants seem to fare better. Widows and orphans are never stuck by these operators, who avoid them like the plague, not because of innate decency, but because widows scream to the authorities and the press. The professional or businessman rarely publicly complains, because he cannot bear to have his own greed and stupidity exposed.

And indeed there is no limit to the greed and stupidity of these lambs who think they are wolves. At 11 p.m. one very cold January night, I received a phone call from a lawyer friend who said he had to see me that night on a very urgent financial matter. He explained that he had two clients with him, dentists who had invested their entire savings of $85,000 in a fantastic once-in-a-lifetime proposition, and that he intended to invest his own modest savings in the morning but first wanted my opinion.

Twenty minutes later, three excited men arrived at my home and poured forth this fantastic story: An unbelievably large iron ore deposit had been discovered in Liberia; the Sheik of Kuwait had agreed to put up twenty million dollars to finance the development and production of the ore, which was then to be shipped to Kuwait, where it was to be used in a new process for refinement of oil under the Kuwait desert. The twenty million was already in deposit in a Liberian bank, and the deal was to be closed in just five days, but the promoters and developers of the property had run short of ready cash and needed just $30,000 to pay the legal fees and close the deal. In return for loaning this $30,000, the two dentists had been given the secret information that Ross Metals,* an unlisted penny stock trading at 30¢, was for tax reasons to be given full title to the iron property. When this news was released to the public, the stock would be worth about $50 per share. To prove the truth of all these statements, the previous week one of the dentists had actually been flown to Liberia and had not only seen the property but had been introduced to the Sheik of Kuwait himself (or a reasonable facsimile). That week the dentists had purchased 200,000 shares of Ross Metals at 30¢.

When I expressed, as gently as possible, my doubts about this "deal of the century", the dentists' reaction was violent. They jumped to their feet, accused me of wanting to discourage them so that they would sell their stock cheaply while I bought it up, then stamped angrily from the house. I learned that night never to try to talk sense to individuals in love with their dreams. They will not tolerate anyone's shattering them.

One month later the promoters of Ross Metals had sold all their stock, and it quickly fell to 2¢. The property in Liberia unfortunately did not have enough ore to warrant going into production, and the pseudo-Sheik of Kuwait had disappeared. Interestingly enough, the two dentists are still mad at me. I guess they have to blame someone other than themselves.

Fortunately, not all penny stocks are swindles. But, as a general rule, if the stock is being sold over the phone, the chance of the client's making money is about nil.

* Name changed.

Even those promoters who are honest (and most promoters and honesty have difficulty going together) cannot offer their clients a decent break. For even if every penny that goes into the company's treasury is spent on exploration and development, the chance of producing a mine is close to nil. Of the thousands and thousands of penny prospects that have been explored in all of North America since the war, less than half a dozen have ultimately turned into a mine and paid dividends greater than their cost. Unfortunately, even the most conscientious promoter must siphon off over half of the money he receives in order to pay the fringe expenses involved in promotion and sale of these mining stocks.

It is, of course, far easier to give advice than to follow it, and although I have no trouble turning down the phone promoter, I find it very difficult to say no to the friend with the "hot tip"; and money is usually just as lost on a hot tip as with the promoter. The information is all too often either false or planted. A recent personal experience illustrates the temptations and pitfalls of the hot tip, even when, as in this case, the stock being tipped was an honest, legitimate one.

One evening John Hay, a mining engineer friend, phoned excitedly after the market had closed. "Mort, I have exciting news! International Copper is trading in Vancouver at 65¢. Tomorrow at two o'clock the company is going to announce a 2% copper find plus an 85¢ underwriting, and the stock is going to be listed on the Vancouver exchange. I have the information straight from a director of the company. I'd like you to buy some stock first thing in the morning, and we'll split the profits. There's no chance of this information being wrong, because he knows I can't afford to lose and he wouldn't give me bad information."

It would be a rare individual who could refuse such a story, apparently straight from a director of a mining company, and next morning I purchased one thousand shares of International Copper at 60¢.

By 11 a.m. the stock was down to 55¢, and I was mentally

berating my own ignorance when John phoned to reassure me that all was well and that at 2 p.m. the announcement would be made. Sure enough, at 1:30 the stock began to move up, and at 2 p.m. I sold it at 84¢.

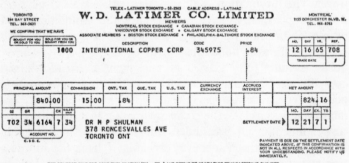

At 2:15 John Hay phoned frantically, "I've made a terrible mistake, I gave you the name of the wrong company! Let's get out and take our loss!" When I told him that I had already sold at a profit we both broke up with laughter.

The moral is that if you make money on a hot tip, it's an accident.

What about those penny mines that do find ore and go up so beautifully? Five years ago a typical penny dreadful was being sold over the phones at 35¢ while drilling was being done on the property. To the amazement of the promoter, a huge ore body was found, which meant that the stock was worth 20 or 30 times the price it was being sold for. No news of this strike was released by the promoter, because to his dismay he had sold almost all his stock. Instead, he went to work buying back all the stock from the phone customers at 50¢ per share. After he had it all back, he released the news, and the stock moved up to its present level of $45.

At least the clients made a little money on that one!

There is thus one general rule in relation to penny mining stocks. *Don't buy them.* The odds are impossible.

There is, however, one exception to this rule. It is a very important one and should not be overlooked.

There are some low-priced mining stocks that have made spectacular market moves and in which no promotion was involved; for example, Pine Point went from $2 to $83, and Mattagami from $3 to $22. The trouble with this type of stock is that it is uncommon; the move is gradual, unspectacular, unadvertised; and the public never buys it until *after* it has made the big move. How can these situations be recognized early? A description of such an issue will show the points to look for.

A typical example was Newconex Holdings. This was a company formed in 1962 by giant Consolidated Goldfields of South Africa. Goldfields had been increasingly nervous about their concentration of funds in South Africa and England and, deciding to place some of their funds in safer political areas, created subsidiaries in the United States, Australia, and Canada. These subsidiaries were set up in such a way that their shareholders literally could not lose.

Newconex originally issued 700,000 shares of stock at $5 each, of which 450,000 were purchased by Goldfields themselves, and the remaining 250,000 were sold to the public by a highly reputable Canadian stock broker, Nesbitt Thomson & Company. The $3.5 million thus raised was all placed in the

Newconex treasury. Each of the 700,000 shares carried as a free bonus two options (warrants) entitling the holder to purchase 2 additional shares of Newconex at $5 at any time within a five-year period.

Simultaneously, Goldfields concluded a unique agreement with Newconex which ensured Newconex's financial success. This unprecedented agreement obliged Goldfields through a wholly owned subsidiary to begin an active program of exploration in Canada. All losses were to be borne by Goldfields, all worthless properties were to be kept by Goldfields, but Newconex was given the right to take over any successful finds from Goldfields within one year, at cost! This meant that Newconex was now an exploration company with all the possibilities of sudden upward surges in the stock that could occur with an ore find, but without any of the dangers of attrition of capital through exploration expense. In other words, this was a company that could not lose!

One would have expected a tremendous rush from the public to buy the stock, for it is not too often that a speculator is given the chance to gamble without any risk of loss. There was no rush; in fact, there was no public buying at all. Nesbitt Thomson & Co. sold the 250,000 shares available to their clients, arranged for the stock to be listed on the Toronto Stock Exchange, and then worried no further about it. Newconex stock slowly drifted downward and in a few weeks was trading at $4.25 with the two warrants still attached. The warrants themselves were trading at $1.00, and so the stock alone was valued by the buying public at only $2.25. Yet this stock had $5 in cash behind every share, plus a guarantee against loss by Goldfields.

During the next three years, Goldfields spent close to one million dollars on exploration and found nothing. Newconex was sitting with $3.5 million dollars, which they invested in stocks and bonds following the advice of Nesbitt Thomson and Company. They invested the funds remarkably well and within three years had increased their assets by over 50%. Each share now had cash and liquid assets behind it of $8.00. The disinterest of the public continued and the stock offered on the exchange was slowly bought up by two or three wealthy, knowledgeable investors and investment funds. The warrants continued to trade around $1 while the stock hung being between $4 and $5. It is interesting to note that even experts find difficulty in buying value when no promoter is spreading glamour about, and by the end of 1964 practically all of Nesbitt Thomson's clients had sold their stock. Goldfields, however, was not unaware of the tremendous value building up in Newconex, and they purchased 50,000 more shares of the company stock from Canadian Gas and Energy, a closed-end mutual (see Chapter 1) fund that had purchased the stock near its lowest prices on the Toronto stock exchange.

Goldfields now compared the results Newconex had achieved in comparison with the other subsidiaries in the United States and Australia and decided that the Canadian company had not done well enough. They requested the president's resignation and brought in Mr. Bill Robinson from Canadian Gas and Energy as the new president. By September, 1965, Newconex had become a beehive of activity. It had crews exploring in many areas of Canada (at Goldfields' expense), and it was busy examining many companies offered to it for sale.

One company that approached Newconex was Pyramid Mining, who owned a very strategic piece of ground in the North West Territories, right next to the huge Pine Point Mine. Pyramid needed money to explore this property, and Newconex agreed to supply this in return for a block of Pyramid stock.

All this activity had not appreciably affected the price of the Newconex stock, which now had liquid assets equal to $8.50 per share but which continued to trade around $5.

There is always a critical point in the stock history of undervalued mining situations like Newconex where the public suddenly sees a situation which has been obvious for years but which no one has looked at. The critical day for Newconex was October 7, 1965. On that day the *Northern Miner* ran this item on the front page:

Newconex, Conwest Share At Pine Point

Newconex Canadian Exploration, exploration a r m of Newconex Holdings, is getting into the Pine Point area in a big way.

At mid - week, the Northern Miner was able to confirm with company officials that it now holds about a 50% participation with Conwest and Central Patricia in that team's substantial and well regarded holdings which almost surround Pine Point Mines.

Conwest, which will continue as the operator, has been carrying out extensive geophysical work on this key ground all summer. Tentative plans are to drill this winter.

This was the first public notice that Newconex was busily searching for a mine, and the following week the *Miner* wrote up as exciting news what the whole mining fraternity had been ignoring for three years.

The **Conwest-Central Patricia** team, starting this week to drill some well regarded anomalies in the Pine Point area on ground they have held for years, new-highed at $6.75 and $1.82 respectively. But the market didn't take too much note of an exclusive story in this paper last week which revealed that Newconex Holdings as a full partner, now probably holds the largest single interest in this project, although it did gain 45¢ to reach its former all-time high of $6.15. This figure is still well below its liquid breakup value which now stands at about $8.50 per share. A unique feature of the New-conex set up permits the company to purchase anything found by its exploration arm for $15,000. The tab for this arm, Newconex Canadian Exploration, is picked up by the parent Gold Fields Mining & Industrial Ltd. of London, Eng. In other words, New-conex Holdings, the T.S.E. listing, doesn't have to spend its money on exploration. And it has a pretty capable associate in Conwest. On the other hand, this association could make available almost unlimited funds in the event of a success at Pine Point or elsewhere. Newconex Warrants, which give the right to buy Newconex stock at $5 per share till Feb. 28, 1967, gained 40¢ on the week to $1.65 on volume of 79,200 shares. Floating supply of both stock and warrants is unusually light, which makes for a rather explosive situation marketwise.

* * *

That did it! First the mining people, then the public, jumped in. The two contracts below illustrate the effect the sudden awakening produced:

HECTOR M. CHISHOLM & CO. LIMITED

MEMBERS
TORONTO STOCK EXCHANGE
MONTREAL STOCK EXCHANGE
CANADIAN STOCK EXCHANGE

GROUND FLOOR
82 RICHMOND STREET WEST
362-4731

BRANCH OFFICE
KING EDWARD SHERATON HOTEL
363-3074

TORONTO 1, CANADA

TO: Dr. M. Shulman,

WE HAVE THIS DAY BOUGHT FOR YOUR ACCOUNT ON ☑ THE TORONTO STOCK EXCHANGE ☐ THE CANADIAN STOCK EXCHANGE ☐ THE UNLISTED MARKET   DATE Sept. 30/65 VALUE Oct. 5/65

BROKERS ON REQUEST	SHARES	DESCRIPTION	PRICE	AMOUNT	COMMISSION	TAX	TOTAL
Daly	200	Newconex Holdings	5.10	1020.00	30.00		1050.00

E. & O.E.

PURCHASES OR SALES ARE MADE WITH THE DISTINCT UNDERSTANDING THAT ACTUAL DELIVERY IS CONTEMPLATED, AND ARE SUBJECT IN ALL RESPECTS TO THE BY-LAWS, RULES AND CUSTOMS OF THE STOCK EXCHANGE WHERE THE ORDER IS EXECUTED AND TO THE CUSTOMS OF THE BROKERAGE BUSINESS. IT IS AGREED THAT ALL SECURITIES CARRIED FROM TIME TO TIME IN THE CUSTOMER'S MARGINAL ACCOUNT, OR DEPOSITED TO PROTECT THE SAME, MAY BE LOANED BY US OR MAY BE PLEDGED BY US ON OUR GENERAL LOANS, EITHER SEPARATELY OR TOGETHER WITH SECURITIES OR OTHERS, AND EITHER TO SECURE ADVANCES WITHIN OR IN EXCESS OF THE AMOUNT DUE US THEREFOR. IT IS ALSO AGREED THAT WE RESERVE THE RIGHT TO CLOSE TRANSACTIONS (WITHOUT DEMAND FOR ADDITIONAL MARGIN OR ANY OTHER NOTICE WHATSOEVER) ON A STOCK EXCHANGE OR SIMILAR INSTITUTION, OR AT ANY PUBLIC OR PRIVATE SALE, WHENEVER WE DEEM IT NECESSARY FOR OUR OWN PROTECTION BY REASON OF INSUFFICIENT MARGIN OR OTHERWISE.

HECTOR M. CHISHOLM & CO. LIMITED

HECTOR M. CHISHOLM & CO. LIMITED

MEMBERS
TORONTO STOCK EXCHANGE
MONTREAL STOCK EXCHANGE
CANADIAN STOCK EXCHANGE

GROUND FLOOR
82 RICHMOND STREET WEST
362-4731

TORONTO 1, CANADA

BRANCH OFFICE
KING EDWARD SHERATON HOTEL,
363-3074

TO Γ

Dr. M. Shulman,

					DATE Nov. 4/65		VALUE Nov. 9/65
BROKERS ON REQUEST	SHARES	DESCRIPTION	PRICE	AMOUNT	COMMISSION	TAX	TOTAL
Bong	200	Newconex Holdings	9.25	1850.00	40.00	2.00	1808.00

E. & O.E.

PURCHASES OR SALES ARE MADE WITH THE DISTINCT UNDERSTANDING THAT ACTUAL DELIVERY IS CONTEMPLATED, AND ARE SUBJECT IN ALL RESPECTS HECTOR M. CHISHOLM & CO. LIMITED
TO THE BY-LAWS, RULES AND CUSTOMS OF THE STOCK EXCHANGE WHERE THE ORDER IS EXECUTED AND TO THE CUSTOMS OF THE BROKERAGE BUSINESS.
IT IS AGREED THAT ALL SECURITIES CARRIED FROM TIME TO TIME IN THE CUSTOMER'S MARGINAL ACCOUNT, OR DEPOSITED TO PROTECT THE SAME,
MAY BE LOANED BY US OR MAY BE PLEDGED BY US ON OUR GENERAL LOANS, EITHER SEPARATELY OR TOGETHER WITH SECURITIES OR OTHERS, AND
EITHER TO SECURE ADVANCES WITHIN OR IN EXCESS OF THE AMOUNT DUE US THEREON. IT IS ALSO AGREED THAT WE RESERVE THE RIGHT TO CLOSE
TRANSACTIONS (WITHOUT DEMAND FOR ADDITIONAL MARGIN OR ANY OTHER NOTICE WHATSOEVER) ON A STOCK EXCHANGE OR SIMILAR INSTITUTION, OR
AT ANY PUBLIC OR PRIVATE SALE, WHENEVER WE DEEM IT NECESSARY FOR OUR OWN PROTECTION BY REASON OF INSUFFICIENT MARGIN OR OTHERWISE.

As such a story should, this one ended happily. Pyramid drilled their property with the money supplied by Newconex and found a huge ore body. Both stocks passed from being ignored to being market darlings, and all those who bought and had the will power to hold on made huge profits.

How can other Pyramids or Newconexes be recognized before their stock has moved 'way up in price? These mining prospects all have five features in common:
a. They are never sold over the phone.
b. No promoter recommends their purchase.
c. Their treasuries all contain substantial funds.
d. From 25 to 80% of their stock is held by one or more large producing mining firms.
e. The amount of stock issued to the public is small, usually less than one million shares.
f. The market price of the stock is always over one dollar and should be less than $10.

There are always a few such stocks available, trading at very low prices, and their history has been almost universally a good one. But these stocks are purchased primarily by knowledgeable people in the mining business and not by the public. These are the only situations in the mining market where the purchaser is almost sure of making a profit.

What this chapter boils down to is, never buy tips or promotions; buy value and wait. There will be many more Pine Points and Newconexes.

3

ADVISORY SERVICES

"Our recommendations outperformed the Dow average by 37%."

"Do you own any of the stocks listed below? If so, send for our free analysis."

"Kelly warrants went from 5¢ to $32. You can learn how to make equally large profits."

These are come-ons to lure investors into subscribing to market letters and, more important, into following their advice. Market letters are the prime weapon of so-called advisory services. Many of them are crooked.

Advisory services should not be confused with information services such as Standard & Poor's and/or Moody's. Firms like these specialize in selling detailed information about companies whose stocks are publicly traded. On the basis of this information, the sophisticated investor can invest his money more intelligently. There has never been any suggestion of hanky-panky among the information companies.

The advisory service is an organization presumably set up to dispense unbiased information and advice. Unfortunately, the economics of such an organization make it extremely difficult for it to be run honestly. Membership dues, which run anywhere from $5 to $500 per year, entitle the member to receipt of the weekly or biweekly market letter, plus varying amounts of individual advice on request. The average advisory service has a clientele of approximately 2,000 subscribers, and it immediately becomes apparent that the average fee of $25 per year will not yield enough gross revenue to even pay the advertising expenses.

Advertising costs are terribly high in this field, and there is an average cost of $25 to secure each subscription. Direct mail advertising is the least expensive way to get clients, but 1,000 pieces of mail bring in an average of only 10 one-year subscriptions. Newspaper advertising is even less productive, and full-page ads in the financial section have on occasion brought in only two or three subscriptions. Inasmuch as the owners of these advisory services must make money in order to remain in business, it soon becomes necessary for them to establish new sources of income. Such sources are always available.

It is an interesting fact that the written word is many times more influential than the spoken one, and written words for which clients are paying soon develop awesome powers. It is not unusual for a market letter with a circulation of 2,000 to produce buying of $200,000 or $300,000 in a stock following a one-page recommendation.

The PFR market letter (one of the better letters whose honesty has never been questioned) recommended the purchase of Campbell Chibougamau stock in December, 1965. Campbell is a junior Canadian copper mine listed on the American Stock

Exchange and the Toronto Stock Exchange; it traded then at about $5 a share. Within two trading days, Campbell had traded over 100,000 shares, equivalent to over half a million dollars, and its price had jumped to over $7.00.

With powerful distribution of this type available through market letters, it is not surprising that dishonest promoters with stock to sell are attracted to them.

An additional factor making these advisory services easy marks for the dishonest is the complete lack of training necessary in order to begin an advisory service. Youths with absolutely no market knowledge have been granted licenses to start such services, and as a result their advice has often been quite unusual. It is interesting that mature intelligent investors would carefully read and follow market letters written by boys to whom they would not have given a second of time in person. The casual way in which market letters and advisory services are begun has produced some ludicrous situations. One of the more successful letterwriters developed a large devoted clientele by getting all his market ideas from the comics, and his average was better than many who used more orthodox methods. Another market advisor bases his advice on the current situation of the stars, but he has no more stars in his eyes than have his clients.

This situation in which untrained individuals reached positions of tremendous stock placing power, yet still had difficulty in making money, inevitably resulted in stock promoters paying large sums of money in order to have the advisor recommend the purchase of their stocks. In some cases the promoter actually buys the advisory service and keeps the advisor on as a figurehead.

Before going into the details of this type of swindle, we should draw a distinction between the various types of market letters. There are three:

a. Least effective is the type which is distributed free by an individual promotion broker in an attempt to sell his own stocks. These letters may describe other stocks, but only as a

come-on to show the great profits which the promoter inti-
mates can be made in his own issue. (See Chapter 2 on penny
stocks for details about this type of letter.)

b. Individual reputable stock brokers often issue free to their
clients an advisory letter, distributed at regular intervals, recommending the purchase of individual stocks that the broker
feels are undervalued. As a general rule, such recommendations
are honestly given, and the stocks often do merit purchase.
Unfortunately, a very serious abuse of these letters is now a
common occurrence. Because advice of this type will often be
sent to thousands of clients simultaneously (particularly when
issued by the larger stockbrokers), there is often a rapid pouring into the exchange of buy orders for the stock involved,
producing an immediate rise in its price. Knowing that this
will occur, certain junior employees (and some not so junior)
have developed a substantial sub rosa income by phoning a
friend the day before the recommendation is issued to the
firm's clients and having the friend purchase a block of the
stock, which is sold the following day after client buying begins
and the stock moves up. Because this practice has now become
so very common, investors should beware of such recommendations, particularly if they have had a recent price rise.

c. The other form of market letter is the one which creates
the most abuse. Subscriptions to the service are purchased on
a yearly basis. The service represents itself as doing independent research and supplying unbiased advice which theoretically
should enable the purchaser to improve his market performance. Humbug! Occasionally one of these services will publish
a report showing that its recommendations have outperformed
the market, but often these apparent good results are achieved
by comparing a stock at its bid price the day before a recommendation (and no client is able to buy it at this price) with
its price after it has been recommended and considerable buying has forced the price up.

Incidentally, there is one way that the nimble trader can

make money from the very large advisory services. Some of the largest ones will forward their recommendations to clients by telegram in return for an additional fee. Because there is usually a price rise following these recommendations, immediate purchase of small quantities of the stock when the telegram arrives with sale the next day, regardless of the price, is often profitable. During a bull (upgoing) market, a doctor friend managed to perform this trick once a month for a year, showing a profit on eleven of the trades. Two of the trades are illustrated below. This practice is not recommended to the average speculator, however.*

Delivery Phone: EMpire 8-7137 EMpire 4-9986		TELEX - LATIMER, TORONTO - 02-2565				TORONTO, ONT. Confirmation Phone: EMpire 3-8921	
		W. D. Latimer Limited Security Dealers 244 BAY STREET Date			Nov. 2-61		

We have this day SOLD TO YOU

				Please have cheques made payable at par in Toronto			
Broker	Quantity	Security	Price	Amount	Brokerage	Tax Que. Prov.	Total
	500	Steadmans	8½	4250.00			4250.00
	700	"	8 5/8	6037.50			6037.50

Delivery Phone: EMpire 8-7137 EMpire 4-9986		TELEX - LATIMER, TORONTO - 02-2565				TORONTO, ONT. Confirmation Phone: EMpire 3-8921	
		W. D. Latimer Limited Security Dealers 244 BAY STREET Date			Nov. 2-61		

We have this day BOUGHT FROM YOU

				Please have cheques made payable at par in Toronto			
Broker	Quantity	Security	Price	Amount	Brokerage	Tax Que. Prov.	Total
	1000	Steadmans	9.00	9000.00		10.00	8990.00
	550	"	9 1/8	5018.75		5.50	5013.25
E.&O.E.							

* These two legitimate companies were recommended by an honest advisory service.

A	AS PRINCIPAL WE HAVE SOLD TO YOU
B'	AS AGENT WE HAVE SOLD THROUGH/FROM YOU
C	AS AGENT YOU HAVE SOLD FOR US
D'	AS AGENT WE HAVE PURCHASED FOR YOU

R. A. DALY & COMPANY

MEMBERS
TORONTO STOCK EXCHANGE
THE INVESTMENT DEALERS' ASSOCIATION OF C

R. A. DALY & COMPANY LIMITED HAVE PLEASURE IN CONFIRMING THE FOLLOWING TRANSACTION EFFECTED WITH YOU SUBJECT TO THE RULES AND R

CODE	ARRANGED BY	MARKET	DATE		NO. OF SHARES OR PAR VALUE	DESCRIPTION OF SECURITY	PRICE	GROSS AMOUNT	ACCRUED INTEREST	C
			TRADE	SETTLEMENT						
D	OFFICE	NYOC	MAR 30 61	APR 7	1 00	INSTRUMENTS FOR INDUSTRY	6 ½ U.S. FUNDS	650 00		

E. & O. E.

PLEASE NOTE ➤

1. IF FUNDS ARE NOT ALREADY IN OUR POSSESSION. PLEASE ARRANGE FOR PAYMENT DIRECT OR AGAINST DELIVERY
2. WHEN CARRYING SECURITIES FOR CLIENTS WE RESERVE THE RIGHT OF PLEDGING THE SECURITIES AND RAISING M CONVENIENT TO US. CHARGING INTEREST ACCORDINGLY.
3. THIS CONTRACT SHOULD BE PRESERVED FOR TAX PURPOSES AS INTEREST PAID BY YOU MAY BE OFFSET AGAINST
4. WHEN ACTING AS AGENT WE WILL FURNISH THE NAME OF THE OTHER BROKER OR BROKERS INVOLVED IN THE TRA
SETTLEMENT MAY BE EFFECTED AT THE BRANCH THROUGH WHICH YOU ARE DEALING. STREET ADDRESS OF WI

W'	AS PRINCIPAL WE HAVE PURCHASED FROM YOU
X'	AS AGENT WE HAVE PURCHASED THROUGH/TO YOU
Y	AS AGENT YOU HAVE PURCHASED FOR US
Z	AS AGENT WE HAVE SOLD FOR YOU

R. A. DALY & COMPANY

MEMBERS
TORONTO STOCK EXCHANGE
THE INVESTMENT DEALERS' ASSOCIATION OF CA

R. A. DALY & COMPANY LIMITED HAVE PLEASURE IN CONFIRMING THE FOLLOWING TRANSACTION EFFECTED WITH YOU SUBJECT TO THE RULES AND RI

CODE	ARRANGED BY	MARKET	DATE		NO. OF SHARES OR PAR VALUE	DESCRIPTION OF SECURITY	PRICE	GROSS AMOUNT	ACCRUED INTEREST	C
			TRADE	SETTLEMENT						
Z	OFFICE	NY	MAR 30 61	APR 7	1 00	INSTRUMENTS FOR INDUSTRY	0.00 U.S. FUNDS	1 000 00		

E. & O. E.

PLEASE NOTE ➤

1. IF NOT ALREADY IN OUR POSSESSION PLEASE ARRANGE FOR DELIVERY OF THE RELATIVE STOCK CERTIFICATES OR (
2. ANY EXPENSE INCURRED THROUGH FAILURE TO DELIVER SECURITIES IN PROPER TRANSFERABLE FORM SHALL B(
3. THIS CONTRACT SHOULD BE PRESERVED FOR TAX PURPOSES, AS INTEREST PAID TO YOU MUST BE REPORTED TO T.
4. WHEN ACTING AS AGENT WE WILL FURNISH THE NAME OF THE OTHER BROKER OR BROKERS INVOLVED IN THE T(
SETTLEMENT MAY BE EFFECTED AT THE BRANCH THROUGH WHICH YOU ARE DEALING. STREET ADDRESS OF W(

This type of advisory service can be subdivided into four subtypes:

1. The strictly honest service giving honest advice for a fee. There are a few of these in existence, but unfortunately it is impossible for the ordinary investor to distinguish them from their not-so-honest cousins. The problem facing the honest service is that, in order to make a financial go of the business, it must develop a large paying clientele, and the cost of so doing is prohibitively high.

One of my friends, thinking that a strictly honest letter *had* to be a success, opened such a service. After two years he found that he had recommended 40 stocks of which 36 had gone up. He had 800 clients and he was earning $20 a week. He closed the service and took a job as a customer's man. During the two years he was publishing, he had over one dozen offers of financial support from various promoters. The honest advisor either does not buy any securities or else lists any securities which he purchases in his advisory letter.

2. The semi-honest service giving what they consider to be good advice on a variety of industrial and mining securities. This type of advisor never takes a payoff, but he ensures his financial success by buying up blocks of the stock he intends to recommend and then resells it to his own clients. He never does this under his own name but hides the transaction by using a friend or relative. This type of advisor never gets rich, because he usually recommends basically sound issues which rarely have a large percentage improvement in price in such a short interval.

Occasionally one of these services gets its comeuppance. In 1957 the owner of Strang Advisory Service purchased a block of stock in Webb & Knapp (Canada) at $2.00 and then recommended its purchase to his clients. It immediately jumped to $2.50, and the advisor was happy to dump his stock and make a nice $15,000 profit. In the following weeks Webb & Knapp continued to move higher, and when it reached $3, the advisor began to sell it short, knowing that it had gone up only because of his recommendation and so expecting an imminent drop. When it reached $3.50 he sent out an urgent telegram to all his clients, recommending profit-taking through immediate sale of Webb & Knapp. His clients sold all right, but the stock continued to move higher, reaching $4.75 one week after his urgent sell advice. Unfortunately for our advisor, what he did not realize was that a much larger New York based service had just recommended purchase of Webb & Knapp!

The stock that had been sold short was bought back at a net loss of just under $20,000. After the advisory services and the short selling were finished, the stock gradually slipped back to $2, which was what it was worth through all the gyrations.

A surprising number of these advisors are chartists, who choose their recommendations by study of the volumes traded and prices recorded of an individual stock over a period of time. A chartist will make a daily record of many stocks, in each case producing a graph showing volume and price. He will study those graphs, looking for certain telltale signs which will indicate to him a "breakout is coming" or "topping is occurring" or "the long-term trend line has been broken". On the basis of this "information" he will recommend purchase or sale of the security involved. This method of forecasting price movements has proven almost as accurate as that of studying the stars or the comics, but unlike these latter methods, charting has thousands of adherents. The theory upon which charting is based is that the market itself cannot be fooled, and all future price movements are forecast by increased or decreased buying and selling. By studying past price movements, they believe that they have discovered certain repeating patterns. It's something like the man who says that since there were 25 years between the beginning of the first and second world wars, a third war should have started in October, 1964. The fact that it didn't doesn't shake his conviction. He believes that this is just an exception.

Chartists have an equally blind faith, and some of them are so blinded by their delusion that they will actually buy stock in a company after studying a chart without knowing the company's earnings or even what business it is in! This mass delusion has been instrumental in producing several millionaires; not the chartists, but those who prey on them. One wealthy New Yorker who runs the markets on several stocks has carefully studied the chart system and has developed a specialty of trading his controlled stocks so as to produce the patterns which a chartist believes indicates a move upwards. Using this unique method, he has sold several million dollars worth of overvalued stocks. He is the only person I have ever met who boasts of the value of charts and can prove it!

3. The individually owned advisory service in which the majority of the recommendations are legitimate, except that every few weeks a "clinker" is thrown in. This clinker is a stock in which a promoter wishes to produce buying in order to sell some of his own position. He will pay the advisor either on a volume basis or a flat rate. The flat rate can vary anywhere from a few hundred dollars up to $25,000 for an all-out recommendation in a well-regarded advisory sheet. The volume basis used to be the most popular method; the promoter was required to pay a fee varying from 15 to 25% of the price of the stock on every share traded in the four days following the recommendation. This method fell into disuse because, alas, there is truly no honour amongst these gentlemen, and the promoters soon found that a great deal more stock was trading than they were selling. What was happening was that the advisor had placed a number of phoney buy and sell orders which cancelled each other out but increased the volume of trading tremendously.

Inasmuch as these advisory services intended to remain in business and hoped to sell a great many more stocks to the same clients, they naturally did not wish to see their recommended stocks collapse, for this would make future sales immeasurably more difficult. Thus the price paid for the recommendation would vary a great deal, depending on who was the promoter. One gentleman still active in the promotion field was well known for selling every possible share after a service had recommended one of his stocks and then letting the price of the stock collapse. He managed to get control of a wide group of companies, varying all the way from furniture stores to mining prospects, but every one of his enterprises ended disastrously for the shareholders. In one case he paid $25,000 to a flourishing advisory service to recommend the purchase of one of his mining prospects trading at 80¢. Over the next two days he sold out his entire position, pocketed over a quarter of a million dollars, and made no further effort to support the price of the stock. It rapidly declined to 10¢, and the advisory service never completely recovered from the loss of confidence which resulted.

On the other hand, there are other promoters who look at the longer picture, and who will at least make some effort to support their stocks after a recommendation is made. These men find it cheaper to do business with owners of market letters than do the more ruthless operators. One of these promoters owns about a dozen small mining companies, each in a different branch of the industry—silver, gold, copper, lead, and zinc. Because each of these different metals has its periods of popularity, he concentrates on selling the particular group which is then "hot". He describes himself whimsically as, "Just a grocer. When they want apples I sell them apples, and when they want bananas I sell them bananas. I keep them all on the shelves, and sooner or later someone wants to buy them." This man uses advisory services frequently and for several years paid a weekly retainer of $300 to one service to ensure that the owner did not close any deals with other promoters!

The various companies owned by this last promoter are all basically sound, none of them have collapsed, and actually the buyers of these stocks would not be making nearly as bad an error as most persons buying through the advice of a market letter. The real trouble is that the stocks are all overpriced when they are recommended.

4. The type of advisory service most dangerous to the public is the one that is deliberately set up by a promoter as a "front" to get rid of worthless or overpriced stocks. Sometimes huge sums of money are spent in building up such a service through widespread advertising, or alternatively, a well-established service may be purchased outright. In either case the story is the same—several weeks or even months of carefully restrained recommendations of a large number of high-grade securities followed by an all-out recommendation of the stock that the promoter wishes to sell.

These tactics can be very effective, and although it may take

$100,000 or more to build up such a service, it is possible for the organizers to take in in excess of a million dollars in a matter of two or three days.

Jerrett Motors stock was distributed in just such a way. This was a company set up to market a new type of low gas-consumption automobile engine that the promoter, Henry Severn, claimed would revolutionize the market. Severn was a handsome, charming man with considerable experience in distribution of stocks in various companies in Europe and the Middle East. When he arrived in New York, he was on the wanted list of the police of France and Turkey for stock fraud. His first step was to buy control of Jerrett Motors, a small, privately owned firm that had been supplying automobile parts to several auto manufacturers for years. Their sales had never exceeded $1,000,000 per year, and net profit had been only $15,000 in the preceding year. Management was happy to sell control of the company for $120,000.

Henry Severn now "went public". He announced that Jerrett Motors had purchased for $500,000 the North American rights to distribute a new type of automobile engine that provided the same service as current models, consumed one-tenth the gasoline, and would sell for less than $100. The business world was electrified by this announcement, and Severn had no difficulty in persuading Lawford and Company, a small but reputable broker, to underwrite and distribute a public issue of one million shares of stock at $1.75 per share. The 1¾ million dollars thus placed in the treasury was immediately depleted by $500,000, which Severn said was being forwarded to the inventor in France. The vice-president of Lawford and Company went on the board of Jerrett to represent and protect Lawford's customers.

Eddy Collins (remember him from the penny stock frauds?) meanwhile had set up a stock advisory service whose market letter was mailed from London. In dozens of European and U.S. newspapers, ads appeared offering an all-encompassing advisory service for only $10 per year. The advertisements listed ten stocks that "Heather Investment Services" had recommended in the past year which had doubled in price.

Collins offered as a "free" service to evaluate all stocks held by new clients and promised that those who followed his advice would double their money by spring.

The response to the series of ads was phenomenal, and within four months Heather Investment Services had a paid circulation of over 5,000. The service then began to recommend the purchase of Jerrett Motors. In the advisory letters, the history of I.B.M. was related in detail: How the company had brought new inventions to the marketplace and how their stock had gone from $5 to $800. Every week this line appeared: "An investment of $1,000 in I.B.M. grew in 10 years to $200,-000." Heather Investment Service stressed that Jerrett Motors now had a new invention that was going to capture the entire automotive market; they suggested that the large auto manufacturers were desperately trying to buy control, and that the stock could very easily go to $100 per share in weeks.

The clients bought, and Jerrett stock went up in a few weeks to $4 per share. Now Collins was able to write in his bulletin, "I said Jerrett Motors would double in 2 months and it has. Now I say that it will double again in the next month. This is the I.B.M. of 1964, and before this year is out the stock may very well trade at $1,000." This brought in about 200,000 shares of buying, and within three weeks the stock was up to $10.

By now the directors of Lawford and Company were becoming nervous. Their persistent requests to see the invention were answered by a private showing of a small automobile engine, which because of "technical difficulties", they were not allowed to operate. They were promised, however, that there would be a public demonstration within a few days. Their requests for an accounting as to where the million dollars withdrawn from the treasury for "development purposes" had been spent received only vague answers, and their representative was voted down when he demanded an outside audit. Lawford and Company had no choice. Their vice president resigned from Jerrett's board, and Lawford phoned all their clients to whom they had sold Jerrett stock and advised them to get rid of it. They could have saved themselves the trouble; their clients were all sophisticated investors and had already sold practically all of their holdings. Strange rumours of looting of the company's treasury and a question as to the actual existence of the engine itself were already circulating on Wall Street, and Lawford's clients had been happy to triple their money and get out.

Now began the most reprehensible part of the whole scheme. Eddy Collins had a list of the securities held by 4,000 of his subscribers, and he began a mail and then a phone campaign to urge them to sell all these excellent securities and replace them with stock of Jerrett Motors, which had quadrupled just as he had predicted and which he said was certain to move up astronomically during the next few weeks. His campaign was highly successful, and a deluge of buying of Jerrett stock followed. It continued to move higher, reaching $24 by late spring.

Henry Severn was meanwhile selling his stock as fast as the orders poured in and had by now disposed of close to 1 million of his 1½ million shares. He had now run into a problem in the form of short selling. This is the sale of stock not owned by the seller in the belief that the stock will go down and can be repurchased at a lower level. The rumours about the company had increased to loud rumbles after the resignation of Lawford's vice president, and professional traders were selling Jerrett stock short at a rapidly increasing rate. There was now a total short position of over 200,000 shares, and the short selling was now almost equal to the buying pouring in from the Collins subscribers. In order for Severn to get rid of the remaining half million shares he now took a final two steps. He placed full-page ads in the financial press, announcing the placing of the engine on retail sale the following month, and he announced that Jerrett Motors had received a takeover offer equivalent to $110 per share from Instrument Controls, a Canadian firm. Instrument Controls was a dummy corporation with no assets that Severn had set up for this very purpose a year earlier.

Although the announcements brought in about 100,000 shares of buying, to Severn's dismay it also produced almost as much short selling, and he now decided to take one final irrevocable step before closing down the operation.

Severn took a one-day trip to Nice which he spent in consultations with Collins. When he returned to New York the following morning, the plans had been settled. Three days later twenty-four stock exchange members received special delivery letters from Geneva. Enclosed in each was a certified cheque for $120,000 on the nonexistent "Royal Bank of Geneva" plus a letter ordering the immediate purchase of 4,000 shares of Jerrett Motors. The letters were signed "Henry Da Silva, Royal Bank of Geneva". Five of the brokers were sufficiently suspicious to phone or wire Geneva before placing the orders. The other nineteen, unfortunately, were not so cautious. By 11 a.m. they had bought 76,000 shares of Jerrett at $25 per share. At 11:10 a.m. the exchange, now aware of the fraud, began to phone every member to warn them. The brokers tried to dump the Jerrett stock, and by 11:30 a.m. it was down to 75¢.

The next day Henry Severn disappeared, and three months later Jerrett declared bankruptcy. The company had been thoroughly looted and had no assets. The miracle engine had never existed. Henry Severn has not been heard from since, but is believed to be living in Rio de Janeiro. Edward Collins closed down his London advisory service and returned to Nice. He has purchased his villa and is reported anxious to invest in any promising business.

The clients who bought Jerrett have surprisingly little bitterness toward Collins. A number of them have remarked, "We had received good advice—after all, the stock did go up tenfold. If only we had sold out!"

In summary, it is too difficult for the ordinary investor to tell the good letter from the dishonest one and the good recommendations from the bad, so the best advice that can be given in connection with advisory letters is *Don't:*

Don't subscribe.

Don't read them.

Don't follow their advice.

If an investor or speculator needs advice, the place to go is to a reputable broker. The New York exchange is now policing its members sufficiently closely that membership in that exchange is the best guarantee of impartiality in giving advice.

4

CONVERTIBLE BONDS

What must we seek in order to find the ideal investment?

First, there must be absolute security of capital.

Second, there must be an adequate yield of dividends or interest.

Third, there must be the possibility, or better still, the likelihood, of large capital gains.

Fourth, this security must be one that can be easily sold very quickly and turned into cash; that is, it must be liquid.

This ideal investment is found *only* in the field of convertible bonds. The convertible bond is the single most important type of investment possible, for it combines the best features of both the bond and stock markets.

A stock represents ownership in a firm and as such will vary in value, depending on how well the firm is doing. A bond, on the other hand, is a loan from the bondholder to the firm, and unless the firm goes bankrupt, the bond will always be worth its face value. It may not always be possible to sell it for its face value, but every bond is a loan for a fixed period of time, and when that time has run out, the firm must repay the face value of the loan.

The advantages of a bond over a stock are safety of capital and a sure income. The disadvantages are the absence of any hope of capital gain plus the lack of protection from inflation, or devaluation of the dollar. The advantages of stock over bonds are the excellent possibility of capital gains plus the protection against inflation or devaluation. The disadvantages are the complete lack of safety of capital and the absence of a sure income. The convertible bond is an amalgam of the advantages of both bond and stock with elimination of the disadvantages.

What is a convertible bond? It is a bond with the added feature that it can be changed into stock at the holder's option at any time; in other words, it is convertible. It is easiest to explain by taking a specific example. Rittersporn Dairies wishes to raise $10 million and issues ten-year convertible bonds to that total face value. The bonds pay 5¾% annually. Each $1,000 bond is convertible into one hundred shares of Rittersporn Dairies at any time during the bond's life. Rittersporn Dairies stock was selling at $8 per share at the time of the bond issue. Inasmuch as the $1,000 bond can be changed into one hundred shares of stock, this would put a cost of $10 per share on each share of stock, so obviously there is no point in making the conversion if the stock is selling at less than that on the open market. If, however, a year later Rittersporn has used the $10 million dollars judiciously, the company's earnings may well have had a very big jump, and the stock that was selling at $8 previously now may have moved up to $15. Because each bond can be converted into one hundred shares of stock, the bond which cost $1,000 a year earlier is now worth 100 × $15 or $1,500—a capital gain of 50% in one year. If, on the other hand, things do not go well with Rittersporn and the stock sells down to $2 per share, the bondholder has lost nothing, for he is still holding his bond and drawing his 5¾% interest.

Thus the holder of a convertible bond can gain if the company's stock goes up but cannot lose if it goes down. Many a stockholder would like to be in this happy position. I know of several millionaire investors who buy only convertible bonds. They are the only investors or speculators who can honestly say, "I have never lost on an investment."

What firms issue convertible bonds and why? Dozens of issues of this type come out yearly. There is not an industry that has not had convertible bonds, and there is hardly a leading corporation that has not issued them at some time. There are three reasons for issuing a convertible bond rather than an ordinary one. The first is to enable the issuer to pay a lower interest rate. Naturally a convertible bond is easier to sell than an ordinary one, and so it is possible to pay an interest rate ½% or even 1% lower than otherwise. This can mean a saving of millions of dollars over the life of the bond. Second, the overall trend of stock prices is upwards, resulting in conversion of most of these bonds into stock before they become due. It is, of course, not necessary for the borrowing firm to repay any bonds that are converted, and so this is often a way to avoid raising the money to redeem the bonds. Third, many firms have a small stock capitalization and a large bond debt. By issuing convertible bonds that are ultimately changed into stock, they succeed in increasing the size of their stock base; they have more stock and thus more shareholders. Any firm interested in public relations is anxious to have as many shareholders as possible, because shareholders tend to be very faithful customers.

Examples of convertible bonds that have proven very profitable to their owners are shown below. The best type of convertible bond is one in which there may be a wide fluctuation in the price of the stock, such as a pipeline, as this will make it more likely for the bond to go up.

In this particular example the Westcoast bonds went up on the day of issue and there was a sizeable profit without any investment. On other convertible pipeline bonds large fortunes have been made from small investments.

(It should be noted that although bonds are issued in denominations of $1,000, they are always quoted in units of 100 for brevity. Thus on the previous contract, although the bonds

were sold for $1,052.50 each, the sale price was quoted at
105¼.)

A few years ago Interprovincial Pipeline made an issue of
convertible debentures at $1,000 each before the company be-
gan to pipe oil. After four years the company's earnings were
zooming upwards, as was the bid on the stock, and the convertible debentures sold up to $5,000 each. Because the risk on
these bonds is minimal, they can be purchased by putting up
only a 10% deposit (or margin) instead of the 50% required
on stocks. Thus each bond can be purchased with a $100 down
payment. At the time of issue, a Toronto gynecologist invested
$5,000 in these bonds on margin, for which he received a face
value of $50,000 worth of bonds. The remaining $45,000 was
supplied by the bank. When the doctor sold out five years later,
he made a net profit of $200,000 from his $5,000 investment.

Pipeline convertibles have proven to be tremendous financial
successes, and the result is that they all become hot issues
when first brought out, a happy situation for those who do not
wish to keep the bonds but are pleased to make an immediate
profit without any investment.

STATEMENT
AND
CONFIRMATION

SALE TO

NESBITT, THOMSON AND COMPANY, LIMITED

220 BAY ST.,
TORONTO 1, ONT.   December 5, 1957

SETTLEMENT DATE   December 10, 1957

WE HAVE ACTED AS PRINCIPAL IN THIS TRANSACTION

SALESMAN   5-T-1775   J.A.McMillan

PAR VALUE	SECURITY	PRICE	AMOUNT	INTEREST	TAX	TOTAL	CONTRACT
22,000	Pembina Pipe Line Limited, 6% Dec. 1 1975 Conv. Deb. if as & when issued.	100.00	22,000.00	32.55		22,032.55	1279

INTEREST FROM   Dec. 1   TO   Dec. 10   DAYS   9

DELIVERY

A prospectus descriptive of this issue was mailed to you on Dec. 4, 1957

REGISTRATION

STATEMENT
AND
CONFIRMATION

NESBITT, THOMSON AND COMPANY, LIMITED

215 BAY ST.,
TORONTO 1, ONT. December 5, 1957.

PURCHASE
FROM

SETTLEMENT DATE   December 10, 1957

WE HAVE ACTED AS PRINCIPAL IN THIS TRANSACTION

SALESMAN   5-T91775   J.A.McMillan

PAR VALUE	SECURITY	PRICE	AMOUNT	INTEREST	TAX	TOTAL	CONTRACT
35,000	Pembina Pipe Line Limited 6% December 1, 1975 Convertible Debentures Series "C"	106.50	37,275.00	51.78	10.50	37,316.28	677

INTEREST FROM December 1   TO December 10   DAYS   9

In this example the Pembina bonds went up 6½% in the
hour after being issued, and there was a $2,000 profit without
any investment.

In some cases where no investment is made the profits can
be amazingly high. White Weld underwrote an issue of convertible bonds of International Minerals and Chemicals in

BACHE & CO.
INCORPORATED
Founded 1879
MEMBERS NEW YORK STOCK EXCHANGE
AMERICAN STOCK EXCHANGE · TORONTO STOCK EXCHANGE
AND OTHER LEADING STOCK AND COMMODITY EXCHANGES

36 WALL STREET
NEW YORK, N. Y. 10005

NOTIFICATION OF PURCHASE OR SALE

In accordance with your instructions and subject to the terms
of transaction shown on the reverse side hereof, we have
made for your account the purchase or sale described below

TRADE DATE	BOUGHT	SOLD	DESCRIPTION		PRICE
12/21/65	4000		INTL.MINERLS&CHEM CV JJ . 4%	1/01/1991	102.00
			NET		

SETTLEMENT DATE	AMOUNT	INTEREST STATE TAX	COMMISSION	FEDERAL TAX	REG FEE POSTAGE	CANADIAN NET AMOUNT	AMERICAN NET AMOUNT
01/04/66	4,080.00	1.33				$	$ 4,081.33

R. A. DALY & COMPANY
LIMITED

44 KING ST. WEST
TORONTO
TELEPHONE 364-4441

836 DORCHESTER BLVD. W.
MONTREAL
TELEPHONE: 861-9751

MEMBERS THE TORONTO STOCK EXCHANGE . MONTREAL STOCK EXCHANGE . CANADIAN STOCK EXCHANGE . THE INVESTMENT DEALERS' ASSOCIATION OF CANADA

BOUGHT FOR YOU OR SOLD TO YOU	SOLD FOR YOU BOUGHT FROM YOU	DESCRIPTION	CODE	PRICE	MO.	DAY	YR.	REF.
	4000	INTL.MINERAL & CHEMICAL CV.SUB.DEB. 4 %JAN 1/91 INTEREST FLAT AS OF DEC 21 IF AS AND WHEN	H 959643	109 3/4 US	12	30	65	007

TRADE DATE

PRINCIPAL AMOUNT	COMMISSION	ONT. TAX	QUE TAX	U.S. TAX	CURRENCY EXCHANGE	ACCRUED INTEREST	NET AMOUNT
4,390.00							4,390.00 US

| 81 | 84 | CX | SMN | | | | | | | | | | | MO. | DAY | EX. | TB |
| T81 | 54 | 4180 | 3 | 25 | | | | | | SETTLEMENT DATE | 01 | 04 | 8 | 5 |

T. & O.E.   ACCOUNT NO.

January, 1966. They were issued at $1,020 each and within half a day were trading at just under $1,100.

Although clients of other firms received small allotments, the best allotments went to the customers of the various underwriters. An individual ordering and receiving $50,000 worth of these debentures would have made a one-day profit of $4,000.

Another excellent reason to buy convertible bonds is their resistance to decline even when all other bonds are falling. During recent years there has been a steady rise in interest rates. This in turn has produced an equally steady fall in the market price of outstanding bond issues, with the prominent exception of most convertible bonds. The very fact of their convertibility tends to hold up their price level even when all other bonds fall.

Below is a list of outstanding convertible bonds quoted in a recent paper:

CONVERTIBLE ISSUES		
Abitibi 4½, 1966	98½	100½
Canadian Util. 5¾, 1977 144		
Federal Farms 7, 1976	100	110
Home Oils 5½, 1984	114½	116½
Loblaws 4⅛, 1976	163	
Pacific Pete 5, 1977	99½	103½
Shawinigan 5½, 1972	96	98
Silverwood 5¼, 1972 127		132
Simpsons 5½, Sept. 15, 79 ..	133	
Sussman C. 7, July 15, 67 ..	99	103
Tr Canada 5, June 1, 88	144½	147½
Triad Oils, 4¾, 1971	92½	95
Westcoast Tr. 5½, 88 C	101½	103½

Unlike ordinary bond lists in the same paper, not a single convertible bond in the list has had a serious drop.

Convertible bonds in less seasoned enterprises are naturally more volatile. In 1962 Commodore Business Machines issued 7% debentures that were not only convertible but also carried a bonus of warrants. These soared upwards in the first month of January, gaining 16% as illustrated on the following page:

MEMBERS:
MONTREAL STOCK EXCHANGE
CANADIAN STOCK EXCHANGE
VANCOUVER STOCK EXCHANGE
CALGARY STOCK EXCHANGE

TELEX - LATIMER, TORONTO - 02-2565

W. D. LATIMER CO.
LIMITED
244 BAY STREET, TORONTO 1, CANADA
TELEPHONE 363-8891
MONTREAL OFFICE: 1155 DORCHESTER BLVD. W.
TELEPHONE 866-8763

TELEPHONES:
CONFIRMATIONS
363-8921
DELIVERIES
363-7137
363-8825

DATE

Jan. 17-63

WE HAVE THIS DAY | SOLD TO YOU ☐
| BOUGHT FOR YOUR ACCOUNT AND RISK ☐

PLEASE HAVE CHEQUES MADE PAYABLE AT PAR IN TORONTO

BROKER	QUANTITY	SECURITY	PRICE	GROSS AMOUNT	BROKERAGE	PROVINCIAL TAX		AMOUNT PAYABLE
						ONT.	QUE.	
	5000	Commodore Debs	103¼	5162.50			Int.	5162.50
		7% Nov. 1-74						78.63
		82 Days Intl						5241.13

HECTOR M. CHISHOLM & CO. LIMITED
MEMBERS
TORONTO STOCK EXCHANGE
MONTREAL STOCK EXCHANGE
CANADIAN STOCK EXCHANGE
82 RICHMOND ST. WEST
TORONTO 1, CANADA
TEL. 362-4731

TO ⌐

THE TORONTO STOCK EXCHANGE   DATE Feb. 6/63
THE CANADIAN STOCK EXCHANGE
WE HAVE THIS DAY **SOLD** FOR YOUR ACCOUNT ON   X THE UNLISTED MARKET   VALUE Feb 11/63

BROKER	SHARES	DESCRIPTION	PRICE	AMOUNT	COMMISSION	TAX	TOTAL
Annett & Co.	$5000.	Commodore Business Machines 7% due Nov. 1,1974 Series "A"	119.75	5987.50			5987.50
		Interest from Nov. 1 to Feb 11 - 102 days					97.81
							6085.31
					Commission		12.50
					Tax		1.50
							6071.31

E. & O.E.

PURCHASES OR SALES ARE MADE WITH THE DISTINCT UNDERSTANDING THAT ACTUAL DELIVERY IS CONTEMPLATED, AND ARE SUBJECT IN ALL RESPECTS TO THE BY-LAWS, RULES AND CUSTOMS OF THE STOCK EXCHANGE WHERE THE ORDER IS EXECUTED AND TO THE CUSTOMS OF THE BROKERAGE BUSINESS. IT IS AGREED THAT ALL SECURITIES CARRIED FROM TIME TO TIME IN THE CUSTOMER'S MARGINAL ACCOUNT, OR DEPOSITED TO PROTECT THE SAME, MAY BE LOANED BY US OR MAY BE PLEDGED BY US ON OUR GENERAL LOANS, EITHER SEPARATELY OR TOGETHER WITH SECURITIES OR OTHERS, AND EITHER TO SECURE ACCOUNTS WITHIN OR IN EXCESS OF THE AMOUNT DUE US THEREON. IT IS ALSO AGREED THAT WE RESERVE THE RIGHT TO CLOSE TRANSACTIONS WITHOUT DEMAND FOR ADDITIONAL MARGIN OR ANY OTHER NOTICE WHATSOEVER ON A STOCK EXCHANGE OR SIMILAR INSTITUTION, OR AT ANY PUBLIC OR PRIVATE SALE, WHENEVER WE DEEM IT NECESSARY FOR OUR OWN PROTECTION BY REASON OF INSUFFICIENT MARGIN OR OTHERWISE.

HECTOR M. CHISHOLM & CO. LIMITED

Subsequently these $1,000 debentures sold as high as $3,000, and very large profits were made by a number of speculators.

The convertible bonds of more seasoned companies are a much more preferable investment, however, because although the profits may be somewhat less, the risks are almost nil.

Greyhound Coach Lines in March, 1958, issued 5½% convertible debentures at $1,000 each.

In the next six months the stock market action was poor; Greyhound did not appear to be doing any better, and its stock dipped downwards. Yet the bonds held up and were worth $1,020 at the end of this difficult period.

In September of 1958 a widow friend purchased ten of these

BRANCH OFFICES

. OHIO	CLEVELAND, OHIO	MINNEAPOLIS, MINN.	SCRANTON, PA.
Y, N. Y.	COLUMBUS, OHIO	NEW HAVEN, CONN.	ST. PETERSBURGH, FLA.
THC CITY, N. J.	DETROIT, MICH.	NEW YORK CITY	SYRACUSE, N. Y.
LV HILLS, CAL.	ERIE, PA.	OIL CITY, PA.	TROY, N. Y.
ANTON, N. Y.	FORT WORTH, TEXAS	PALM BEACH, FLA.	TULSA, OKLA.
N. MASS.	GREENSBORO, N. C.	PHILADELPHIA, PA.	UTICA, N. Y.
LO. N. Y.	KANSAS CITY, MO.	RALEIGH, N. C.	WASHINGTON, D. C.
OTTR, N. C.	MIAMI, FLA.	ROCHESTER, N. Y.	WHEELING, W. VA.
GO, ILL.	MIAMI BEACH, FLA.	SAN ANTONIO, TEXAS	WILKES-BARRE, PA.
INATI, OHIO	MILWAUKEE, WISC.	SCHENECTADY, N. Y.	WINTERHAVEN, PA.

TORONTO, CANADA

LONDON, ENGLAND
GENEVA, SWITZERLAND

BACHE & CO.

MEMBERS NEW YORK STOCK EXCHANGE AND OTHER
LEADING STOCK AND COMMODITY EXCHANGES

36 WALL STREET   NEW YORK 5, I

THIS CONFIRMATION IS ISSUED BY OUR OFFICE /

360 BAY STREET   TORONTO, CAN/

Tel. EMpire 8-4871

HAVE/ TO-DAY **SOLD** TO YOU, AS PRINCIPALS:

	QUANTITY	DESCRIPTION	PRICE	AMOUNT	INTEREST	COMMISSION	DOMINION TAX	PROVINC TAX
	85,000	GREYHOUND LINESOF CDA LTD	5½/MAR 15/78 100.00		IF AS AND WHEN ISSUED			

NAME ON REQUEST

.T.

em TNI

& O. E.—Printed in Canada

CONDITIONS

IT IS AGREED THAT ALL TRANSACTIONS ARE SUBJECT TO THE RULES AND CUSTOMS OF THE EXCHANGE OR MARKET WHERE COUNTER MARKET, TO THE BY-LAWS, RULES OF FAIR PRACTICE AND CUSTOMS OF THE NATIONAL ASSOCIATION OF SECURIT AND, (AS TO ACCOUNTS ON MARGIN), OUR MARGIN CUSTOMER AGREEMENT, AND OF ALL WRITTEN AGREEMENTS BETWEEN STANCES WHICH WILL PERMIT THE COMMINGLING THEREOF WITH SECURITIES OF OTHER CUSTOMERS, AND THAT, IN THE A DELIVER TO YOU THE IDENTICAL SECURITIES PURCHASED, HELD, OR CARRIED FOR YOUR ACCOUNT, AND THAT ALL SUCH SE IS CONTEMPLATED BY BOTH PARTIES, AND PAYMENT FOR THE SECURITIES BOUGHT MUST BE RECEIVED BY US NOT LATER INTEREST IS CHARGED FROM THAT DATE TO THE DATE OF PAYMENT. IF THIS TRANSACTION IS A SALE AND DOES NOT REPR SECURITIES ARE NOT ALREADY IN OUR POSSESSION, PLEASE FORWARD THEM IMMEDIATELY TO THE OFFICE SERVICING YOUR TAX ON SECURITIES BORROWED. THIS AGREEMENT SHALL ENURE TO ANY SUCCESSORS OF BACHE & CO. RESULTING MERG CUSTOMER DOES NOT INDICATE HIS NONACQUIESCENCE IN SUCH AGREEMENT, THE NAME OF OTHER PARTY OR BROKER B

MEMBERS
TORONTO STOCK EXCHANGE
THE INVESTMENT DEALERS' ASSOCIATION OF CANADA

DOHERTY ROADHO

HEAD OFFICE

335 ▓ BAY STREET — TORON

1. TORONTO STOCK EXCHANGE   2. MONTREAL STOCK EXCHANGE - CANADIAN STOCK EXCHANGE   3. CALGARY STOCK EXCHANGE   4. V

ACTING AS AGENT WE HAVE THIS DAY **SOLD** FOR YOUR ACCOUNT AND RISK:

DATE AY MONTH	FOR VALUE DAY MONTH YEAR	SHARES	SECURITY	PRICE	AMOUNT
10 9	15 9 58	8000	GREYHOUND DEB 5½ 78 42441 INTEREST FLAT DAYS	102.00	8160

07 0450.2 07~

THIS AND ALL OTHER TRANSAC
EXECUTED AND TO THE FOLLOWING (
1. WE SHALL HAVE THE RIGHT
AMOUNT DUE BY YOU THEREON OR PC
SEPARATELY OR TOGETHER WITH OTI
2. ANY AND ALL SECURITIES AND

debentures, for which she paid $10,200. She drew 5½% interest for three years and then resold them for $17,000. This was truly the ideal investment for "widow and orphan".

Some first-grade companies have seen their convertible debentures do even better. A Simpsons (Sears Roebuck) convertible issued in 1959 for $1,000 and paying 5½% was worth $1,800 six years later.

One less common type of convertible debenture is occasionally issued by the company which is just beginning to have public ownership. Because no one is quite sure how much the stock will earn, it may be difficult to sell stock publicly at a reasonable price. The issuing corporation gets around this by issuing convertible debentures.

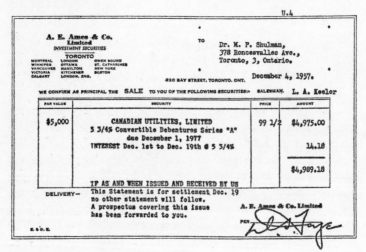

STATEMENT
AND
CONFIRMATION   NESBITT, THOMSON AND COMPANY, LIMITED

SALE TO

Dr. Morton P. Shulman,
378 Roncesvalles Ave.,
Toronto, Ontario.

290 BAY ST.,
TORONTO 1, ONT.

SETTLEMENT DATE   Aug 28/59
                  Sept 15/59

WE HAVE ACTED AS PRINCIPAL IN THIS TRANSACTION

SALESMAN AND CODE NO.
5-T-1775 J.A.McMillan

PAR VALUE	SECURITY	PRICE	AMOUNT	INTEREST		TOTAL	CONTRACT
1000	Simpson's Ltd.Conv. Debs.Ser."C" 5½% Sept 15/79.. I.A.& W.	100.00	1000.00			1000.00	P597

INTEREST FROM   TO   DAYS
          Flat as at Sept 15

DELIVERY   Cash

REGISTRATION Bearer

NESBITT, THOMSON AND COMPANY, LIMITED

PER

A COPY OF THE PROSPECTUS DESCRIBING THIS ISSUE HAS BEEN MAILED TO YOU

For example, in 1957 Canadian Utilities, the Manitoba
Power Company, decided to seek public shareholders in order
to have funds for expansion. 5¾% convertible debentures were
issued at $995 each.

U.4

A. E. Ames & Co.
Limited
INVESTMENT SECURITIES
TORONTO

MONTREAL   LONDON   OWEN SOUND
WINNIPEG   OTTAWA   ST. CATHARINES
VANCOUVER HAMILTON   NEW YORK
VICTORIA   KITCHENER BOSTON
CALGARY   LONDON, ENG.

TO

Dr. M. P. Shulman,
378 Roncesvalles Ave.,
Toronto, 3, Ontario.

820 BAY STREET, TORONTO, ONT.   December 4, 1957.

WE CONFIRM AS PRINCIPAL THE SALE TO YOU OF THE FOLLOWING SECURITIES:-   SALESMAN. L. A. Keeler

PAR VALUE	SECURITY	PRICE	AMOUNT
$5,000	CANADIAN UTILITIES, LIMITED 5 3/4% Convertible Debentures Series "A" due December 1, 1977 INTEREST Dec. 1st to Dec. 19th @ 5 3/4%	99 1/2	$4,975.00
			14.18
			$4,989.18

IF AS AND WHEN ISSUED AND RECEIVED BY US
DELIVERY— This Statement is for settlement Dec. 19
           no other statement will follow.
           A prospectus covering this issue
           has been forwarded to you.

A. E. Ames & Co. Limited

PER

Because this was a utility, earnings did not move up spectacularly as did some of our other examples, but they did move up slowly and steadily. By 1959 the debentures were worth $1,145 each, plus interest.

STATEMENT AND
CONFIRMATION

NESBITT, THOMSON AND COMPANY, LIMITED
350 BAY ST.

PURCHASE FROM
Dr. Morton P. Shulman,
378 Roncesvalles Ave.,
Toronto 3, Ontario.

TORONTO 1, ONT.

SETTLEMENT DATE   Aug 5/59
                   Aug 10/59

WE HAVE ACTED AS PRINCIPAL IN THIS TRANSACTION

SALESMAN AND CODE NO.
5-T-1775 J.A.McMillan

PAR VALUE	SECURITY	PRICE	AMOUNT	INTEREST	TAX	TOTAL	CONTRACT
10,000	Canadian Utilities Ltd. 5 3/4% Dec 1/77 Conv.	114.50	11,450.00	110.27	3.00	11,557.27	2539

INTEREST FROM June 1   TO Aug 10   DAYS 70

REGISTRATION
DELIVERY &

Growth continued at the same rate of 7% per year plus the 5¾% interest, and the same widow described earlier sold her Canadian Utilities debentures in 1962 for $1,360 each. Some widows do better than their advisors!

There is really only one pitfall to watch for in investing in a convertible bond. It must be remembered that when any bond is bought, money is being loaned by the purchaser to the corporation issuing the bond. Therefore, one should not purchase a convertible bond from any corporation from whom one would not purchase an ordinary bond, because the danger in any loan is that the borrower will not be able to repay his loan. As in any other business, an excellent criterion of whether a loan will be repaid is whether previous loans have been repaid.

A simple yardstick by which to judge a company's convertible bonds is the name of the underwriting broker. If he is a member of a major stock exchange who is doing a moderate amount of underwriting, he will not imperil his reputation by issuing stock in an unsound corporation.

One other important matter to consider is the conversion

price of the stock, that is, how many shares are received if the bond is converted into stock. If the figure is ten shares per $1,000 bond, the purchaser will be paying $100 per share if he converts. This conversion figure is usually 10% to 15% above the current price of the stock. If it is more than 20% above the current stock price, then the stock must move up a long way before the conversion feature will have any value, and the bond should not be bought. The closer the conversion figure to the current price of the stock, the more attractive is the bond.

Thus the basic rules in buying convertible bonds are as follows:

1. The underwriter should be a member of a major stock exchange.

2. The company should have a record of earnings and should have assets well in excess of the face value of the bonds.

3. The company should be in an industry where there is a possibility of growth.

4. The conversion price of the bond should be within 15% of the current price of the stock.

5. The interest paid by the bond should be within 1% of that paid on non-convertible corporation bonds.

There are several dozen such issues every year. When buying them you cannot lose. By confining your investments only to this type of issue and diversifying among a number of convertible bonds, you are certain of large profits plus good income. *Buy them!*

5

THE STOP LOSS

Several years ago a book was written about stop loss selling that became a best-seller. It purported to show how judicious use of the stop loss would minimize losses and maximize profits. The theory is very simple, and on paper it appears so certain of success that thousands have attempted to emulate the example described by the writer.

The stop loss is a requirement that a stock *must* be sold if it sells at a certain price. Thus if a stop loss order is placed to sell General Motors at $100, the broker must sell it when it reaches that price. Normally the stock would be priced higher than $100 when the order is placed, although this is not always so. Thus a broker holding such an order would not check with his client even if the order had been placed months before, but would automatically sell the General Motors at the best bid as soon as one sale had occurred at the $100 figure. The client who had placed the stop loss order may not receive $100 per share, however, for the stock will be immediately sold at the best bid then available, which might be lower than $100.

The stop loss theory is that stocks will either go up or go down and that, of course, the investor wishes to keep the ones which will go up and get rid of the ones which are going down. Therefore, at the time of purchase of each stock, a stop loss open order is placed, so that if the stock were to decline a certain percentage, the broker would automatically sell it. For example, one buys 100 shares of General Motors at $105 per share and simultaneously puts in a stop loss order at $100. If the stock reaches that point, it will be automatically sold, producing a loss of $500 plus commission and thus preventing a larger loss if the stock continues to decline. On the other hand, if the stock does not go down to $100, it will not be sold, and if it begins to climb, new stop losses are put in at higher figures. Thus if the stock reaches $110, a stop loss is put in at $105 so that the worst that can happen is that the stockholder breaks even; if the stock reaches $115, a stop loss is put in at $110, thus guaranteeing a profit, and so on upwards. It certainly sounds like an excellent idea, and it can be summed up in an old market maxim, "Cut your losses and let your profits ride." Unfortunately, as with so many other theories and maxims, if one attempts to follow this one, disaster may result.

The stop loss is a very handy tool under certain circumstances, but to base a whole stock market philosophy upon it is equivalent to giving an army an unlimited supply of anti-tank guns but no other weapons and then directing it to fight a war. It may win, but it probably won't.

There are two circumstances in which the stop loss will work; these are the stocks that go straight up and the stocks that slowly go straight down. Unfortunately, they form a very small minority of the many securities traded.

Most stocks follow a zigzag pattern, with an overall trend in one direction or another, and in these cases, which unfortunately form the vast majority, the stop loss system leads straight to bankruptcy.

Let us take an example. In early 1965 Molybdenum, listed on the American exchange, appeared to have very bright prospects. The company was the largest producer of molybdenum in the world, and it appeared that its earnings were due to take a sharp move upward. It was predicted that within one year new mine and company developments would justify a price over $60 for the stock, which was then trading at $40. The individual who purchased the stock at that time and put in a stop loss was quickly sold out, for the stock slipped to $33. If our stop loss believer tried again when the stock rallied to $35 he would once again lose, for Molybdenum then slipped to $28. In the latter part of the year the company's predicted boom did occur, and the stock did sell up over $60. Lots of people made money. A very, very few lost; they had used the stop loss system and in effect they had been whipsawed.

If one looks over the entire list of stocks on the New York exchange the pattern we find is up-down-up-down with some stocks ending much higher than they began, some much lower, and most a little higher or lower. This whipsaw action results in the stop loss believer being sold out on any weakness and not being in on the recovery. Those who follow the system faithfully, selling on weakness and buying on strength, can actually buy a stock like Brunswick, which after one year is at exactly the same price, and yet find themselves having lost their entire capital through the repeated whipsaw action.

If a security has been purchased for yield and safety there is, of course, no reason to put in a stop loss. The stop loss is normally considered when a stock has been bought in the hope of making a capital gain.

Presumably before buying such a security the prospective buyer will have decided why he is buying it; his reasons would normally be either that the company stock is reasonably priced in relation to its earnings with the prospect of further growth and increase in earnings, or else that the price of the stock is low in relation to its assets. In either case there is no reason to put in a stop loss, for if the company stock was attractive for either of the above reasons when trading at $50, it should be even more attractive at $45. Rather than selling out in panic, the investor should be buying more at the lower price and averaging down his cost.

If thus the stop loss can be eliminated from stocks purchased for safety, yield, or capital gain on a reasoned basis, there is only one group left where it should be used. This is the stock purchased for capital gain on hope and whose current price cannot be justified on known facts. These are the stocks bought on hot tips or because of rumours of a takeover. Inasmuch as the person buying for these reasons is going to lose his money anyway, he might just as well use the stop loss. After all, it doesn't matter much how you lost it after it's all over.

If all this hasn't been enough to discourage the use of the stop loss, there are three further reasons which can be added:

1. The first is human forgetfulness. There is not a broker in North America who has not had the distressing experience of phoning a client to tell him that an old stop loss order has just been exercised and having the client cry, "Oh no, I sold that stock weeks ago and forgot all about the stop loss!" The person using many stop losses needs a secretary to keep track of them, for there is nothing easier to forget than an unexecuted order which has been placed months earlier. In such cases the broker will buy back the stock, but the client must bear the loss.

2. Stop loss orders must be executed immediately when the stated selling price has been reached. Often there is not a good bid available, and the order must be executed at the best available bid. If the stock is inactive or there are a number of stop loss orders at the same price, the stock may be sold far below the stop loss figure. When Rollins Broadcasting was whipsawing in 1964, its overall upward move took it from $14 to $150, but in the middle of this upward move there was a one-day reaction from $64 down to $55. A stop loss put in at $61 was actually executed at $57, because the few other bids between $61 and $57 were filled by other orders. Thus the person who

thinks he is protecting a profit may actually be ensuring a loss.

This same experience has occurred with many other stocks. Shortly after being listed on the American Exchange, Computer Application tumbled from $30 down to $15¾. A stop loss put in at $21 was executed at $18½. The stock subsequently recovered its entire loss, but this didn't help those poor speculators who had been wiped out by relying on the stop loss.

3. Stop loss sales can be cumulative, and this is their greatest evil. Stock exchanges attempt to prevent too many stop loss orders accumulating in any one stock, but periodically such a disaster does occur in stocks that have had large percentage rises. The usual story is that in a company like Rollins, there will be a radical change which produces greatly increased earnings plus a large, rapid increase in the price of the stock. Because the market action appears so exciting, many stockholders hang on past the point where reason tells them the stock is fully priced. On the other hand, because current earnings and assets cannot possibly justify such a price for the stock, these shareholders attempt to protect themselves by putting in a stop loss order slightly under the current market price. As the stock continues to move up, more and more stop loss orders come in until there is at last a ladder of stop loss orders which may look like this on the floor of the exchange:

Current price of Rollins—$150.

Stop Loss Orders:

700	$149½
1,000	149
400	148
2,000	147
1,000	146
8,000	145
2,000	144
1,200	143
900	142
600	141
10,000	140

The specialist running the market on that particular stock at the exchange is very aware of the powder keg he is sitting on. If selling begins to come in at $150, rather than attempt to support the stock and take the risk of large financial loss, he may very well let it fall. Now the nightmare that stop losses can produce develops rapidly. The moment that Rollins trades at $149½, seven hundred shares must be automatically sold at the best possible price. As this stock is sold it produces a sale at 149, which thus automatically requires the immediate dumping of another thousand shares, and so on down the ladder. At round numbers like 145 or 140 huge amounts of stock are poured in to be sold, because it is more common for an individual to enter a stop loss at a round number.

When a stop loss order binge like this is completed, the stock may have lost one-third of its value and its shareholders up to two-thirds of their capital. Now a new evil enters the picture. Because the stock has fallen so far in price, all those shareholders holding their stock on margin will now receive a call from their brokers demanding more margin. (Margin buying of stock means that the shareholder does not have enough money to buy all the stock he wishes, and so he puts up only a certain amount, usually 50%, and borrows the rest from the broker.) This call for margin in turn produces more selling from those shareholders not wishing or able to put up more capital, and this in turn sets off more stop losses, which in turn produce more margin calls, which in turn set off more stop losses. It can be a pretty horrible picture, and although no one likes to remember it, it has happened before and can happen again.

The moral is, beware of stop loss orders.

There is only one circumstance in which the use of a stop loss can be truly justified—when the individual is leaving the country on vacation and cannot remain in touch with his investments.

With this sole exception, *do not use stop loss orders.*

6

PUTS AND CALLS

Puts and calls are options to buy or sell stock. They are the wildest form of gambling possible in the stock market. Two-thirds of those purchasing options lose their entire investment within six months. One-sixth make rapid profits unimaginable in any other field, sometimes multiplying their investment thirtyfold within a year.

Even though puts and calls offer such possibilities of riches or ruin, they are the least-understood branch of the stock market and are too often used when they should be ignored and forgotten when they are most useful. To explain puts and calls it is first necessary to define a few terms.

A call is an option to buy a stock at a predetermined price

for a definite period of time. This can vary anywhere from ten days to one year, but most calls are sold for six months and ten days, with a minority sold for 95 days or 35 days.

A put is an option to sell a stock and can be sold under the same time period as a call.

A straddle is a put and a call on the same stock at the same price.

A spread is a put and a call on the same stock at different prices.

A strap is two calls and a put on the same stock at the same price.

A strip is a call and two puts on the same stock at the same price.

These options are sold to the public through put and call brokers, most of whom are located in New York. These firms specialize only in puts and calls and normally do not handle any other form of brokerage. There is a bitter rivalry between the dozen put and call brokers because of a shortage of sellers of these options. The only thing that brings these brokers together is outside criticism, which they will band together to ward off. The rest of the time they vie strongly with one another in the keenest of competition.

Ninety-five percent of options sold are calls. The remaining 5% are puts. Spreads, straddles, straps, and strips are rarely sold to the public. Put and call brokers normally do not finance their own options; they are not selling options to the public on stocks they own themselves, but they primarily sell options which they have purchased from other members of the public.

These firms do not work on a commission like most other brokers, however. Instead they buy options and resell them for as high a markup as possible. In order to conceal from their clients the size of the markup, they have developed a stratagem known as conversion. They rarely buy puts or calls, which is what they sell. Instead they purchase primarily straddles, but also straps, strips, and spreads, and they change these into calls.

The mechanism by which this is done is highly ingenious. If

a put and call broker has received an order for two six-month calls on Ampex, he will sell them for $500 each. He will then buy from a client one six-month straddle on Ampex, for which he will probably pay $575. A straddle consists of one call and one put. He has an order for two calls so he must change the one put into a call. He does this by simultaneously purchasing one hundred shares of Ampex stock, which he holds until the option runs out. If the Ampex goes up, the two calls will be exercised; the broker already owns one call, and he also owns 100 shares of Ampex, which he gives up at the option price to satisfy the second call. If Ampex goes down the calls are, of course, not exercised. The broker gets rid of his 100 shares of stock by exercising the put which he received when he bought the straddle. Thus it doesn't really matter to the put and call broker whether the stock goes up or down. At the end of the six months, regardless of what Ampex is selling for, the calls will have run out and he will be rid of the stock either through its being called from him or by his selling it to the individual who sold him the straddle. In either case his profit is exactly the same—the $1,000 he received for the two calls, less the $575 paid for the straddle, less the carrying charges for the money spent on buying and holding the Ampex for six months. In other words there is a net profit of about $350.

The reason that the broker does not just buy two calls from a client when he receives an order to sell two calls is that, in order to make the same profit, he would only be able to pay the client $325 for each call, and the advertised sale price of $500 would soon cause cries of outrage. The broker persuades his client to sell the straddle by pointing out that in six months the Ampex will be either higher or lower; it obviously cannot be both and therefore the client is receiving the $575 for only one option, as the other will not be exercised. In effect he says, "Ampex is $25 today. If you buy the stock today and the call is exercised you will end up having sold your stock for $30.75. If, on the other hand, the put is exercised, you will end up buying another 100 shares of stock for only $19.25. In either case you must be ahead of the game." This sounds very logical, but unfortunately there are flaws in the logic.

Who buys puts and calls and why? The various put and call brokers all issue a little booklet explaining the uses and values of these options. They list a number of reasons to purchase options, most of which are not too sensible. "To protect profits after a long rise buy a put. If the stock continues to rise you will still participate in the profit. If, on the other hand, it should fall you are completely protected." Completely true, but there are much cheaper ways to protect your profits, for example, by selling if the stock dips to a certain predetermined figure. Because the premium for a put is quite prohibitive for profit protection purposes, less than 1% of options are sold for the numerous reasons listed in the booklets. The two reasons which are not listed and which actually produce 99% of option buying are these:

1. 5% of option buying comes from employees, officers, or directors of firms who may have information of a favourable nature concerning major progress or increases in profits, before such information is generally available to shareholders and the public. The advantage of buying options instead of stock is tenfold, for by laying out the same amount of money much higher profits can be made. In 1962 Shell Oil decided to expand in Canada by taking over the Canadian Oil Company. Canadian Oil was then trading for $35 per share, and the Shell board of directors had voted at their directors' meeting to offer the equivalent of $55 for every share of Canadian Oil.

At that time I was a partner in a firm which had sold large numbers of options to put and call brokers in previous years. Suddenly we were swamped with requests to buy thirty-day calls on Canadian Oil for which we were offered $3.50 per share, a huge sum when considering that a ninety-five-day call normally would sell for about that figure. These orders all emanated from New York and were unlimited; that is, they offered to buy any size.

The advantage to the buyer was obvious. If he bought 1,000

shares of Canadian Oil, his outlay would be $35,000. When the offer was announced he would get $55,000 for his stock, making a $20,000 profit. On the other hand, if he were to spend the same $35,000 for options on Canadian Oil at $3.50 each, he could buy options on 10,000 shares, on which his profit would now be 10,000 × the rise in price of the stock: $16.50 or a profit of $165,000.

This is actually what did happen. Options were purchased on many thousands of shares. The profits were immense.

A more recent example caused considerable public furor. Texas Gulf Sulphur made a huge copper discovery near Timmins. The first hole was drilled in November, 1963. Between November, 1963, and March 30, 1964, a number of calls on Texas Gulf Sulphur stock were purchased by employees. A statement was made by the company on April 12, 1964, that the drilling was too preliminary to make a decision as to whether or not an ore body existed. On April 16 the company reported 25,000,000 tons of indicated ore. During this four-day period, no calls were purchased by insiders. The stock went from $20 to $80. The option purchasers made $60,000 for every $3,000 investment. If they had bought the stock, they would have made only $9,000 on the same investment.

2. The second buyer, who produces the vast majority of option volume, is a gambler. This is the individual who, for one of a hundred different reasons, believes that a stock will go up. He has no inside knowledge, but from his studies of the particular company or stock he thinks that a move in the stock is imminent. Often he does not have the funds to purchase the stock itself but can afford the much smaller price for an option. For example, Brunswick in 1965 had had severe setbacks due to the collapse of the bowling industry, and the Brunswick stock slipped to an all-time low of $7.00. Thousands of options were now sold to various speculators who either felt that the company was going to go completely under and bought puts or else believed that the company would successfully diversify and overcome its troubles and so bought calls.

It is one of the sad facts of the market that these option buyers are more often wrong than right. It has been my experience that over two-thirds of option buyers are wrong, and the stock goes in the wrong direction. Thus two-thirds of the capital spent in buying options goes straight down the drain. This is not as bad as it seems, however, for the individual option represents only a small portion of the price of the same amount of stock, and the dollar loss on an option is often much smaller than the loss on an equivalent amount of stock, even though the percentage loss may be higher.

To take an example, Universal Match in 1960 was trading at $50 per share. Those who bought six-month calls, for which they paid $800 per one hundred shares, lost 100% of this, or $800. If, however, the same purchaser had bought one hundred shares of stock that slipped all the way from $50 down to $15, he would have lost $3,500. This case illustrates the one great honest advantage of options. They should be purchased in cases where the company under consideration is undergoing a massive expansion or other change which may or may not work out well. In these cases it is better to gamble a little money through a call than to buy the stock itself and risk losing much more.

Syntex at the beginning of 1966 was in exactly the same position. The stock, because of its birth control pill, moved vigorously from $70 to $210 and was then split. Earnings were increasing astronomically, and the future of the company appeared bright indeed. It was expected that the Vatican would shortly announce permission for Roman Catholics to use the Pill, and Syntex would be the prime financial gainer in such a change. But what if the Vatican decision was to put off, or worse, to turn down the Pill? In such a case a six-month call option is the ideal compromise. Rather than invest $21,000 in buying one hundred shares of stock, the cautious speculator bought an option for $2,000, thus limiting his loss but not hindering his possible profit.

This is the sensible use of options, to enable a speculator to gamble in highly volatile stocks while at the same time limiting the risk to small amounts of capital.

Who sells stock options? This is the best-kept secret of the business, and put and call brokers guard the names of their sellers as closely as the United States government guards Fort Knox. Sellers are the lifeblood of puts and calls; there are not enough of them, and the few sizeable ones are continually courted by the brokers as Guinevere was by Lancelot. In 1958 a young broker, Wilfred Posluns, formed a partnership with me to sell these options. Soon several New York put and call brokers were phoning long distance each day, forwarding expensive presents, and offering invitations to visit New York and indulge in the various pleasures available in that city. In our innocence we thought that this was because of our delightful personalities!

The shortage of sellers is due to three reasons:

The first is the vast amount of money necessary to sell options. Let us suppose that a new seller wishes to sell only one option per day. Before his first option runs out in six months he will have sold 135 options, for which he will have received $25,000 in premiums. At this point he will have sold options on $285,000 worth of stock, which he will either have bought or must remain prepared to buy.

The second reason is that an option seller must enjoy the ancient art of bargaining. Because there is no fixed price for options, put and call brokers will try to buy from their sellers as cheaply as possible. Thus for a straddle on Ampex for which they could afford to pay up to $800 and make money and which they really expect to buy for $600, they will initially bid $400 and will then bargain with their seller until they finally agree on a price. In today's fixed price society this bargaining is almost impossible for many people. We complained many times to the New York dealers that this method was demeaning and undignified. We begged them to give us their best price at once so as to save time, but they just laughed and continued as before. I really think that the striking of the bargain gives them as much pleasure as the actual profit.

One day I accepted a price as initially offered by a partner of one of the largest New York put and call brokers. The dismay in this man's voice was equivalent to that of the hawker in an Arabian bazaar whose first price has been accepted—perhaps a little more profit but not nearly so much fun.

The third reason is that, despite the huge investment in selling puts and calls, there is no guarantee of financial success. In fact it is just as easy to lose money as make it in this risky business. The reason is that most options are sought on highly volatile stocks, and the seller of options soon finds that some of his stocks go 'way up and some go 'way down. Unfortunately unlike the buyer of these stocks or options, the ones that go up do not counterbalance the ones that go down, because the option seller does not get the profit on the ones that do go up. Regardless of how much a stock goes up or down, the seller receives only the option price. But in those stocks that go 'way down, the seller can be stuck with his original stock purchase, which he dare not sell until the option has run out and in which he can take a very severe loss.

In order to successfully sell options of this type, the seller must have an intimate knowledge of the market and must also keep in close touch with the individual stocks on which he has sold options in order to protect his investments. Thus most option sellers, if they have sold a call on, say, Ampex at $25 for a premium of $2 per share, and if the price falls the full limit of their option, will sell their stock, hoping to at least break even on that particular deal. They hold their position on the stocks that go up and make the full option as profit.

This system works fairly well most of the time. When it doesn't work, the results can be disastrous, as in whipsawing stocks. Whipsawing occurs when a stock moves up and down over a broad price range several times during the life of an option. Although the stock price may finally end up exactly where it started, the option seller can lose huge sums in the meantime. Molybdenum is the horrible example that always comes to my mind. In 1958 I was the veteran of two years of option selling and had quite convinced myself that I knew all there was to know about the business. Molybdenum was trading quietly at $45 on the American exchange, and I was very happy to sell puts and calls on the stock, slowly at first, and then when the weeks went by, much more rapidly. Then slowly but steadily Molybdenum began to slip, going down at the rate of 50¢ per day. When it got to $40 I began to unload my stock. When it reached $35 I got rid of all of it. Then to my dismay the stock began to climb again at the same rate. When it reached $40 I started to buy again. At $45 I was buying rapidly. At $50 I completed my buying. Now with only one month left for the options to run, to my horrified disbelief the stock began to fall. When the options finally all ran out Molybdenum was $45, exactly where it had started. The balance sheet was somewhat depressing. Premiums taken in $12,000—Carrying charges $2,000—Loss on trading $36,000. Overall loss $26,000. To my partner's credit he didn't say a word. I learned the most important single fact to be remembered when selling options. Never sell an option in a company with whose stock and business you are not familiar.

The one group who can make money by selling options are very wealthy people who have a constant large portfolio. By selling options against this portfolio, they can significantly increase their earnings without increasing their risk.

All others would do well to avoid this very dangerous speculation. There have been some very spectacular bankruptcies occur as a result of large-scale option selling.

In summary, leave option selling for someone else. Option buying can be very profitable under certain limited circumstances, but in general puts and calls can be summed up in one word: *Avoid!*

7

CONVERTIBLE PREFERRED

Convertible bonds are ideal investments. Convertible preferreds are *almost* ideal, and they should not be overlooked, for they offer great possibilities of capital gains with a very limited risk.

Ownership of a company is represented by common stock, which gives both the privileges and danger of ownership. The privileges are the right to vote and appoint the management of the company plus the reward of participating in increased profits. The danger is the possibility of losing money if the company does not do well and earnings fall. Preferred stock is a compromise security between high risk common stock and low or no risk bonds. Preferred stockholders receive a fixed annual dividend, which is usually higher than the yield paid to the company's bondholders, but they do not have a vote unless their dividend is in arrears, and they do not participate in any increase in earnings. Unlike a bondholder, a preferred stockholder cannot be certain of getting his capital back on a fixed date, for preferred stock does not run for a specified length of time, although it can be redeemed if the company so decides. Normally preferreds are only redeemed when money is freely available and can be borrowed by the company for less interest than is being paid on the outstanding preferred.

The preferred shareholder has two advantages over the common stockholder. The preferred dividends must be paid every year before the company considers any payment to its common shareholders. These preferred dividends are usually cumulative, and if one year a firm cannot pay its preferred dividend, it must save up the missed money in succeeding years and pay off all missed preferred dividends before beginning any payments on its common stock. The other advantage is that in any windup, bankruptcy, or dissolution of the company, preferred shareholders must be paid the value of their stock in full before anything can be paid to the common stockholders. However, preferred shareholders rank behind bondholders and all other creditors in such a windup.

Thus the preferred share has two real advantages:

1. Temporarily increased yield.
2. Preference over the common share in receipt of dividends and in case of a windup of the company.

These relatively minor advantages do not compensate for the very serious disadvantages:

1. No participation in increased company earnings as with common stock.
2. No certainty of capital return as with bonds.
3. The likelihood of preferred stock being redeemed if interest rates fall.
4. No protection against inflation.

Therefore, the wise investor will normally completely avoid

preferred stocks, with one major exception, the convertible preferred.

Just as the convertible bond was developed to meet some of the drawbacks of bonds, similarly convertible preferred stock was developed for the company that wished to issue preferred stock but found that to do so would require a terribly high interest rate. Instead, prospective buyers can be attracted by the lure of convertibility. A convertible preferred stock carries the right to convert it into common stock, thus giving the relative safety and assured yield of the preferred stock plus the possibility of making capital gains if the common stock goes up.

A typical example of a convertible preferred was issued by Allis Chalmers in May 1965. Money was becoming tighter at that time and yields were rising. Rather than pay 5% or more for the necessary money, Allis Chalmers issued a 4.2% convertible preferred at $100 per share.

Each share of this new preferred was convertible into three and a half shares of Allis Chalmers common stock, which was then trading on the New York Stock Exchange at $28 per share. If the common stock were to move up in price over $30 per share, it is clear that the convertible feature would have given the preferred an increased value over its $100 issue price. If, for example, the Allis Chalmers common stock doubled to $56 per share, the convertible preferred would be worth almost $200 per share.

What happens to convertible preferreds when the common stock goes down?' Immediately after Allis Chalmers made their issue, the general stock market weakened, and Allis Chalmers common stock quickly lost 20% of its value. The preferred certainly went down, but not nearly as much, and at its worst it lost only 6%, going to $94 per share. This is because the assured 4.2% dividend plus the convertibility feature put a floor on the stock price and acted to retard its fall.

However, the delightful feature of convertible preferreds is that although they do not fall nearly as fast as their common stock, they do go up just as quickly. Thus when the Allis Chalmers common stock recovered to $34, the preferred quickly jumped to $120 per share.

This is a perfect example of how, by buying a convertible preferred, one can enjoy a good yield, relative safety, and still make a capital gain. In other words, it is possible to have the advantages of common stock without the very serious risks normally entailed.

There is one pitfall which buyers of convertible preferreds must avoid——the purchase of common stock disguised as convertible preferred. This not uncommon ploy is used to issue a so-called preferred stock that carries the same high risk as ordinary common stock. It must be remembered that preferred stock is preferred only in relation to the company's common stock and is safe only in relation to the financial worth of the common stock. If a company's net worth is $100,000,000 after the value of all outstanding debts including bonds is deducted, and if in addition there is outstanding $20,000,000 worth of preferred stock, this leaves a value of $80,000,000 to the common stock. This $80,000,000 serves to protect the preferred shareholders and would have to be dissipated before there was any risk to the preferred. In such a circumstance, the preferred is quite safe. On the other hand, if a company's net worth is $25,000,000 after the face value of all debts is deducted and there is the same $20,000,000 worth of preferred outstanding, then the common stock has a value of only $5 million. In this case a loss of $5 million by the company would immediately imperil the preferred, which has very little protection. Preferreds of this type will fluctuate just as wildly and widely as any common stock. There are certain circumstances under which common stocks can be very profitable, but it should be remembered that the risk is just as great as any possible profit and that such risk is unnecessary when so many other safe, high-potential profit situations are available.

An example of a convertible preferred which carried all the risks of common stock was the issue of Rockower 6% cumulative redeemable convertible 1st preferred on November 8, 1961, at $10 per share.

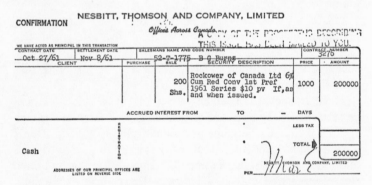

This company was engaged in the sale of clothing through outlets in the Tower Discount Stores. There was no common stock in the hands of the public, as it was all held by principals and management of Rockower. The equity represented by the common stock was very small, so that the convertible preferred behaved as irrationally as any common stock could. In late 1961 the stocks of discount houses were behaving very well; their sales and stocks were soaring, and optimism for the future was unlimited. Within two months Rockowers preferred stock soared up over $28.

CONFIRMATION

NESBITT, THOMSON AND COMPANY, LIMITED

Offices Across Canada

WE HAVE ACTED AS PRINCIPAL IN THIS TRANSACTION

CONTRACT DATE	SETTLEMENT DATE	SALESMANS NAME AND CODE NUMBER		CONTRACT NUMBER
Jan 4/62	Jan 9/62	B.G. Burns 52-T-1775		11303

CLIENT	PURCHASE	SALE	SECURITY DESCRIPTION	PRICE	AMOUNT
	100		Rockower of Canada Ltd. 6% Cum Red Conv 1st Pref 1961 Series $10 p.v.	2815	281500

ACCRUED INTEREST FROM ____ TO ____ — DAYS

LESS TAX 200

TOTAL 281300

ADDRESSES OF OUR PRINCIPAL OFFICES ARE LISTED ON REVERSE SIDE

PER

In retrospect it is quite clear that Rockower was never worth anywhere near $28, but excesses of enthusiasm had made investors and speculators lose their heads. Suddenly everyone was shaken back to reality by the sudden collapse of many discount chains.

JACKSON, McFADYEN SECURITIES LI

MEMBERS:
TORONTO STOCK EXCHANGE
MONTREAL STOCK EXCHANGE
CANADIAN STOCK EXCHANGE
THE INVESTMENT DEALERS' ASSOCIATION OF CANADA
11 ADELAIDE ST. WEST — TORONTO 1, ONTARIO

TELEPHONE
EM. 4-5161.   No. 7479

WE HAVE THIS DAY **BOUGHT** FOR YOUR ACCOUNT AND RISK ON THE TORONTO STOCK EXCHANGE
(SUBJECT TO THE RULES AND REGULATIONS OF THE EXCHANGE WHERE EXECUTED)   DATE

VALUE DATE	CLIENT'S NAME	SHARES	SECURITY	PRICE	AMOU
FEB 6 6		200	ROCKOWER OF CDA-PFD	5.3/8	1 C

Although this did not really affect Rockower in any way, the loss of optimism for the stock engineered a rapid rush to sell, and within a year Rockower preferred was down to $5.

Interestingly, those who sold Rockower at $5 were just as wrong as those who bought at $28. Rockower itself was never in danger of going bankrupt and it gave a 12% yield when selling at $5. Gradually confidence returned, and the stock slowly moved upward to its current level of $15.

This story has been related only to show what should *not*

happen with a preferred. If a preferred is really preferred as to safety and earnings, it can fluctuate upwards as did Rockower but should never plunge to 50% of its issue price. Let us now look at a proper convertible preferred. There are hundreds to choose from.

In late January, 1964, Federal Pacific Electric, a large U.S. manufacturer of heavy electrical equipment, decided to sell off part of their Canadian subsidiary, F.P.E. Pioneer Electric, as requested by the Canadian Minister of Finance of all U.S. parent firms. Federal Pacific intended to keep control of the subsidiary, so they retained all of the B common stock and issued to the public A, or partially preferred, stock plus a 5½% $50 convertible preferred. This issue was initially made in the form of units consisting of 2 convertible preferred shares at $50 and 5 shares of Class A at $10, each unit selling for $150.

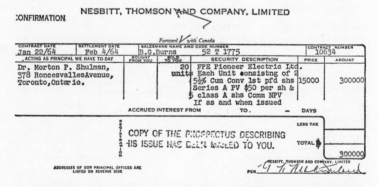

This issue illustrates a number of basic points in investing in the market, particularly in the preferred field, and it is the perfect illustration of a "can't-lose" situation. It involved free riding, hot issues, and spinoffs, which are discussed in other chapters, and it presented an ideal convertible preferred which could only go up.

An examination of the prospectus when the company first made this issue was an unusual delight. The company stock had been previously held completely by its U.S. parent, which had had some troubled years. The Canadian subsidiary, however, had had only good years, and each year its earnings increased. In addition future prospects were excellent, and the company had a large backlog of orders.

The capitalization of F.P.E. was very unusual. It consisted of common shares called B shares; A shares, which were preferred as to a 56¢ dividend; and a 5½% convertible first preferred.

The A shares held preference to the B shares in initial dividends, being entitled to 56¢ per share per annum before the B received any payment. If the company declared dividends on the B shares in excess of 56¢ per year, the A had to receive an equal amount above this preferred 56¢. Thus the A stock was actually a participating preferred—preferred as to dividends, but participating in increased earnings if the company did well.

The B stock was all held by the parent U.S. company; the parent company was taking the primary and major risk. This in itself was a good reason to buy the A stock.

There were, however, far more important reasons. In 1963 the company had earned 90¢ per combined A and B share. Of this, the A shares had been paid 56¢ each, while the B shares received only 4¢. The excess 52¢ the B had not received was returned to the company's treasury where it was of value to both classes of stock, thus increasing the true earnings of the A stock to about $1.50.

Thus the A stock was preferred as to dividends, would participate in any improvement in the company's fortunes, paid a 5.6% dividend, and yet was being issued at only $10, less than seven times earnings. Common stocks in growth companies like this one usually trade at twenty or twenty-five times earnings and give a yield of between 3 and 4%. Therefore this A stock was an outstanding buy.

The convertible preferred was even more outstanding. This stock, issued at $50 per share, gave a yield of 5½% and was convertible into 4 shares of Class A stock. Earnings of the company per preferred share was $12, so the stock was being issued at less than five times earnings. So here we had a preferred whose earnings were so high that there was literally no risk in its purchase, giving a 5½% yield and, even more remarkable, being convertible into a Class A participating stock.

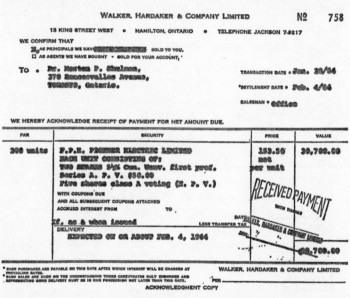

It was obvious that these stocks were being issued at prices far below their true worth, yet the public interest was almost nil. I think the reason is that this type of issue is considerably more complicated than the average type of glamour stock which the public flocks to buy in order to get "action" more quickly. Unfortunately, the action is often in the wrong direction.

The units were traded for only a very few days before being split up into their A stock and convertible preferred components. During these few days the free riders who had bought the units in order to grab a quick profit dumped them, thereby giving long-term investors a wonderful chance to buy them cheaply.

In February the units ceased to trade and their two components began to sell separately, the Class A at $10⅛ and preferred at $52¾. Although these prices were higher than the issue price, they were still very obviously ridiculously low to anyone who had taken the trouble to study convertible and participating preferreds. Fortunately for the rest of us, the public ignored these stocks completely, and they continued to be available at these very low prices for months.

HECTOR M. CHISHOLM & CO. LIMITED

MEMBERS
TORONTO STOCK EXCHANGE
MONTREAL STOCK EXCHANGE
CANADIAN STOCK EXCHANGE
82 RICHMOND ST. WEST
TORONTO 1, CANADA
TEL. 362-4731

TO┌ Dr. M. Shulman,

				THE TORONTO STOCK EXCHANGE	DATE	Mar. 10/64
XX				THE CANADIAN STOCK EXCHANGE		
WE HAVE THIS DAY **BOUGHT** FOR YOUR ACCOUNT ON				THE UNLISTED MARKET	VALUE	Mar. 13 /64

BROKER	SHARES	DESCRIPTION	PRICE	AMOUNT	COMMISSION	TAX	TOTAL
	100	FPE Pioneer Electric					
		"A" Common	10 1/8	1012.50	25.00		1037.50

IF THIS TRANSACTION HAS BEEN EXECUTED ON A STOCK EXCHANGE IT IS SUBJECT TO THE BY-LAWS, REGULATIONS AND CUSTOMS OF SUCH STOCK EXCHANGE AND OF ANY CLEARING HOUSE INVOLVED.

NESBITT, THOMSON AND COM

WE HAVE ACTED AS AGENTS IN THIS TRANSACTION

Forward with Canada

DATE CONTRACT NO.	*	BOUGHT FOR YOUR ACCOUNT	SOLD FOR YOUR ACCOUNT	DESCRIPTION	PRICE	AMOUNT DEBIT	CREDIT
MAR 12 64 35564-3	32		50	F.P.E. PIONEER PFD.	52¾	2637 50	

NAME OF BROKER SUPPLIED ON REQUEST

ADDRESSES OF OUR PRINCIPAL OFFICES ARE

By the end of 1964 the company's sales and earnings had jumped considerably. Earnings per Class A and B shares were now up to $1.10. True earnings per Class A share were actually much higher, because the B shares were still not receiving an equal share of the dividends. The original underwriting broker now began to recommend the purchase of these stocks to its clients, and they began to creep higher. The public, however, continued to ignore F.P.E., and by May, 1965, the Class A was still available at $13 per share and the preferred at $58.50.

By the summer of 1965 considerable buying began to come

HECTOR M. CHISHOLM & CO. LIMITED
MEMBERS
TORONTO STOCK EXCHANGE
CANADIAN STOCK EXCHANGE
82 RICHMOND ST. WEST
TORONTO 1, CANADA
TEL. 362-4731

TO⌐ Dr. M. Shulman

		XX	THE TORONTO STOCK EXCHANGE			DATE	May 14/65	
WE HAVE THIS DAY **BOUGHT** FOR YOUR ACCOUNT ON			THE CANADIAN STOCK EXCHANGE					
			THE UNLISTED MARKET			VALUE	May 19/65	

BROKERS ON REQUEST	SHARES	DESCRIPTION	PRICE	AMOUNT	COMMISSION	TAX	TOTAL
Midland	25	FPe Pioneer Electric					
		Pref.	58.50	1462.50	10.00		1472.50
	75	"	59.00	4425.00	30.00		4455.00

into F.P.E. from a number of friends to whom I pointed out
this great opportunity, and the Class A moved up to 15½ and
the preferred to $62.

HECTOR M. CHISHOLM & CO. LIMITED
MEMBERS
TORONTO STOCK EXCHANGE
CANADIAN STOCK EXCHANGE
82 RICHMOND ST. WEST
TORONTO 1, CANADA
TEL. 362-4731

TO⌐ Dr. M. Shulman

		XX	THE TORONTO STOCK EXCHANGE			DATE	Aug. 9/65
ᴡE HAVE THIS DAY **BOUGHT** FOR YOUR ACCOUNT ON			THE CANADIAN STOCK EXCHANGE				
			THE UNLISTED MARKET			VALUE	Aug. 12/65·

BROKERS ON REQUEST	SHARES	DESCRIPTION	PRICE	AMOUNT	COMMISSION	TAX	TOTAL
Chis	50	F.P.E. Pioneer Electric Pref.	62.00	3100.00	22.50		3122.50

E. & O.E.   HECTOR M. CHISHOLM & CO. LIMITED

At the end of 1965 F.P.E. brought out its annual report,
showing that earnings per combined class A and B shares were
now at a record $1.60, while sales were at a new peak and the
company now had a backlog of orders larger than ever before.

Suddenly and belatedly, as always happens with these issues,
the general public became aware of F.P.E. Pioneer Electric,
and generalized buying poured into the stock. The Class A
sold up to $19 and the preferred to $75.

At these levels the Class A stock had given a capital gain of
90% in less than two years and the preferred 50%. Yet during

this time both stocks had given a yield of 5½%, and even more amazing, the Class A carried very little risk and the preferred absolutely none. Here was another situation where everyone made money.

The free riders made a profit without any investment; speculators in hot issues did the same; those who bought early made money; those who bought late made money; those who held on made more; those seeking income received a high yield; those seeking security ran no risk; those seeking capital gains did many times better than those who bought the average common stock. Unusual? Yes—but not unique. There are opportunities like this every year in the United States and Canada. In some cases the profits are unbelievably high. In no case should the risk involve more than 10% of the invested capital.

In May, 1959 Massey Ferguson, the huge farm implement manufacturer, issued a 5½% convertible preferred stock at $100 per share.

Each preferred share was convertible into 5⅞ shares of common stock, which was then trading at $13.

Inasmuch as through conversion the common stock would cost $17.50 per share, there was no point in immediate conversion unless the common moved above $17.50 per share. Actually the common languished, because Massey Ferguson's earnings did not immediately expand, and the common stock

Guaranty Trust Company of Canada
Toronto, Ontario   OFFICE DATE   May 1/59   19

PARTICULARS	AMOUNT
Purchase for your account 40 shrs. Massey-Ferguson 5½% Pfd. Stock @ $100.	.4,000.00

┌ ┐
Dr. Morton Shulman   TOTAL
378 Roncesvalles,   ADVICE ONLY   THIS IS A DUPLICATE OF A CHARGE
Toronto, Ontario   MADE TO YOUR ACCOUNT
                              Account No.   9610
└ ┘
                                             TRUST OFFICER OR ACCOUNTANT

FORM 48

IN ACCOUNT WITH

price drifted downwards, losing over ½ of its value to $5.50 per share. The preferred was protected by its dividend and conversion feature from such a collapse, although it did at its worst sell down to $90. Then the expected growth in sales and expansion in earnings began, and the common moved up all the way to $35. Ultimately all of the preferred was converted into common stock, but patient holders found that each preferred share, which had cost an original $100, was worth $200 six years later. In addition it had given a yield of 5½% while this excellent capital gain had occurred.

Because convertible preferreds offer all the best features of investments with few of the drawbacks, they are eagerly sought after when new issues appear. As a result there are great opportunities to make an immediate capital gain without taking any risk or making any investment, because regardless of their ultimate course, these stocks usually sell up to a premium immediately after being issued.

In this case there was an immediate profit of $148 without a cent having been invested.

Because of the likelihood of large capital gains without the danger of loss of capital, convertible preferreds are ideal subjects for free riders (see Chapter 9) as well as for investors and speculators. Intelligently chosen, such a purchase must be a successful one.

HECTOR M. CHISHOLM & CO. LIMITED
82 RICHMOND ST. WEST
TORONTO 1, CANADA
EMPIRE 2-6731

TRADE DATE - Apr. 19/65
SETTLEMENT DATE - Apr. 22/65

AS ARRANGED THROUGH

/E HAVE PLEASURE IN CONFIRMING THAT
- ☒ AS PRINCIPALS, WE HAVE TODAY SOLD TO YOU
- ☐ AS AGENTS, WE HAVE TODAY PURCHASED FOR YOU
- ☐ AS AGENTS, WE HAVE TODAY SOLD TO YOU

AMOUNT	SECURITY	PRICE	VALUE
100	Columbia Cellulose $1.20 Cum. Red. Conv. Pref.	26.00	2600.00
	INTEREST FROM TO *DAYS		
			2600.00

DELIVERY

Retain this statement for income tax purposes—under the act, accrued
interest received must be included in taxable income and accrued
interest paid may be deducted from the relative interest when received.

E. & O.E.

WE ASSURE YOU OF OUR APPRECIATION OF THIS BUSINESS

HECTOR M. CHISHOLM & CO. LIMITED

GREENSHIELDS INCORPORATED
GREENSHIELDS LTD.

WE CONFIRM THAT YOU HAVE
BOUGHT   SOLD

	SOLD	DESCRIPTION	CODE	PRICE	NO.	DAY	YR
	100	COLUMBIA CELL.1.20 CV PR IF, AS, AND WHEN ISSUED	169524	27 1/2	04	22	65

PAYMENT IS DUE
ON
SETTLEMENT DATE

PRINCIPAL AMOUNT	COMMISSION	PROVINCIAL TAXES ONT. QUE.	U.S. TAX	EXCHANGE	INTEREST		
2,750.00	2.00					2,748.00	04 29 65
							MO. DAY YR

EX   YR
4 6 72 47 2910 9 AT

71/72   ACCOUNT NO.   SLMH.

ABE MARKET AND TRANSACTION CODES

NET AMOUNT
538

ALL CHEQUES, INSTRUCTIONS, ETC.
SHOULD BE SENT TO THE OFFICE
SERVICING YOUR ACCOUNT.

In summary, convertible preferreds can be ideal investments. Here are the points to look for in such a purchase:

1. The company must have a large common stock investment so as to give safety to its preferred.

2. The conversion price should be no more than 15% higher than the current price of the common stock.

3. The yield of the convertible preferred should be a reasonably high one—certainly no more than 1% below current yields on non-convertible preferreds.

4. The company must be a sound one with a record of earnings and possibilities of growth.

If these four factors are present, large profits will result.

8

WARRANTS

Warrants are options to buy stock. They differ from calls in that calls are short-term options which are created and sold by individuals, whereas warrants are longer-running options issued by a company itself. Another major difference is that warrants are usually listed on a stock exchange and can always be resold, but calls once purchased normally cannot be resold. The advantage of a call is that it can be purchased on any stock; the advantage of a warrant is that because it was not created to satisfy an individual request, it is much cheaper.

Warrants are without doubt the most volatile security that can be purchased. It is not uncommon for the warrant on a stock to go up as much as tenfold while, during the same period, the stock itself has merely doubled. In Chapter 2 there was a detailed write-up on Newconex, showing how the stock went from $5 to $9 in one month. Yet in the same period Newconex warrants went from $1 to $5. It is this rapid jump in price that gives warrants their great attraction, for it presents the possibility of huge profits from small investments. The rapid price gain is due to *leverage*.

Leverage is the first thing to look for in assessing a warrant; leverage refers to the amount that a warrant will move up if the stock doubles in price. For example, when Newconex stock was trading at $5, its warrant was trading at $1 and presented the right to buy stock at $5. At this level the warrant had no real value but presented a potential value if the stock moved above $5. When the stock moved up to $9, the warrant now had a real value of the market price ($9) less the option price of $5; in other words the warrant now had a real value of $4. If the stock moved to $10, the warrant would have a real value of $5. Thus if the stock doubled from $5 to $10, the warrant would go up at least five times, from $1 to $5. Its *leverage factor* would be 5:1.

The major reason for buying a warrant is its leverage. The leverage figure should never be less than 2:1. Ideally it should be at least 3:1 or 4:1. Normally the highest leverage is found in warrants that have no real value; that is, where the stock is trading at or below the option price of the warrant (for example, Newconex before it moved up above $5). Once the warrants develop real value, their leverage rapidly disappears. If the leverage is less than 2:1, the warrant should not be bought, regardless of all other circumstances.

Let us now consider Newconex stock at $9 while the warrant is at $5. If the stock doubles to $18, the warrant would be worth $13, so the leverage is now less than 3:1. On higher-priced warrants there may be no leverage at all, in that a doubling of the stock price will no more than double the warrant price.

Volatility is the second thing that should be considered in assessing a warrant. There is no sense in buying a warrant with excellent leverage if the stock is a very stable one with no chance of moving up in price. The stock must have potential volatility, in that there must be a good possibility of a fast upward move due to increased earnings or some major change in the company's business. If the company stock does not have volatility or potential volatility, the warrant should not be bought, regardless of how cheaply it is priced.

Time is the third factor to consider in buying a warrant. Practically all warrants have a fixed life and are due to expire on a certain date, varying anywhere from one to twenty years after issue, although a very few are perpetual and never expire. The longer the warrant has to run, the more valuable it is, and as the time of expiry approaches the warrant will gradually lose any premium in its price and slip downward to its real value. If that real value is zero, the warrant may expire without having any value, and so this pitfall must be avoided. *When a warrant is purchased, there should be sufficient time remaining in its life to allow its stock to move up enough to increase the value of the warrant by at least 100%.* As a general rule it is unwise to purchase any warrant that has less than two years to run, and it is best to purchase warrants that have a minimum of five years of life remaining.

If these three factors are all considered before a warrant is purchased, financial profits are certain. Members of the public lose vast sums every year by ignoring one or more of these factors. Warrants present the greatest financial opportunities in the market and also the greatest risks. The risks are unnecessary ones.

An ideal example of the perfect warrant was that of the Investment Company of America. This is a mutual fund which has perpetual warrants outstanding, each of which allows the purchase of eleven shares (approximately) at the price of $10.48 each. In 1954 these warrants were trading at $3¼, having moved up from 50¢. The three factors of leverage, volatility, and time were all favourable, and the warrants were an obvious buy.

IN ACCOUNT WITH

DOHERTY ROADHOUSE & CO.

−1

255 BAY STREET
TORONTO

DR. M. SHULMAN
378 RONCESVALLES AVE.
TORONTO   ONT.
109-B.

DATE	NO. OF SHARES BOT. OR RECEIVED	NO. OF SHARES SOLD OR DELIVERED	S T O C K	PRICE	DEBIT	CREDIT	BALANCE
1954 MAY- JUNE			BALANCE				5,968 00
16,	100,		INV. CO. OF AMER. WTS.	3¼	326 79		
	200,		DO	03¾	727 88		
,	100,		DO	03¾	363 94		
.	400,		DO	03¾	1,455 76		14,260 45
17,	200,		INV. CO. OF AMER. WTS.	03¾	777 44		
		200	ONT. JOCKEY CLUB WTS.	74		144 00	14,893 89
21,	200,		INV. CO. OF AMER. WTS.	400	802 00		

FOR AUDIT PURPOSES—Please communicate full particulars of any difference in the above account direct to Audit Department, Box 67, General Delivery, Toronto, Canada

B.S.LTD. 26424
E.'& O. E.

THIS ACCOUNT WILL BE CONSIDERED CORRECT IF NO REPORT IS RECEIVED WITHIN TEN DAYS

404

The leverage in this warrant was truly outstanding. The stock was then trading at about $8. If it were to double to $16, the warrant would have a real value of $16 less $10.48 (the option price) multiplied by 11, because each warrant allowed the purchase of eleven shares of stock. This would give a real value of $60.50. The warrant was then trading at $3.25, so the leverage factor was an amazing 18:1. I have never seen a higher leverage factor.

The time factor was also the best possible one, for the warrants were perpetual; they would never run out. This is very rare.

The volatility factor was the weakest of the three in this case. Because the Investment Company of America is a mutual fund, its value would, of course, move up with a strong market. However, the company follows the practice of paying out all its realized gains in distributions to its shareholders. This slows the rate of growth but does not completely remove the volatility, because gains are not paid out until realized, that is, until or unless the stocks on which there are profits are sold by the fund. In any case the reduced volatility was certainly overshadowed by the tremendous leverage and time factors.

When warrants are bought in this scientific manner it is almost impossible for the purchaser to lose, and within two years, although the stock of Investment Company of America had moved up less than 20%, the warrants had jumped to four times their 1954 price, and I was happy to sell many of my warrants between $14 and $15.

JN30   56   DR MORTON P SHULMAN

DATE	BOUGHT, RECEIVED, OR LONG	SOLD, DELIVERED, OR SHORT	DESCRIPTION	PRICE OR REFERENCE #	DEBIT
MY 31			BAL FWD 05 31 56		
JN O 1	1 5		UTS WESTCOAST TRANSM	126¼	1922 27
JN O 1			100DEB3CAP 88 5½ A20		
JN O 4		100	WTS INVESTMENT CO AM	14¼	
JN O 4		100	WTS INVESTMENT CO AM	14¼	
JN O 4		200	WTS INVESTMENT CO AM	14¼	
JN O 4		100	WTS INVESTMENT CO AM	14½	

Actually, looking back, I realize that I was very wrong to sell, because even when the warrants were up to $14, the three factors were still very favourable. The time and volatility factors had not changed, of course, and the leverage was still very good. The stock was at $10, so if it doubled to $20 this would put a value of $20 − $10.48 × 11 on the warrant or a value of $104.50 for each warrant. Divide this by $14 and the leverage factor is 7:1 which is much better than can usually be found.

At the time of writing, the stock is $14 and the warrant has jumped to $32. Even at this $32, a figure up tenfold from my original purchase, these warrants are a tremendous buy. The volatility and time factors are still the same, so the leverage is the crucial factor. If the stock doubles to $28 the warrant will be worth $28 − $10.48 × 11 or $192. Divide this by $32 and we get the leverage figure of 6:1 which is higher than can be received on any other long-life warrant.

Thus we have the amazing situation where a stock has gone from $8 to $14 in a decade and yet its warrant has jumped from $3.25 to $32 and still remained a bargain. The Investment Company of America warrant truly exemplifies the romance and rewards possible in warrant purchases.

Where do warrants come from? Why do companies issue them? What is the cheapest way to buy them?

Many warrants were legacies of the depression and a few of these are still trading. In the early thirties, when thousands of companies went bankrupt and were reorganized, in many cases not only was there no equity for the shareholders, but in addition many bondholders were left with nothing. In the attempt to give these unfortunate investors something for their lost money, newly reorganized companies often set up warrants which were given to the former stock and bondholders and which at least offered some hope of someday getting some money back. The Investment Company of America warrant was set up in just such a way. The predecessor mutual fund had gone broke, and in the reorganization the shareholders of the predecessor company were thrown a bone in the form of these perpetual warrants. It took thirty years, but if anyone had been able to wait, he would have got his money back plus interest!

Fortunately warrants issued today are not produced as the result of such unhappy financial situations. Practically all of today's warrants are issued as a "sweetener" with a bond or stock issue. They cost the company nothing and will facilitate the sale of a bond that otherwise might have required much higher interest rates. Most corporations would much rather give away warrants, which cost nothing, than pay the higher interest which comes out of earnings.

A typical example of such an issue was made in 1960 by the Canadian Chemical Company. In 1960 there was a temporary shortage of funds available for bonds and mortgages, and the resulting competition for the available money produced a sizeable increase in interest rates. At the height of the shortage Canadian Chemical needed to borrow 15 million dollars, and in order to sell this quantity of bonds they were forced to pay the unheard-of rate of 7% on a twenty-year bond. In addition they gave a bonus of fifty warrants with every $1,000 bond.

These warrants appeared very interesting. They had a ten-year life and so were not due to expire until 1970. Their option price was not constant but on a rising scale; that is, they were an option on Canadian Chemical stock at $7¼ until 1964, then if not used would be changed into an option at $8½ until 1967, then if not used would be changed into an option at $10 until 1970. This type of rising scale is not uncommon with long-term warrants and is used as an encouragement to early exercise of the warrants, for if a warrant is going to be exercised sometime it is to the company's advantage to have it done as soon as possible so as to clear the decks for future issues.

The company appeared to be a very volatile one. It is engaged in the production and marketing of industrial chemicals, some of which it subsequently uses in the production of cellulose acetate fibres and yarns. Most of its stock is owned by Celanese Corporation of America, whose huge research facilities are available to Canadian Chemical. In 1960 the company appeared to be on the verge of a huge earnings breakout.

Thus we had a long-life warrant on a highly volatile company. What was the leverage of this warrant? The company stock was then trading at $7 per share and initial sales of the warrant occurred at $2. If the stock were to double to $14, the warrant would be worth $6¾, giving a leverage of about 3½:1 —not nearly as good as the Investment Company of America warrants. But this factor was overshadowed by the tremendous volatility.

Under these circumstances the warrants were a tremendous buy, as were the Canadian Chemical bonds. However, as so often happens with wonderful issues of this type, the public completely ignored it, and the underwriting brokers had difficulty selling their bonds. In less than a week the bonds were actually selling for less than their issue price of $1,000 each.

Delivery Phone:			TORONTO, ONT.
EMpire 8-7137	TELEX - LATIMER, TORONTO - 02-2565		Confirmation Phone:
EMpire 4-9986			EMpire 3-8921

W. D. Latimer Limited
Security Dealers
244 BAY STREET

Date Feb. 24-60

We have this day SOLD TO YOU

				Please have cheques made payable at par in Toronto			
Broker	Quantity	Security	Price	Amount	Brokerage	Tax Que. Prov.	Total
	$5000	Cdn. Chemicals Debs 7% Mar.1/80 Delivery Mar.8-60	99.5/8	4981.25 Interest for 7 days			4981.25 6.71
							4987.96

E.&O.E.

KINDLY NOTE TERMS: 1. In buying stock outright no certificates are transferred into a client's name until payment is made in full.
2. On receipt of confirmation of stock purchased immediate payment should be made to us.
3. When selling stocks, immediate delivery of certificates should be made upon receiving confirmation sale.
4. Purchase or sales are made subject in all respects to the rules, by-laws and customs existing at the time where the order is executed. In carrying stocks for clients we reserve the right to pledge same from time to time on such terms as lenders may require, either separately or together with securities of others, to secure advances on the amount due to us on stock securities, or to secure our general loans, and to buy or sell any or all of such securities by public or private sale, without notice, when margins are running out or when such sale or purchase is deemed necessary by us, for our protection, and to settle contracts in accordance with the rules and customs of any exchange or market on which the transaction may be made.
5. All information given by us or our representatives as to the financial or other responsibility of individuals, firms or corporations, or as to values or prospects of stocks, bonds or other property, or similar information, is based on opinion only, and is given as a courtesy to our customers and we assume no responsibility of any kind therefor.

W. D. LATIMER Limited

BY _____

These sales showed a lack of foresight equal to that displayed in the sale of New York by the Indians.

A triple market now developed. First was the selling of these bonds by the ignorant. Second was the purchase of the warrants themselves by speculators who hoped to double their money or better, and third was the purchase and sale of bonds "ex warrants"—the purchase of the bonds at issue price of $1,000 and their resale at $900 without the warrants to clever investors who wished to own these high-yield bonds and make a sure capital gain when they moved back up to $1,000.

Everyone who bought in any of these three ways made a great deal of money.

Those who bought the original bonds (as shown in the preceding illustration) made an almost immediate profit. Within a few days the panic sellers were bought out and the bonds began to move upward, reaching $1,042 each within one month. Some profit taking immediately occurred.

Those who were more patient made commensurately higher profits, for within one year these bonds sold at $1,200 each, giving a 27% return for one year on a conservative investment!

Those who bought the bonds stripped of their warrants made a very good investment. They paid $900 each and within one year they sold at $1,000, receiving an 18% one-year return on a no-risk investment, ⅔ of which was a capital gain.

Those who bought the warrants did best of all, although after initially trading at $2 they quickly slipped down to $1.92, where many thousands were sold.

DOHERTY ROADHOUSE & CO.

MEMBERS
TORONTO STOCK EXCHANGE
CANADIAN STOCK EXCHANGE
WINNIPEG STOCK EXCHANGE

HEAD OFFICE
335 BAY STREET — TORONTO 1 — PHONE: EMpire 8-7411

MEMBERS
VANCOUVER STOCK EXCHANGE
THE INVESTMENT DEALERS' ASSOC. OF CANADA
CALGARY STOCK EXCHANGE

ACTING AS AGENT WE HAVE THIS DAY

BOUGHT	SOLD		PRICE
	50000	CDN CHEM CO A 7½ 80	90 0 0
		INTEREST 7 DAYS	
		EX WTS	

FOR YOUR ACCOUNT AND RISK:

GROSS AMOUNT	COMMISSION	ONT. TAX	OTHER TAXES	INTEREST OR EXCHANGE	AMOUNT PAYABLE AT THE OFFICE SERVICING YOUR ACCOUNT	EX.
4500000		1500		6712	45052 12	6

TRADE DATE
R 3 60

VALUE DATE
R 8 60

7 0 450 2 07
BRANCH   ACCOUNT   SSN

Delivery Phones:
EMpire 8-7137
EMpire 4-9986

TELEX - LATIMER, TORONTO - 02-2565

TORONTO, ONT.
Confirmation Phone:
EMpire 3-8921

W. D. Latimer Limited
Security Dealers
244 BAY STREET

Dr. M. Shulman

Date   Feb 24/60

We have this day SOLD TO YOU

Please have cheques made payable at par in Toronto

Broker	Quantity	Security	Price	Amount	Brokerage	Tax Que. Prov.	Total
	200	Cdn Chemical Wts.	1.92	384.00			384.00

E.&O.E.

KINDLY NOTE TERMS: 1. In buying stock outright no certificates are transferred into a client's name until payment is made in full.
2. On receipt of confirmation of stock purchased immediate payment should be made to us.

A few days later the warrants began to move upward, trading at $2.38 within a few weeks. Foolishly I sold some warrants at that time.

W. D. Latimer Limited
Security Dealers
244 BAY STREET

Dr. M. Shulman

Date   Apr 5/60.

We have this day BOUGHT FROM YOU

Please have cheques made payable at par in Toronto

Broker	Quantity	Security	Price	Amount	Brokerage	Tax Que. Prov.	Total
	400	Cdn Chem Wts.	2.38	952.00			952.00

E.&O.E.

KINDLY NOTE TERMS: 1. In buying stock outright no certificates are transferred into a client's name until payment is made in full.
2. On receipt of confirmation of stock purchased immediate payment should be made to us.

After dipping down in June, the warrants sold up to $2.50 in July, then to $2.60 in September, at which time I am very sorry to say I sold most of my warrants.

GEN. OFFICE—EM. 3-5057   TELEX - LATIMER, TORONTO - 02-2565

IN ACCOUNT WITH

W. D. LATIMER LIMITED
244 BAY STREET
TORONTO, ONT.

Dr. M. P. Shulman   Date Sept.30-60

Date	Bought or Received	Sold or Delivered	Security	Price	Debit	Credit	Balance
			Forward				$53008.50 Dr
Sept.1/29	400		Can. Chemical Wts	2.40	960.00		
2/30	350		"	2.35	822.50		
	500		"	2.40	1200.00		
6/31		19000	Imp. Inv.6½%'80	100 3/8		19065.55	
1	100		Can. Chem. Wts.	2.35	235.00		
		500	"	2.45		1225.00	
2		1000	"	2.43		2430.00	
		800	"	2.48		1984.00	
			Int. Imp.Inv.			20.30	
6	500		Can. Chem. Wts.	2.57	1285.00		
		2200	"	2.58		5676.00	
		500	"	2.50		1250.00	
		1000	"	2.55		2550.00	
		500,	"	2.60		1300.00	

This was probably the biggest stock market error I ever made. Within a year the company began to expand its sales and earnings; its stock went up and the warrants went right along, first to $4 and then higher. Within four years the company's stock was up to $20, and the warrants broke through $11.

This was truly a dream investment. Everyone made money —the bond buyers, the warrant buyers, those who bought in early, those who bought in late, those who sold early, those who held on. Everyone made, but those who made the most were the warrant buyers who bought early and held on, because each $1,000 investment turned into $5,000.

The best brokerage houses find difficulty in putting a value on new warrants. In 1957 the Loblaw Company issued a 6% twenty-year bond carrying a bonus of warrants. Many large institutions were very happy to sell off the warrants so as to get their bonds at a lower price and increase their income yield, but no one was quite sure at what price the warrants should be sold. The underwriting broker thought $4 appeared fair, and this was the price the institutions received. In turn they were resold at $4⅜ to speculators who thought that this price was very cheap.

STATEMENT
AND
CONFIRMATION

NESBITT, THOMSON AND COMPANY, LIMITED

SALE TO

Dr. Morton P. Shulman,
378 Roncesvalles Ave.,
TORONTO 3, Ontario.

100 BAY ST.,
TORONTO 1, ONT.

August 26 1957
SETTLEMENT DATE   August 29 1957

WE HAVE ACTED AS PRINCIPAL IN THIS TRANSACTION

SALESMAN   J.A. McMillan, 5 T 1775

PAR VALUE	SECURITY	PRICE	AMOUNT	INTEREST	TAX	TOTAL	CONTRACT
1,000	Loblaw Companies Limited Stock purchase warrants	4.3/8 net	4,375.00			4,375.00	9482
		INTEREST FROM		TO		DAYS	

DELIVERY   As above, by letter of intent to deliver
as and when available. Street.
REGISTRATION Payment to be made immediately.

Within a few days the brokers realized their error and rushed to buy the warrants back at $6.50.

STATEMENT
AND
CONFIRMATION

NESBITT, THOMSON AND COMPANY, LIMITED

PURCHASE FROM

Dr. Morton P. Shulman & Associates,   September 10 1957
378 Roncesvalles Ave.,
TORONTO, Ontario.

100 BAY ST.,
TORONTO 1, ONT.

SETTLEMENT DATE   Septmeber 13 1957

WE HAVE ACTED AS PRINCIPAL IN THIS TRANSACTION

SALESMAN   J.A. McMillan 5 T 1775

PAR VALUE	SECURITY	PRICE	AMOUNT	INTEREST	TAX	TOTAL	CONTRACT
3,000	Loblaw Companies Limited Stock Purchase Warrants if, as & when issued	6.50 net	19,500.00			19,500.00	5774
		INTEREST FROM		TO		DAYS	

Those of us who had bought at $4⅜ and sold right back at $6.50 laughed at those silly stockbrokers, but not for long. The warrants proceeded to sell up all the way to $30.

Warrants are not always issued with bonds, but sometimes they are used as a sweetener in takeovers (see Chapter 13). In 1962 Shell Oil bought out the Canadian Oil Company, giving shareholders of Canadian Oil their option of two takeover offers. The one that is of importance here consisted of $52.50 in cash plus a warrant to buy Shell of Canada stock.

These warrants had a ten-year life at a fixed option price of $20 per share. Thus, unlike the Canadian Chemical warrant, at any time within ten years the holder of such a warrant had the option to buy one Class A share of Shell for $20.

Shell was and is a very dynamic, expanding oil company, so this warrant obviously had both a long life and volatility. What about its leverage? The trouble was that nobody knew what Canadian Shell stock was worth, because up until 1962 it had all been held by the parent companies, Shell U.S. and Shell Investments. These companies now announced that they were going to distribute six million shares of A stock to their shareholders. The first hint of the value of the stock was the issue by Shell of a preferred stock at $20 that was convertible share for share into Shell's A stock. This meant that the Shell was worth something less than $20, and as most of these convertible issues are issued at ten to twenty per cent above the market price of the stock, it meant that the Shell Co. felt the stock was worth about $16 or $18. Actually the first tentative stock trades took place well below this figure, at $11, but then the stock moved up steadily to $14.

Initially the warrants were available free to all takers! This unique situation occurred because thousands of shares of Canadian Oil stock were bought by speculators prior to the Shell offering being made public, and they rushed to take their profits by dumping their stock the morning after the announcement was made. Thus thousands and thousands of shares of Canadian Oil traded between $52 and $52½ that memorable morning. All those who bought were able to hand in the stock to Shell and get back their $52.50 and be left with a free warrant. All that was necessary was the cash or the bank credit to pay for the stock for the few days before Shell reimbursed the holder. For those who did not have this capital or credit available the first warrants were available at $2.

CONFIRMATION   NESBITT, THOMSON AND COMPANY, LIMITED

Forward with Canada

CONTRACT DATE Oct 23/62	SETTLEMENT DATE Oct 26/62	SALESMANS NAME AND CODE NUMBER B G Burns 52-1775-T		CONTRACT NUMBER 2713	
ACTING AS PRINCIPAL WE HAVE TO-DAY		BOUGHT FROM YOU	SOLD TO YOU SECURITY DESCRIPTION	PRICE	AMOUNT
Dr Morton P Shulman 378 Roncesvalles Avenue Toronto, Ontario			200 Shell Investments Ltd Wts Warrants	200	40000
		ACCRUED INTEREST FROM	TO — DAYS		
DELIVERY	REGISTRATION		· LESS TAX		
			· TOTAL ▶		40000

ADDRESSES OF OUR PRINCIPAL OFFICES ARE LISTED ON REVERSE SIDE

NESBITT, THOMSON AND COMPANY, LIMITED
PER *G. H. McGarland*

At this price the leverage factor was 4:1, and this, associated with the very long life of the warrant and the high volatility of the stock, made the warrant an excellent buy. Close to half a million traded below $3.50 over a six week period. Suddenly toward the end of November, several brokers realized the value of the situation, and they and their clients rushed to buy both the warrants and the stock. The stock moved to $16 and the warrants to $6. At these prices there was absolutely no leverage left in the warrants, and most of the original purchasers sold their holdings.

The correctness of our trading was proven by subsequent developments. Three years later the Shell A stock had moved up to $20, but the warrants were still trading at $6.

This proves the basic rule; if there is no leverage, the warrant should be sold.

Sometimes warrants are issued as a bonus with a new issue of preferred stock. Preferred stock represents ownership in a corporation just as common stock does, but it is preferred inasmuch as it normally receives a fixed dividend annually, even though there may be no dividends paid on the common stock.

HECTOR M. CHISHOLM & CO. LIMITED

MEMBERS
TORONTO STOCK EXCHANGE
MONTREAL STOCK EXCHANGE
CANADIAN STOCK EXCHANGE
82 RICHMOND ST. WEST
TORONTO 1, CANADA
TEL. 362-4731

TO ⌐
  Dr. M. Shulman.

		THE TORONTO STOCK EXCHANGE			DATE	Nov 28/62
WE HAVE THIS DAY **SOLD** FOR YOUR ACCOUNT ON		THE CANADIAN STOCK EXCHANGE				
		X THE UNLISTED MARKET			VALUE	Dec 3/62

BROKER	SHARES	DESCRIPTION	PRICE	AMOUNT	COMMISSION	TAX	TOTAL
Lat.	400	Shell Co. of Can. Wts.	6.00	2400.00	30.00		2370.00

E. & O.E.

PURCHASES OR SALES ARE MADE WITH THE DISTINCT UNDERSTANDING THAT ACTUAL DELIVERY IS CONTEMPLATED, AND ARE SUBJECT IN ALL RESPECTS TO THE BY-LAWS, RULES AND CUSTOMS OF THE STOCK EXCHANGE WHERE THE ORDER IS EXECUTED AND TO THE CUSTOMS OF THE BROKERAGE BUSINESS. IT IS AGREED THAT ALL SECURITIES CARRIED FROM TIME TO TIME IN THE CUSTOMER'S MARGINAL ACCOUNT, OR DEPOSITED TO PROTECT THE SAME, MAY BE LOANED BY US OR MAY BE PLEDGED BY US ON OUR GENERAL LOANS, EITHER SEPARATELY OR TOGETHER WITH SECURITIES OR OTHERS, AND EITHER TO SECURE ADVANCES WITHIN OR IN EXCESS OF THE AMOUNT DUE US THEREON. IT IS ALSO AGREED THAT WE RESERVE THE RIGHT TO CLOSE TRANSACTIONS WITHOUT DEMAND FOR ADDITIONAL MARGIN

HECTOR M. CHISHOLM & CO. LIMITE

In any dissolution of the company the preferred stockholders must be paid the face value of their stock before the common shareholders receive anything. Because preferred stocks do not normally participate in increased earnings, they do not have the glamour of common stocks, and when being issued to the public, they often have a warrant attached as a sweetener.

Such an issue was made by the Alberta Gas Trunkline in 1960. They issued a 6¼% preferred at $100 per share carrying a bonus of 2½ warrants per preferred share. The response to this issue was amazing, and within a very few days the preferred sold up to $108 per share.

The owners of the preferred were happy to sell off the warrants at $4.50 each. These warrants had a nine-year life and initially allowed the purchase of common stock at $25 per share while the stock was then trading at $20. Alberta Gas Trunkline was engaged in the piping of natural gas and obviously was a growth stock with great volatility. The leverage factor was over 3:1, which is quite satisfactory, and the warrants were obviously a good buy at $4.50.

Within two weeks the warrants had sold up to $5.40. This brought the leverage factor down to less than 3:1. With a long-term warrant of this volatile nature such leverage is still very

STATEMENT
AND
CONFIRMATION

SALE TO

NESBITT, THOMSON AND COMPANY, LIMITED

290 BAY ST.,

TORONTO 1, ONT.

SETTLEMENT DATE May 2/60
May 17/60

WE HAVE ACTED AS PRINCIPAL IN THIS TRANSACTION

SALESMAN AND CODE NO.

5-T-1775 J. A. McMillan

PAR VALUE	SECURITY	PRICE	AMOUNT	INTEREST		TOTAL	CONTRACT
50 Shs	The Alberta Gas Trunk Line Co.Ltd 6½% Cum.Red.Pfd Shs Series "A" (of the P.V. of $100 each)(accompanied by Class "A" Common Share Purchase Wts) I.A.& W.	100.00	5000.00			5000.00	P2577
				INTEREST FROM	TO ✓	DAYS	

DELIVERY

Bank of Montreal, Adelaide & Spadina Ave., Toronto, Ont.

REGISTRATION
Street

NESBITT, THOMSON AND COMPANY, LIMITED

PER

Delivery Phone:
EMpire 8-7127
EMpire 4-9986

TELEX - LATIMER, TORONTO - 02-2565

TORONTO, ONT.
Confirmation Phone:
EMpire 3-8921

W. D. Latimer Limited
Security Dealers
244 BAY STREET

Date May 2/60

We have this day BOUGHT FROM YOU

Please have cheques made payable at par in Toronto

Broker	Quantity	Security	Price	Amount	Brokerage	Tax Gov. Prov.	Total
	200	Alberta Gas Trunk Line 6½% Pfd. - Cum Wts.	108.10	21620.00		8.00	21,612.00

E.&O.E.

KINDLY NOTE TERMS: 1. In buying stock outright no certificates are transferred into a client's name until payment is made in full.
2. On receipt of confirmation of stock purchased immediate payment should be made to us.
3. When selling stocks, immediate delivery of certificates should be made upon receiving confirmation sale.
4. Purchases or sales are made subject in all respects to the rules, bylaws and customs existing at the time where the order is executed. In carrying stocks for clients we reserve the right to pledge same from time to time on such terms as lenders may require, either separately or together with securities of others, to secure advances on the amount due to us on stock securities, or to secure our general loans, and to buy or sell any or all of such securities by public or private sale, without notice, when margins are running out or when such sale or purchase is deemed necessary by us, for our protection, and to settle contracts in accordance with the rules and customs of any exchange or market on which the transaction may be made.
5. All information given by us or our representatives as to the financial or other responsibility of individuals, firms or corporations, or as to values or prospects of stocks, bonds or other property, or similar information, is based on opinion only, and is given as a courtesy to our customers and we assume no responsibility of any kind therefor.

W. D. LATIMER Limited

BY

---

good, but on this occasion I allowed my better judgment to be overruled by such a rapid profit and I sold my warrants.

One year later the warrants traded over $17.

There are two pitfalls a warrant purchaser must avoid. These are callability and dilution.

Callability is a strange provision carried by some warrants that they may be called (cancelled) at the company's option

STATEMENT AND
CONFIRMATION

NESBITT, THOMSON AND COMPANY, LIMITED
350 BAY ST.

TORONTO 1, ONT.

SALE TO

SETTLEMENT DATE   May 3/60
                   May 17/60

SALESMAN AND CODE NO.

WE HAVE ACTED AS PRINCIPAL IN THIS TRANSACTION

5-T-1775 J.A.McMillan

PAR VALUE	SECURITY	PRICE	AMOUNT	INTEREST		TOTAL	CONTRA
3000 Warrants	The Alberta Gas Trunk Line Co. Ltd. I. A.& W.	4.50	13,500.00			13,500.00	9059
		INTEREST FROM		TO		DAYS	

REGISTRATION   Street

DELIVERY   Bank of Montreal,
            Adelaide & Spadina Ave.,
            Toronto, Ont.

NESBITT, THOMSON AND COMPANY, LIMITED

PER

by some minor payment to the warrant holder. Such warrants
should never be purchased.

Dilution means increasing the amount of outstanding stock
without receiving equivalent value for the stock. For example,
if a company were to split its stock two for one, this would

ANNETT PARTNERS LIMITED
MEMBER TORONTO STOCK EXCHANGE
220 BAY STREET
TORONTO 1

TELEPHONE
EM. 3-7361

BOUGHT FROM YOU

WE HAVE THIS DAY

CLIENT	DATE		SHARES	SECURITY	PRICE	AMOUNT	COMMIS
	TRADE	VALUE					
Dr. M.P. Shulman, 378 Roncesvalles Ave., Toronto, Ont.	17/5	20/5	100	Alberta Gas Wts.	5 3/8	537.50	
	IF AS AND WHEN ISSUED						

CASH SALES ARE MADE ON THE UNDERSTANDING THAT CERTIFICATES (DULY ENDORSED AND WITNESSED) WILL BE RECEIVED BY PHB
THIS OFFICE BY VALUE DATE, AFTER WHICH PAYMENT WILL BE FORWARDED.
THE NAME OF THE OTHER BROKER IN THIS TRANSACTION WILL BE FORWARDED ON REQUEST.
E. & O.E.

automatically halve the stock's value. If the warrant holder
were not protected against such dilution, he could easily see
his investment wiped out overnight. Never buy a warrant that
is not protected against dilution. (The warrant certificate
states whether it is protected.)

In summary, warrants are possibly the most important single type of security available to the speculator. By carefully choosing warrant purchases, the buyer should on average double his money annually. The risk is, however, greater than with stocks, and warrants are not meant for the investor who cannot afford the occasional loss. The four basic points to seek in buying warrants are:

1. The warrant must have a long life ahead of it.
2. The leverage factor must be a minimum 2:1 and preferably much higher.
3. The warrant should be on a stock with high volatility and a prospective expanding future.
4. The warrant should be non-callable and protected against dilution.

When these four rules are followed, large profits will result.

9

THE FREE RIDERS

Free riding is the purchase and sale of stock without putting up any money. Mentioning the free rider to a stockbroker elicits the same infuriated response as praising term insurance to an insurance executive, and for equally bad reasons. Stockbrokers certainly approve of buying stocks and bonds without putting up any money, but most feel that this practice should be restricted to professionals (themselves) and heartily disapprove of any public participation.

The free rider is an individual who purchases stocks or bonds with no intention of paying for them; he avoids this necessity by selling the security before the day arrives on which payment is due. This cannot often be done with ordinary stocks, because payment must be made within three trading days; except in unusual circumstances, this is not enough time for a stock to go up. However, it can very easily be done on the "if, as, and when" market, where payment commonly is not required for many weeks or months.

The "if, as, and when" market normally begins when a new equity is issued. This can be a true new issue of stock or bonds, which has been announced and sold; it can be a spinoff from an established company; or it can even be a new stock resulting from a stock split.

1. *"If, As, and When" Warrants*

The best opportunities arise when bonds or debentures are issued that carry a bonus of warrants. It is common practice to immediately issue interim bonds; actual physical delivery of the bonus warrants cannot be made until they are printed and delivered with the definitive bonds some three to six months later. These warrants are traded in the interval, however, on an "if, as, and when" issued basis. This means that delivery is not effected and payment is not made until the warrants are available some months later. Before the delivery day arrives, the purchaser can sell the warrants, taking his profit (or loss) without having made any initial investment. Because of the very special circumstances involved here, there is usually a profit to take rather than a loss.

This is because purchasers of such bonds are normally large institutions or investors. The small investor or speculator has usually neither the capital, the knowledge, nor the desire for the small sure profit shown by these bonds. Since these institutions are primarily interested in safety and yield, they are quite happy to sell off at low prices the bonus warrants from their bonds, thus reducing their cost per bond and raising their investment yield. This is well illustrated by an issue in November, 1965. The Traders Finance Corporation issued $10 million worth of 6½% five-year debentures carrying a free bonus of 25 warrants per $1,000 bond. The company is large, well managed, and showed excellent earnings; it had to give such a large yield because of a temporary market shortage of loan money for finance companies. The institutions that purchased the bonds were happy to sell the warrants at $2.50 each, thus reducing their cost per bond to $937.50 (i.e., $1,000 − 25 × $2.50). This meant that they now received a yield of over 8% on their perfectly safe investment, and they were happy to have sold their warrants.

The warrant purchasers received a seven-year warrant (see the preceding chapter), giving an option on Traders Finance A stock at $15, while the market value of the stock was $12.50. Similar warrants from other similar companies listed on various stock exchanges were then trading at prices considerably higher than $2.50. One of Traders Finance's competitors, for example, had a similar warrant outstanding, which was trading at $3.10, even though its terms were less advantageous than those of the Traders warrant.

So here we had a situation in which one could buy a warrant with a probable true value of about $4 for $2.50, and it was not necessary to invest a penny. Reproduced below is a copy of a purchase made at that time. You will note that although the sale took place on November 22, 1965, payment was not required until the settlement date of May 15, 1966.

This was truly a free ride, in which almost everyone made money. The insurance companies received 8% on their investment plus a capital gain to be received in 1970 when the debentures would be redeemed. The finance company that borrowed the money did not pay 8% on the money they received, but only 6½%. The issuing stockbroker made a profit of $250,000 for distributing the issue. Other stockbrokers charged a commission or markup for handling the sale of the warrants, varying from two to five cents per warrant. Finally, the warrant purchaser ended up with an item worth much more than the $2.50 purchase price and without having invested a penny.

In the stock market, items do not often remain on the bargain counter for very long. Thus, within a very few days, investors began comparing the price of these Traders warrants with other similar issues and began bidding up the price. Within a week, the bid rose to $2.75, and the original free riders were able to sell out a profit of $230 per thousand warrants (see illustration below).

Members of The Investment Dealers' Association of Canada	WALKER, HARDAKER & COMPANY, LIMITED	15 KING STREET W. HAMILTON, ONTARIO 527-9217

WE CONFIRM THE FOLLOWING TRANSACTION FOR YOUR ACCOUNT

CONTRACT NO.	SALESMAN	TRANSACTION DATE	SETTLEMENT DATE
6987	Office.	Nov. 29/65.	If As & When Issued

CODE	SOLD TO - BOUGHT FOR	BOUGHT FROM - SOLD FOR	DESCRIPTION	PRICE
2		4,700	TRADERS FINANCE CORPORATION "AA WARRANTS	2.75

PRINCIPAL AMOUNT	COMMISSION	ONTARIO TAX	OTHER TAX	ACCRUED INTEREST	NET AMOUNT
12,925.00					12,925.00

Dr. Morton P. Shulman,
378 Roncesvalles Avenue,
TORONTO, Ontario.

All transactions subject to the rules and regulations of the exchange where executed. All securities carried at any time when indebted to us for your account may be loaned or pledged by us on our general account. Such securities may be bought or sold by us when such transaction is deemed necessary for our protection. All statements of acc'unts are deemed to be correct unless written notice is given within five day, after their receipt. The name of the other broker in any transaction will be provided upon request.

WALKER, HARDAKER & COMPANY, LIMITED

PER *W.Walker*

1. OUR SALE TO YOU AS PRINCIPALS.	3. AS AGENTS, OUR SALE FOR YOUR ACCOUNT.
2. OUR PURCHASE FROM YOU AS PRINCIPALS.	4. AS AGENTS, OUR PURCHASE FOR YOUR ACCOUNT.

It is interesting to note that even though our original purchaser at $2.50 on November 22 sold his warrants a week later at a profit of $600, he did not receive this profit until the warrants were actually printed and delivered many months later. Until that time it was a bookkeeping entry. A minor nuisance indeed in such a lovely situation!

Unfortunately, all warrant buyers do not make money, and

in market panics, warrants will fall percentage-wise much more rapidly than stocks or bonds. Thus, in the great market shakeup of May, 1966, the Traders' stock fell only from $12.50 to $10.75, but the warrants lost nearly half of their value, trading as low as $1.50 at time of writing. They are, however, worth almost twice that figure and undoubtedly will rebound. But this volatility illustrates the great danger of warrants as well as their largest virtue.

It is obvious that the early bird gets the worm in these "if, as, and when" situations. One does not have weeks or even days to consider one's purchase. When such opportunities arise, they must be quickly taken advantage of. Happily, this specific type of situation becomes available surprisingly often. The three basic factors to be considered when making a purchase are:

1. Is the warrant being offered for a lower price than similar outstanding warrants?
2. Is the free-ride period sufficiently long to allow time for the warrants to receive distribution and rise in price?
3. Is the company that is issuing the debenture sound?

There is one small flaw in this situation. A broker selling warrants on an "if, as, and when" basis obviously must know his customers; he must be sure that they or their estate will be available in six months to complete the transaction. Therefore, in order to protect themselves, such brokers normally require that the purchaser deposit some other stock in their account as security. Inasmuch as most clients normally leave stocks on deposit with their brokers, this produces little difficulty.

2. *Government Bonds.*

Without question, this is the area of the "if, as, and when" market which is most lucrative; in addition it has the advantage of having probably the lowest risk of any form of investment anywhere. Unfortunately free riding in government bonds increases the government's difficulty in distributing its bonds and so cannot be recommended.

Many free riders have been drawn to government bonds, however, because the bonds are freely available and it is not necessary to scramble with other would-be buyers, as the bonds can be ordered at any bank or brokerage house in almost any quantity.

The free-ride time is much less than in the previous example, usually running around two or three weeks. But this is quite sufficient in this type of ride, and in fact riders here usually sell after three or four days. The size of the profit is usually small, often only $2.50 per $1,000 bond or even less, but inasmuch as large numbers of the bonds are available the overall profit may be substantial.

The reason for the free availability of government bonds is very simple. Unlike corporations, governments must raise vast amounts of money, and so their smallest issues are in the hundreds of millions of dollars. To raise such moneys, they distribute the bonds widely through innumerable banks and brokers. Because printing and distribution of these bonds takes time, there is always a free ride of two or three weeks available to initial purchasers. (These bonds should not be confused with savings bonds available only in limited quantities per individual and which cannot fluctuate in price.)

The reason that free riders almost always make money on government bonds is that, in raising such large amounts of money, the government must price their bonds sufficiently low to attract buyers, and this in effect means putting a slightly higher interest rate on this new issue than is prevalent on outstanding similar bonds. After such an issue has been announced, yields must come into line, and so either the new issue must rise in price or else all similar outstanding issues must fall in price. In actuality both usually occur, and within a very short time the bond prices will come into line with one another.

The free riders have a built-in safety factor in these bonds, because the government will not stop raising money after this issue but must continue to bring out bond issues ad infinitum. Thus they tend to price the bonds sufficiently attractively to ensure their success and, more important, they normally will support the bonds at issue price or slightly below it, at least until distribution has been completed. Thus after a bond has been issued, even if international events should force a fall in general bond prices, new issues normally have sufficient support to allow a free rider to get out with his money. If he is willing to take a small profit and sell after two or three days, the rider can be certain of taking a profit seven times out of ten and of breaking even in two of the remaining times. Because all this is done without investing a penny, patriotism has not been sufficient to slow the pace of free riding in government bonds.

Banks, dealers, and government are extremely loath to see free riders buy these bonds because, when the bonds are unloaded, it puts pressure on the market and in effect they must be sold twice by the dealers, once to the original purchaser and a second time to another person or institution. Therefore, if a free rider is so blatant as to buy and sell his bonds through the same broker or bank, he will soon find that his orders for subsequent issues are either not filled or else are drastically cut. Thus in order to avoid putting any money up (if he does that he is no longer a free rider) he uses the stratagem of "delivery against payment". This means that the rider instructs the broker from whom he purchased the bonds to deliver them to his bank (where he has already sold them) against payment or vice versa. Brokers are quite happy to make such deliveries because they are a normal part of stock business and are usually not associated with free riding.

The free rider's rule for profit in government bonds is to quickly compare new government bond issues with similar outstanding bonds and to buy in large quantities those that compare favourably, selling them three days later regardless of whether or not they have gone up. It means sure profits but no popularity with the brokers or the country's treasury department.

3. *New Stock Issues.*

This is the ideal place for the free rider to make money, but it must be done with circumspection, because brokers hate free riders in this field and will do anything possible to prevent riding. Basically the same factors apply as with government bonds; new stock issues must be attractively priced in order to pull in buyers, and there is usually a one- to two-week lag between confirmation of purchase and payment date, and the issuers normally support the stock at its issue price for some days or weeks after issue. Normally the underwriter will oversell his stock inventory, so that he will have a short position from which he can support the issue. He is naturally not anxious to buy back the stock he has just gone to such trouble and expense to distribute—and so free riders never sell their stock back directly. Instead they sell through a bank or an over-the-counter broker. Otherwise they would quickly be blackballed from receiving future issues.

There is a very simple rule for the free rider in such issues, and it should be strictly followed, because unlike government bonds there is no government behind these issues, just a broker. If the issue starts to go down, it can go down fast. Also it is much more difficult to evaluate the true demand for and value of these issues before they come out than it is in the bond field. The rule is this: after a new stock issue is released *if it trades at or below its issue price, sell it immediately.* This is because the "hot" issues will go to an immediate premium, and it will be perfectly safe to ride them until payment is demanded, whereas those issues that were overpriced to start, or which were not well sold, or which have not caught the public imagination, will begin trading at their issue price with a so-called "penalty" bid. A penalty bid is one that is made by the underwriting broker at issue price for a few days after the issue, and its purpose is to attempt to stabilize the stock price. The "penalty" involved does not affect the speculator but in effect represents a loss of the original selling commission by the broker. This is why brokers hate free riders.

The perfect example of a "hot" new issue was the issue of Comsat in 1965. Coming out at $20, the stock immediately sold at $22, then fell back to 20½ but did not sell at or below issue price. Almost every broker in the United States had blocks of this stock to distribute to its clients, and those who either paid for the stock and kept it or alternatively sold it when payment was demanded made excellent profits, for the stock went up to over $70 per share. There are literally dozens of similarly profitable issues every year where no funds need be invested. An example is shown below:

Note that the Global Marine was purchased December 16, 1964, for $133.50 per unit, and payment presumably should have been made or the stock sold by December 22, 1964. In actuality, physical delivery was not made until December 30, 1964, by which time the stock had moved up to $149 per unit, where it was sold. This is an interesting and profitable characteristic of new issues. Because of the delays and red tape attendant upon a new issue, often there is a two- or three-week delay in actual physical delivery, and this means a longer ride and larger profit for the free rider. It is, of course, essential that at the time of purchase the broker be instructed to deliver the stock against payment to a bank or Canadian broker, for this delay allows the free ride. The broker must be a Canadian one, because U.S. brokers will not co-operate with free riders, but any American citizen can open a U.S. account with a Canadian broker.

Occasionally a broker will attempt to minimize or prevent free riding by issuing a contract of sale like the one below:

HECTOR M. CHISHOLM & CO. LIMITED

MEMBERS
TORONTO STOCK EXCHANGE
CANADIAN STOCK EXCHANGE
82 RICHMOND ST. WEST
TORONTO 1, CANADA
TEL. 362-4731

TO

BROKERS ON REQUEST	SHARES	DESCRIPTION	PRICE	AMOUNT	COMMISSION	TAX	TOTAL
	200	Union Carbide Canada Ltd.,	24	4,800.00			4,800.00

SOLD TO
WE HAVE THIS DAY BOUGHT for YOUR ACCOUNT ON

THE TORONTO STOCK EXCHANGE
THE CANADIAN STOCK EXCHANGE
X THE UNLISTED MARKET

DATE Oct 6/64
VALUE Oct 9/64

NOTE : Our agreement with the underwriters states that this stock is not to be sold during period of Primary Distribution.

The agreement referred to, however, is between two brokers and does not involve either the purchaser or any third broker with whom he consummates the ultimate sale. Indeed, the broker issuing such a contract often knows perfectly well that the stock will be immediately resold, but prints the contract as illustrated so as to satisfy the original underwriters. There is no problem in making the sale.

TORONTO 344 BAY STREET TEL.: 363-4591	TELEX - LATIMER TORONTO - 02-2565 CABLE ADDRESS - LATIMAC **W. D. LATIMER CO. LIMITED** MEMBERS			MONTREAL 1155 DORCHESTER BLVD., W. TEL.: 866-8763

MONTREAL STOCK EXCHANGE • CANADIAN STOCK EXCHANGE
VANCOUVER STOCK EXCHANGE • CALGARY STOCK EXCHANGE
ASSOCIATE MEMBERS • BOSTON STOCK EXCHANGE • PHILADELPHIA-BALTIMORE STOCK EXCHANGE

WE CONFIRM THAT WE HAVE
BOUGHT FOR YOU OR SOLD TO YOU / SOLD FOR YOU OR BOUGHT FROM YOU

DESCRIPTION	CODE	PRICE	MO.	DAY	YR.	REF.
200 UNION CARBIDE CANADA LTD. IF, AS, AND WHEN ISSUED	688374	25 5/8	10	02	64	566

TRADE DATE

PRINCIPAL AMOUNT	COMMISSION	ONT. TAX	QUE. TAX	U.S. TAX	CURRENCY EXCHANGE	ACCRUED INTEREST	NET AMOUNT
5,125.00		4.00					5,121.00

GI	BR	CK	SALES MAN					SETTLEMENT DATE ▶	MO.	DAY	EX.	TB
T02	34	6164	7	50					10	07	3	6

ACCOUNT NO.

4. *Secondary Issues.*

A secondary stock issue is a distribution of stock in a company that already has outstanding stock, which is usually listed and trading on an exchange. The new stock is either from the treasury of the company and is being issued to raise money for corporate purposes, or else is a distribution of stock previously held by one or more large shareholders. (Brokers define secondary issues as stocks that have already been sold once to the public and which are being resold in a large block by their current owner.) Possibilities of profit are much more limited here than in new issues, and as a general rule the free rider would be well advised to avoid such issues. There are exceptions, however.

The mechanism of a secondary issue is such that after the market closes the underwriting broker will announce the price of the secondary issue, other details of which have been previously announced, and will then distribute it to his clients at the announced price and with *no* added commission.

If the announced issue price is well below the price at which the stock was trading on the exchange, there is a good opportunity for the rider, because in the days or weeks before physical delivery is made and payment demanded, the stock is very likely to bounce back to its original price. An example of such a trade is given below:

In this case the Ethyl stock moved up within two days to its previous level, giving a very rapid profit. Actually it moved much higher in subsequent days, and the patient rider would have made very much larger profits.

5. Outstanding Stocks.

Prolonged free riding in the normal stock purchase is not as easy as in previously described groups, but it is even more important because opportunities arise daily.

At the time of purchase the broker should be instructed to register the stock in his (the broker's) name and then forward it against payment to the client's bank or a Canadian broker. Such registration and delivery instructions are very common.

If an actively traded stock has been purchased, very often within the one to two weeks required for delivery the stock will have fluctuated sufficiently to ensure a profit.

On the American exchange there are large price movements and many such opportunities.

Thus in one day the Syntex moved substantially, giving a $260 profit.

Even more striking is the example shown on the following page.

In four days Rollins moved up over $10, giving a profit of almost $1,000 on the purchase of 100 shares——without any investment.

Although these opportunities are not as common on the New York exchange, even the big board does give the occasional free-ride profit. Last year, for example, R.C.A. became very active (see page 122).

Not a large profit, but after all, there was no investment!

I have an acquaintance who, using the above method, last year traded over one million dollars' worth of listed stocks, never put up any money, and showed a net profit of $28,000. He had 130 trades and showed a profit on 94 of these. He warns that this method is not suitable for a bear market.

In summary, free riding is the purchase of securities for which no payment is required.

In successful free riding:

1. The free period should be as long as possible, preferably at least one month.
2. Other securities must be deposited with your broker to protect him.
3. No security should be purchased just because it involves free riding, but it should present the same value and potential as if cash were being paid.

The experienced free rider can proceed to the ultimate in free riding, which is the investing of imaginary money in order to earn real interest from it.

The mechanism is simple. The rider makes an initial deposit of a few thousand U.S. dollars to open a new account, preferably with a Canadian broker. He then proceeds to order new issues of European or U.S. convertible bonds through his regular American or Canadian brokers, with instructions that they be delivered against payment to the broker where the cash deposit has been made. Although he may have only deposited $5,000, he will order $100,000 or more of various convertible bonds. Because of the long distances and delays attendant upon new issues, delivery takes many weeks or months, and the rider draws interest on his bonds even though he has put up no money for them. He instructs his new broker to accept the first five bonds and just deposit them in the account, using the original cash deposit to pay for them. Then, as more bonds arrive for payment, the first ones are sold to pay for the new ones.

The results are spectacular, for in addition to making the normal free-riding profit, the rider draws huge amounts of interest on non-existent money. In fact it is possible to earn up to 80% per annum in interest alone by continually ordering more bonds. A typical example is illustrated below. The Reynolds bonds were ordered on March 15, but as can be seen on the sales slip, delivery was not made until April 11. The $7.13 interest from March 23 until April 12 was earned with no investment and was added to the $360 capital gain.

Shown on page 10 is a more striking example, in which interest of $153 was earned on an investment of a non-existent $10,000.

During the same short period when Reynolds issued their convertible bonds, Pepsi-Cola, International Telephone, Marathon Oil, Lear Jet, and Rockwell Standard all made similar issues. Each went up after delivery, and in every case weeks were required for delivery.

To draw real interest on imaginary money is surely the ultimate in free riding.

10

WHICH BROKER SHOULD I USE?

Most people choose a broker because he is a neighbour, an old schoolmate, or belongs to the same golf club. Yet brokers are as different as contractors. There are very good ones and very bad ones, and an individual should choose his broker for the advantages the broker offers. All brokers give service; they execute buy and sell orders. No one broker does this materially better than any other. But there are two advantages some brokers offer and some do not—research and money.

The larger brokerage firms have research analysts who are in close touch with many different corporations. Often they will spot an upward trend in a corporation long before it is obvious to the general public. Several brokers are typical of this group. The analyst for one U.S. broker foresaw the upward earnings boost Meredith Publishing one year before it took place, and their clients made large profits as a result. Similarly, one Toronto broker who was closely connected with Federal Pacific Pioneer Electric, advised their clients to purchase the stock at $10 and saw it go to $18 within a year. Most brokers cannot afford large analytical services, and many have only one man who works at analysis part time. These brokers should be avoided.

For the day trader in U.S. securities (a speculator who buys and resells a security on the same day) there are tremendous advantages to dealing with a Canadian broker rather than with a United States firm. When dealing with a U.S. broker, up to 70% of the value of the stock must be deposited within three days, but if the same trade is made via a Canadian broker, nothing need be put up. At the end of three days, the speculator merely collects his profit or pays his loss. This procedure is perfectly legal, and many shrewd American speculators follow this system. The best firms to deal with for this type of trading are members of the Toronto Exchange who have Telex communications with New York associates.

A typical example, shown below, involved a $19,000 trade without a penny being put up. The $402 profit was forwarded to the New York speculator three days later.

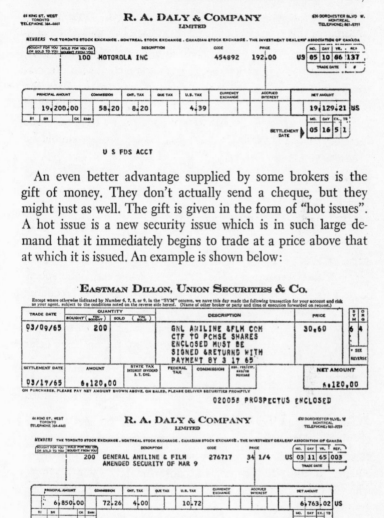

An even better advantage supplied by some brokers is the gift of money. They don't actually send a cheque, but they might just as well. The gift is given in the form of "hot issues". A hot issue is a new security issue which is in such large demand that it immediately begins to trade at a price above that at which it is issued. An example is shown below:

In that particular trade there was an immediate $640 profit without any investment. The same thing often occurs in bond issues with kickers or convertible bonds (see Chapter 4). An example of this type of hot issue is illustrated below:

These sure profits are given out by most brokers to their clients in proportion to the amount of regular business received from each client. However, all brokers do not share equally in these hot issues, and unfortunately some of those who do have a share do not pass them on to their clients but grab the profit themselves.

In the choice of a broker, therefore, the most important single factor is whether the broker has a large participation in hot issues and whether he passes them on to his clients. Some of the largest firms participate in all the hot issues, but because the firms are so very large, the allotments available to any individual client are so small as to be inconsequential.

Examples of how the salesmen of one firm give their customers frequent financial presents are shown below. In a four-month period they forwarded seven different gifts to one physician customer. In each case the stock was part of a "hot issue" which was resold the same day, and the profits ranged from 5% all the way up to 130%.

In addition to intentional gifts of money as described above, brokers occasionally send gifts that are quite unintentional.

For some strange reason, brokers do not appear to take the same care in controlling their cheques as do other financial institutions, and all too often they quite unintentionally send out rather substantial financial bonuses. To draw from my own

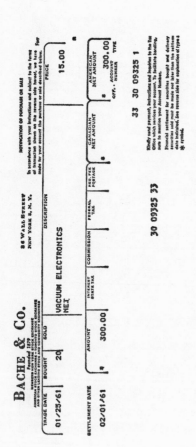

BACHE & Co.

Founded 1879

MEMBERS NEW YORK STOCK EXCHANGE
AMERICAN STOCK EXCHANGE — TORONTO STOCK EXCHANGE
AND OTHER LEADING STOCK AND COMMODITY EXCHANGES

36 WALL STREET
NEW YORK 5, N.Y.

NOTIFICATION OF PURCHASE OR SALE

In accordance with your instructions and subject to the terms of transaction shown on the reverse side hereof, we have made for your account the purchase or sale described below. For

TRADE DATE	BOUGHT	SOLD	DESCRIPTION	PRICE
01/25/61	20		VACUUM ELECTRONICS NET	15.00

	AMOUNT	COMMISSION	FEDERAL TAX	INTEREST STATE TAX	REG. FEE POSTAGE	CANADIAN NET AMOUNT	AMERICAN NET AMOUNT
SETTLEMENT DATE 02/01/61	300.00						$ 300.00

OFF. , ACCOUNT NUMBER   TYPE

33 30 09325 1

30 09325 33

Kindly send payment, instructions and inquiries to the the office which services your account. To facilitate handling, sure to mention your Account Number.

Financial settlement for securities bought and delivery securities sold must be made not later than the settlement date indicated. See reverse side for explanation of type a ⁂ symbol.

R. A. DALY & COMPANY

MEMBERS
TORONTO STOCK EXCHANGE
INVESTMENT DEALERS' ASSOCIATION OF CAN

R. A. DALY & COMPANY LIMITED
TAKE PLEASURE IN CONFIRMING THE FOLLOWING TRANSACTION EFFECTED WITH YOU SUBJECT TO THE RULES AND REG

CONTRACT AS TO NAME OF INDIVIDUAL

CODE	ARRANGED BY	MARKET	DATE TRADE	DATE SETTLEMENT	No. OF SHARES OR PAR VALUE	DESCRIPTION OF SECURITY	PRICE	GROSS AMOUNT	ACCRUED INTEREST	CO
W	AS PRINCIPAL, WE HAVE PURCHASED FROM YOU									
X	AS AGENT WE HAVE PURCHASED THROUGH/TO YOU									
Y	AS AGENT YOU HAVE PURCHASED FOR US									
Z	AS AGENT WE HAVE SOLD FOR YOU	CORRECTED								
Z	WMP	N.Y. OC	JAN 25	JAN 31	20	VACUUM ELECTRONICS 23.¼ U.S. FUNDS		470 00		

E. & O. E.

PLEASE → NOTE

1. IF NOT ALREADY IN OUR POSSESSION PLEASE ARRANGE FOR DELIVERY OF THE RELATIVE STOCK CERTIFICATES OR S
2. ANY EXPENSE INCURRED THROUGH FAILURE TO DELIVER SECURITIES IN PROPER TRANSFERABLE FORM SHALL BE T
3. THIS CONTRACT SHOULD BE PRESERVED FOR TAX PURPOSES, AS INTEREST PAID TO YOU MUST BE REPORTED TO TH
4. AS AGENT WE WILL FURNISH THE NAME OF THE OTHER BROKER OR BROKERS INVOLVED IN THE TR

SETTLEMENT MAY BE EFFECTED AT THE BRANCH THROUGH WHICH YOU ARE DEALING, STREET ADDRESS OF WH

BACHE & Co.

Founded 1879

MEMBERS NEW YORK STOCK EXCHANGE – TORONTO STOCK EXCHANGE
AMERICAN STOCK EXCHANGE AND OTHER LEADING STOCK AND COMMODITY EXCHANGES

36 WALL STREET
New York 5, N. Y.

NOTIFICATION OF PURCHASE OR SALE

In accordance with your instructions and subject to the terms of transaction shown on the reverse side hereof, we have made for your account this purchase or sale described below.

TRADE DATE	BOUGHT	SOLD	DESCRIPTION
02/08/61		50	MIDLAND GUARDIAN CO NET

	AMOUNT	INTEREST STATE TAX	COMMISSION	FEDERAL TAX	MFG. FEE POSTAGE	CANADIAN NET AMOUNT	AMERICAN NET AMOUNT
SETTLEMENT DATE 02/16/61	700.00						700.00

PRICE 14.00

OFF. 33 ACCOUNT NUMBER 30 09325 TYPE 1

30 09325 33

Kindly send payment, instructions and inquiries to the Stat Office which services your account. To facilitate handling, sure to mention your Account Number.

Financial settlement for securities bought and delivery securities sold must be made not later than the settlem date indicated. See reverse side for explanation of type a * symbol.

R. A. DALY & COMPANY

MEMBERS
TORONTO STOCK EXCHANGE
THE INVESTMENT DEALERS' ASSOCIATION OF CANA

R. A. DALY & COMPANY LIMITED HAVE PLEASURE IN CONFIRMING THE FOLLOWING TRANSACTION EFFECTED WITH YOU SUBJECT TO THE RULES AND REG

			DATE							
	PRINCIPAL, WE HAVE PURCHASED FROM YOU									
W										
X	AS AGENT WE HAVE PURCHASED THROUGH/TO YOU									
Y	AS AGENT YOU HAVE PURCHASED FOR US									
Z	AS AGENT WE HAVE SOLD FOR YOU									

CODE	ARRANGED BY	MARKET	TRADE	SETTLEMENT	No. OF SHARES OR PAR VALUE	DESCRIPTION OF SECURITY	PRICE	GROSS AMOUNT	ACCRUED INTEREST	CON
Z	WMP	NY	FEB 16 61	FEB 22	50	MIDLAND GUARDIAN	17⅛ U.S. FUNDS	862 50		

PLEASE → NOTE

1. IF NOT ALREADY IN OUR POSSESSION PLEASE ARRANGE FOR DELIVERY OF THE RELATIVE STOCK CERTIFICATES OR BO
2. ANY EXPENSE INCURRED THROUGH FAILURE TO DELIVER SECURITIES PROPER TRANSFERABLE FORM SHALL BE T
3. THIS CONTRACT COVERING SECURITIES SHOWN AS BEING PAID FOR TAX PURPOSES, AS INTEREST PAID TO THI
4. WHEN ACTING AS AGENT WE WILL FURNISH THE NAME OF THE OTHER BROKER OR BROKERS INVOLVED IN THE TRA

SETTLEMENT MAY BE EFFECTED AT THE BRANCH THROUGH WHICH YOU ARE DEALING, STREET ADDRESS OF WHI

R. & O. E.

BACHE & Co.

Founded 1879

MEMBERS NEW YORK STOCK EXCHANGE
AMERICAN STOCK EXCHANGE • TORONTO STOCK EXCHANGE
AND OTHER LEADING STOCK AND COMMODITY EXCHANGES

36 WALL STREET
NEW YORK 5, N. Y.

NOTIFICATION OF PURCHASE OR SALE

In accordance with your instructions and subject to the terms of transaction shown on the reverse side hereof, we have made for your account the purchase or sale described below.

TRADE DATE	BOUGHT	SOLD	DESCRIPTION	PRICE	For
02/20/61		200	SHORE CALNEVAR INC NET	9.00	

	AMOUNT	COMMISSION	INTEREST STATE TAX	FEDERAL TAX	REG. FEE POSTAGE	CANADIAN NET AMOUNT	AMERICAN NET AMOUNT
SETTLEMENT DATE 02/28/61	$ 1,800.00						$ 1,800.00

OFF. ACCOUNT NUMBER TYPE

33 30 09325 1

30 09325 33

Kindly send payment, instructions and inquiries to the Box Office which services your account. To facilitate handling, be sure to mention your Account Number.

Financial settlement for securities bought and delivery securities sold must be made not later than the settlement date indicated. See reverse side for explanation of type and ✱ symbol.

R. A. DALY & COMPANY

MEMBERS
TORONTO STOCK EXCHANGE
THE INVESTMENT DEALERS' ASSOCIATION OF CANADA

R. A. DALY & COMPANY LIMITED HAVE PLEASURE IN CONFIRMING THE FOLLOWING TRANSACTION EFFECTED WITH YOU SUBJECT TO THE RULES AND REGU

	W	AS PRINCIPAL WE HAVE PURCHASED FROM YOU
::	X	AS AGENT WE HAVE PURCHASED THROUGH/TO YOU
	Y	AS AGENT YOU HAVE PURCHASED FOR US
→	Z	AS AGENT WE HAVE SOLD FOR YOU

CODE	ARRANGED BY	MARKET	DATE TRADE	DATE SETTLEMENT	NO. OF SHARES OR PAR VALUE	DESCRIPTION OF SECURITY	PRICE	GROSS AMOUNT	ACCRUED INTEREST	COM
Z	WMP	NYOC	FEB 20 61	FEB 24	2 00	SHORE CALNEVAR	10.¼ U.S. FUNDS	2050 00		

E. & O. E.

PLEASE → NOTE

1. IF NOT ALREADY IN OUR POSSESSION PLEASE ARRANGE FOR DELIVERY OF THE RELATIVE STOCK CERTIFICATES OR BO
2. ANY EXPENSE INCURRED THROUGH FAILURE TO DELIVER SECURITIES IN PROPER TRANSFERABLE FORM SHALL BE TI
3. THIS CONTRACT SHOULD BE PRESERVED FOR TAX PURPOSES, AS INTEREST PAID TO YOU MUST BE REPORTED TO THE
4. WHEN ACTING AS AGENT WE WILL FURNISH THE NAME OF THE OTHER BROKER OR BROKERS INVOLVED IN THE TRA

SETTLEMENT MAY BE EFFECTED AT THE BRANCH THROUGH WHICH YOU ARE DEALING, STREET ADDRESS OF WHI

BACHE & Co.

Founded 1879
MEMBERS NEW YORK STOCK EXCHANGE
AMERICAN STOCK EXCHANGE · TORONTO STOCK EXCHANGE
AND OTHER LEADING STOCK AND COMMODITY EXCHANGES

36 WALL STREET
NEW YORK 5, N. Y.

NOTIFICATION OF PURCHASE OR SALE

In accordance with your instructions and subject to the terms of transaction shown on the reverse side hereof, we have made for your account the purchase or sale described below.

TRADE DATE	BOUGHT	SOLD	DESCRIPTION	PRICE
03/03/61	15		LEASEWAY TRANSPORT NET	15.00

COMMISSION	FEDERAL TAX	INTEREST STATE TAX	REG. FEE POSTAGE	CANADIAN NET AMOUNT	AMERICAN NET AMOUNT
					$ 225.00

SETTLEMENT DATE		AMOUNT		OFF. ACCOUNT NUMBER	TYPE
03/09/61		$ 225.00		33 · 30 09325 1	

30 09325 33

Kindly send payment, instructions and inquiries to the tax Office which services your account. To facilitate handling, sure to mention your Account Number.

Financial settlement for securities bought and delivery securities sold must be made not later than the settlement date indicated. See reverse side for explanation of type of ⊕ symbol.

R. A. DALY & COMPANY

MEMBERS
TORONTO STOCK EXCHANGE
THE INVESTMENT DEALERS' ASSOCIATION OF CAN.

W | AS PRINCIPAL WE HAVE PURCHASED FROM YOU
X | AS AGENT WE HAVE PURCHASED THROUGH/TO YOU
Y | AS AGENT YOU HAVE PURCHASED FOR US
Z | AS AGENT WE HAVE SOLD FOR YOU **CORRECTED CONTRACT**

R. A. DALY & COMPANY LIMITED HAVE PLEASURE IN CONFIRMING THE FOLLOWING TRANSACTION EFFECTED WITH YOU SUBJECT TO THE RULES AND REG

CODE	ARRANGED BY	MARKET	TRADE	DATE SETTLEMENT	No. OF SHARES OR PAR VALUE	DESCRIPTION OF SECURITY	PRICE	GROSS AMOUNT	ACCRUED INTEREST	CO
Z	WMP	NYOC	MAR 3 61	MAR 9	15	LEASEWAY TRANSPORTATION 24.¼ U. S. FUNDS		363 75		

PLEASE NOTE →
1. IF NOT ALREADY IN OUR POSSESSION PLEASE ARRANGE FOR DELIVERY OF THE RELATIVE STOCK CERTIFICATES OR BC
2. ANY EXPENSE INCURRED THROUGH FAILURE TO DELIVER SECURITIES IN PROPER TRANSFERABLE FORM SHALL BE T
3. THIS CONTRACT SHOULD BE PRESERVED FOR TAX PURPOSES, AS INTEREST PAID TO YOU MUST BE REPORTED TO THI
4. WHEN ACTING AS AGENT WE WILL FURNISH THE NAME OF THE OTHER BROKER OR BROKERS INVOLVED IN THE TRA

SETTLEMENT MAY BE EFFECTED AT THE BRANCH THROUGH WHICH YOU ARE DEALING, STREET ADDRESS OF WHI

E. & O. E.

BACHE & CO.
Founded 1879
MEMBERS NEW YORK STOCK EXCHANGE
AMERICAN STOCK EXCHANGE TORONTO STOCK EXCHANGE
AND OTHER LEADING STOCK AND COMMODITY EXCHANGES

36 WALL STREET
NEW YORK 5, N. Y.

NOTIFICATION OF PURCHASE OR SALE

In accordance with your Instructions and subject to the terms of transaction shown on the reverse side described below have made for your account the purchase or sale described below.

TRADE DATE	BOUGHT	SOLD	DESCRIPTION	PRICE
03/08/61		25	MARLEY CO NET	19 1/2

SETTLEMENT DATE	AMOUNT	COMMISSION	FEDERAL TAX	INTEREST STATE TAX	REG. FEE POSTAGE	CANADIAN NET AMOUNT	AMERICAN NET AMOUNT
03/16/61	487.50						487.50

OFF. ACCOUNT NUMBER TYPE

33 30 09325 1

30 09325 33

Kindly send payment, instructions and inquiries to the Bache which services your account. To facilitate handling, be mention your Account Number.

Financial settlement for securities bought and delivery of se said must be made not later than the settlement date ind See reverse side for the explanation of Type and a symbol.

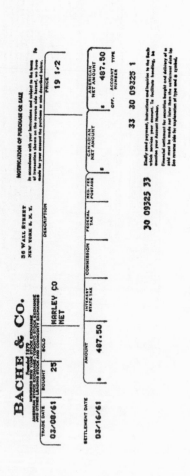

BACHE & CO.
Founded 1879
MEMBERS NEW YORK STOCK EXCHANGE AND OTHER
LEADING STOCK AND COMMODITY EXCHANGES

NOTIFICATION OF PURCHASE OR SALE

In accordance with your instruction and related to the terms of transaction shown on the reverse side described below, we have made for your account the purchase or sale described below.

YOUR ACCOUNT NUMBER	%	QUANTITY 1-YOU BOUGHT 3-YOU SOLD	DESCRIPTION	+ A B	PRICE	AMOUNT	INTEREST ON STATE TAX	Commission	FEDERAL TAX	REG. FEE	NET AMOUNT
30093251S ONTS	.25	25	MARLEY, CO		19.500	57500		400	1075	121	56276

U. S.   F U N D S

30 09325 33

33

Kindly send payment, instructions and inquiries to the Bache Office which services your account. To facilitate handling, please mention your Account Number.

Financial settlement for securities bought and delivery of securities sold must be made no later than the settlement date indicated. See reverse side for explanation of P/C Type and symbol.

TRADE DATE			SETTLEMENT DATE		
Mar. 16/61			Mar. 22/61		
MO.	DAY	YR.	MO.	DAY	YR.

BACHE & CO.
Founded 1879

MEMBERS NEW YORK STOCK EXCHANGE
AMERICAN NEW YORK STOCK EXCHANGE (ASSOCIATE) TORONTO STOCK EXCHANGE
AND OTHER LEADING STOCK AND COMMODITY EXCHANGES

36 WALL STREET
NEW YORK 5, N. Y.

NOTIFICATION OF PURCHASE OR SALE

In accordance with your instructions and subject to the terms of transaction shown on the reverse side hereof, we have made for your account the purchase or sale described below.

TRADE DATE	BOUGHT	SOLD	DESCRIPTION	PRICE
04/05/61	15		ALBERTO CULVER CO NET	10.00

SETTLEMENT DATE	AMOUNT	COMMISSION	INTEREST STATE TAX	FEDERAL TAX	REG. FEE POSTAGE	CANADIAN NET AMOUNT	AMERICAN NET AMOUNT
04/13/61	* 150.00					*	* 150.00

OFF. ACCOUNT NUMBER TYPE

33 30 09325 1

30 09325 33

Kindly send payment, instructions and inquiries to the Main Office which services your account. To facilitate handling, be sure to mention your Account Number.

Financial settlement for securities bought and delivery securities sold must be made not later than the settlement date indicated. See reverse side for explanation of type symbol. ✻ symbol.

R. A. DALY & COMPANY
MEMBERS
TORONTO STOCK EXCHANGE
THE INVESTMENT DEALERS' ASSOCIATION OF CANA

R. A. DALY & COMPANY LIMITED HAVE PLEASURE IN CONFIRMING THE FOLLOWING TRANSACTION EFFECTED WITH YOU SUBJECT TO THE RULES AND REG

CODE	ARRANGED BY	MARKET	DATE TRADE	DATE SETTLEMENT	NO. OF SHARES OR PAR VALUE	DESCRIPTION OF SECURITY	PRICE	GROSS AMOUNT	ACCRUED INTEREST	COM
Z	OFFICE	NYOC	APR 6 61	APR 12	15	ALBERTA CULVER	23.00 U.S. FUNDS	345 00		

W:	AS PRINCIPAL WE HAVE PURCHASED FROM YOU
X	AS AGENT WE HAVE PURCHASED THROUGH/TO YOU
Y	AS AGENT YOU HAVE PURCHASED FOR US
Z	AS AGENT WE HAVE SOLD FOR YOU

PLEASE NOTE →

1. IF NOT ALREADY IN OUR POSSESSION PLEASE ARRANGE FOR DELIVERY OF THE RELATIVE STOCK CERTIFICATES OR BO
2. ANY EXPENSE INCURRED THROUGH FAILURE TO DELIVER SECURITIES IN PROPER TRANSFERABLE FORM SHALL BE T
3. THIS CONTRACT SHOULD BE PRESERVED FOR TAX PURPOSES. AS INTEREST PAID TO YOU MUST BE REPORTED TO THE
4. WHEN ACTING AS AGENT WE WILL FURNISH THE NAME OF THE OTHER BROKER OR BROKERS INVOLVED IN THE TRA

SETTLEMENT MAY BE EFFECTED AT THE BRANCH THROUGH WHICH YOU ARE DEALING, STREET ADDRESS OF WHI

E. & O. E.

experience, about once a year I have received large cheques to which I was not entitled from a number of brokers. These have varied from $500 to $25,000. I have reproduced a copy of one such strange "gift" below. In this case the broker owed me about $50, so it wasn't just a matter of adding a couple of extra zeros.

NEGOTIABLE WITHOUT CHARGE AT ANY BRANCH OF THE ROYAL BANK OF CANADA IN CANADA (FAR NORTHERN BRANCHES EXCEPTED)

Incorporated

TORONTO 1, ONT.   R.2   N° 10318

DATE   PAY TO THE ORDER OF

MAR.5/65   DR. MORTON SHULMAN $10,023.49

$10023 AND 49 CTS

TO:
THE ROYAL BANK OF CANADA
TORONTO, ONT.

AUTHORIZED SIGNATURES

⑈00002⑈003⑈   221⑈197⑈7⑈

Other investors have told me of having this same experience. Of course, the money must be returned eventually, but it certainly can cause excitement for a while.

There is one source of undeserved money that does not always have to be returned—the unearned dividend. A few brokers have built up a substantial extra source of income by registering in their own names all stocks being shipped to other brokers or even to customers. In many cases, particularly if the stock does not pay dividends, the registration will not be changed, and the stock certificate may be put away in a safety deposit box and forgotten. Months or years later when dividends are declared on these stocks, they will be sent to the person in whose name ownership is registered. The dividends must, of course, be given back to the rightful owner if a claim is made by him, but all too often the true owner is unaware of the dividend and makes no claim.

Any person buying and selling securities should at the time of payment instruct his broker that the security be registered in his name before it is delivered. This will ensure that all future dividends are received. In addition it will result in the improper receipt of numerous undeserved dividends. For example, on March 2, 1966, I sold my holdings in Diversified Metal Corporation. Yet on May 2, 1966, I received this dividend cheque.

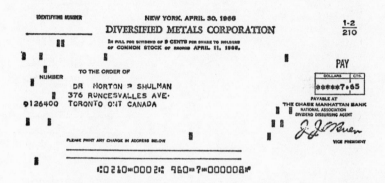

The most honest individual in the world could not return this cheque to its true owner, for his identity is unknown. My stock was sold by one broker to another broker acting for a third broker. It would take a Sherlock Holmes to trace the present holder of the stock. I must, therefore, keep the dividend, and if it is claimed by its true owner or his broker I will forward it to him. Experience has shown that about one-third of these dividends are never claimed. Far better that you should receive these funds than your broker.

The rules in picking a broker who will give the greatest return on your investment dollar are:

1. The broker should be a member of the New York Stock Exchange or the Toronto Stock Exchange.
2. The broker should underwrite stock issues or convertible bonds or "kicker" bonds with reasonable frequency. This can be ascertained by a daily glance at the Wall Street Journal.

3. The broker should give his active clients participation in "hot issues" at least four times a year. If he doesn't, get another broker.

In summary, choosing the right broker is as important as choosing the right lawyer and for the same reason——the best broker means more dollars in the bank. A broker with many hot issues can easily increase one's overall income by 10% to 20%.

11

WHICH TO BUY—
CANADIAN OR U.S. SECURITIES

For the American citizen one would think that this question is
easily answered. President Kennedy, in an effort to ease the
dollar drain, was instrumental in arranging the passage of the
Interest Equalization Tax, which imposes a 15% tax on all U.S.
purchasers of Canadian securities. (There are certain minor
exemptions to this tax.) However, since enactment of this bill,
U.S. markets have been much stronger than Canadian ones,
and American stocks on average now sell at considerably more
than 15% above comparable Canadian securities. So Canadian
stocks would appear to be a bargain.

For the Canadian there certainly should be no problem. In
addition to Canadian stocks being cheaper than American

ones, the Canadian citizen receives a substantial tax credit on dividends received from Canadian stocks.

Alas, the obvious is not always the truth. The fact is that, except in unusual circumstances such as were earlier described, one is better advised to buy U.S. securities. The reason is very simple; when buying a U.S. security, one has more security.

As a government employee it is not proper for me to comment here on Ontario securities legislation. But, in addition to governmental duty there is a heavy responsibility on the various stock exchanges to police their members and maintain high standards among the companies whose stocks they are listing. This responsibility is not always carried out.

In considering their responsibilities, all the Canadian stock exchanges quite properly look to the Toronto Stock Exchange as a model. It is the largest Canadian exchange; it has the most members, the biggest volume, the largest listing and is located on Bay Street in Canada's financial centre. Once a Canadian stock has been listed on the Toronto Stock Exchange it has arrived. If the Toronto Stock Exchange does not face up to its duties, one can hardly expect the smaller regional exchanges to do so.

During the past two years two Toronto Stock Exchange listed companies have collapsed overnight, one in the mining field, the other a finance company. Following these blows the Toronto Stock Exchange have made efforts to tighten up their standards and have delisted a number of inactive penny stocks. Many public investors, including myself, believed that we now could expect that Toronto Stock Exchange listed companies would approach New York standards in their consideration of the shareholder; that management would be more responsible to individual shareholders; and that there would be full disclosure of companies' noncompetitive activities. Numerous articles appeared in the press indicating the reforms being carried out by the Toronto Stock Exchange, and these convinced many people that better and fairer dealings could be expected, at least in securities listed on the Toronto Exchange.

My disillusionment came rapidly. I am a substantial shareholder in an excellent company listed on the Toronto Stock Exchange. At the annual meeting I naively requested a breakdown of the company's investments and also asked which directors had stock options and for how much. When the directors refused me this information, I wrote to the Board of Governors of the Toronto Stock Exchange, who replied two and a half months later, ". . . So far as we can ascertain, ... Limited has not been guilty of a breach of any By-Laws or Regulations of the Toronto Stock Exchange . . ."

The directors of the company should not be too severely criticized. After all, if the Toronto Stock Exchange does not object to directors optioning company stock at prices below the market without shareholder approval, if the Toronto Stock Exchange refuses to compel the company to give the shareholders a breakdown of what the company is doing with its money and to tell who received options and to what extent, one can hardly blame boards of directors for taking advantage of the situation.

Under these circumstances and until such time as the Toronto Stock Exchange raises itself to New York standards, I feel that Canadian stocks in general must remain highly speculative. One reason that stocks in Canada remain at bargain prices is the erosion of public confidence produced by just such incidents.

With the greatest regret I must say that "Buy Canadian" is a great formula everywhere except in the stock market. There are exceptions where stocks are vastly underpriced (Newconex was such an exception), but except for these uncommon securities, it is better to avoid Canadian stocks. It is with difficulty that I as a Canadian must recommend, other factors being equal, "Buy American."

12

GOLD

Must there be a change in price? Will the price be increased? Will this change occur soon? Uninvolved economists answer an unqualified "yes" to these three questions.

When a businessman spends more than he earns, when he has impoverished distant relatives whom he supports, and when in addition he keeps a very expensive mistress, his impending financial downfall is obvious to all. However, when a country spends more than it earns, when it gives millions away to other countries and destroys more millions by keeping an army stationed around the world or by fighting a chronic war, its financial downfall, though not so obvious, is just as inevitable. In such circumstances the only financial cure is to cut expenses and/or raise revenue. The only way the United States can cut its expenses in a meaningful way is to bring its soldiers home from Europe, stop the war, forbid out-of-the-country tourism, or stop foreign aid. It has not done any of these things, but it has imposed an interest equalization tax, and it has cut the tourist's limit on duty free imports. This is equivalent to the businessman's refusing to give up the mistress and the relatives but agreeing to take the subway to work instead of a taxi. The measures are equally ineffective. The United States can meaningfully raise its revenue in only one way, and that is by drastically raising taxes. This the government finds politically impossible, and so the annual deficit is made up by borrowing more funds.

When the improvident businessman carries on like this, his associates soon lose faith in his business. When a country does it, other countries lose faith in its money. The United States has now reached the point of no return. They have found it impossible to take the drastic measures necessary to maintain their solvency, and the rest of the world now is beginning to feel uncomfortable about holding U.S. dollars. Because of this lack of faith in the dollar, other countries and individuals have been selling dollars and buying gold, which the U.S. sells to them at the artificially pegged price of $35 per ounce.

This drain on U.S. gold began immediately after the Second World War, and it has continued and steadily accelerated since then. Because the United States is the most powerful nation in the world, she has from time to time been able to temporarily interfere with and slow down the gold drain by pressure on other countries plus international banking agreements. But each time after a few weeks the countries involved have quietly begun to sell their dollars again. Now the gold supply at Fort Knox has reached a critical level, and something must be done.

Every American president since Franklin Roosevelt has followed the advice of his treasury officials and proclaimed the soundness of the dollar and his determination to maintain the price of gold. Unfortunately, despite the brave pronouncements, the countries of Western Europe, the oil sheiks of the middle east, and the moguls of the far east have continued to sell dollars and buy gold. The situation has now deteriorated to the point where some U.S. importers are now hurrying to pay foreign currency bills, and exporters are delaying payment in U.S. funds, in the belief that devaluation may be near. This in itself tends to aggravate the dollar drain and bring the moment of reckoning closer.

What can the United States do? Short of the drastic political and tax solutions suggested above, which are clearly impossible, there is only one choice, either continue until the dollar becomes worthless outside the United States and there is a raging inflation inside the country as people rush to unload their paper money, or alternatively, drastically raise the price of gold to a point where the backing behind the U.S. dollar is sufficient to satisfy the rest of the world of its soundness. In other words, if today it takes only $35 to buy an ounce of gold, raise that price sufficiently so that other governments will not be willing to pay that many dollars for an ounce of gold and to the point where others will be willing to sell their gold for the increased number of dollars they will receive. The situation is now sufficiently critical that the minimum effective price is probably $100 per ounce.

How can the individual protect himself against an improvident government which has become caught in such a financial tangle? If the dollar is to be devalued, one must own "things" other than dollars, whether they be real estate (but not mortgages), antiques, "wealth in the ground" (oil, copper, or base metal stocks), jewels,—or gold.

In 1933, when the United States went off the gold standard, it became illegal for an American citizen to own gold inside the country. In 1960, when the gold drain was being accelerated by Americans purchasing gold and storing it in Canada, a law was passed making it illegal for American citizens to own gold anywhere. A surprising number are breaking U.S. laws by continuing to purchase and store gold in Toronto, but there are preferable ways of protecting one's investment without breaking the law.

The simplest way to own gold is by buying stock in a producing gold mine; the three favourites are Homestake Mines on the New York Exchange and Dome Mines and Campbell Red Lake on the New York and Toronto exchanges. Unfortunately so many investors want to buy the small amount of stock available that the price of these stocks has moved up drastically. Dome has gone from $11 seven years ago to over $40 today, while the others have acted equally well. Thus even if the price of gold were to be raised tomorrow, much of the increased profits which would be shown by gold mines have already been discounted, and so it is now probably too late to buy these stocks.

Undoubtedly the best way for an investor to protect himself is by owning the gold itself. This is perfectly legal for any non-American and the method is quite simple.

The Bank of Nova Scotia is the largest trader in gold in North America, and they are prepared to handle purchases and sales of any size. The amount of money that must be put up in a down payment is only 3% of the purchase price plus interest for three months at the rate of 7% per year, and this produces the possibility of huge capital gains. For example:

Cost of 400 ounces of gold at $35 per ounce is $14,000.
Down payment of 3% is $420.
Three months interest at 7% is $245.
Therefore the total down payment is $665 plus a small storage charge.

How much can be lost and how much can be made? If the price of gold is not raised at the end of ninety days, $245 will have been lost or $980 over a period of a year. If, however, the price of gold is raised to $100 per ounce the 400 ounces would be worth $40,000, and the net profit is in excess of $25,000.

The ideal speculation is one in which the risk is small and the possible profit large, and so no better speculation can ever be found.

American citizens cannot own gold. However, they can participate in this type of speculation by buying gold options from a Canadian broker. An option holder does not own any gold; he merely has the right to buy the gold at some future date. Provided he does not exercise that right, he has broken no U.S. law. Thus Americans buying gold options pay about 8½% for a one-year option to buy gold bars at $38 per ounce. An option on a 400-ounce bar costs $1,100 for one year. Thus the possible loss is $275 for 90 days or $1,100 for one year if the price of gold is not raised. If the price is raised the U.S. citizen cannot exercise his option, but he can resell it to the broker and take his $25,000 profit in cash without ever taking ownership of the gold.

The French government is so impressed with the likelihood of a rise in the price of gold that they are converting their entire national reserve into bullion. They believe that in order to preserve its economic stability the U.S. government must raise the gold price.

As an example of how a slight fluctuation in the price of gold can produce large percentage profits, see the transaction below. On October 12, 1960, gold began to slowly move up in price. By October 19, it had reached a price of $35.68. On that date 2,000 ounces were purchased. The next day bullion traded as high as $40. An investment of $4,356 on October 19 grew to $14,000 within one day.

When the price of gold is finally changed, there will be a similar overnight rise, and under those circumstances the same $4,356 would grow to $134,000. With that kind of potential profit, it is almost mandatory to own at least a little gold, even if the change should be delayed for some years.

It is unlikely, however, that there will be further intermediate fluctuations in the price of gold similar to that shown in the previous trade, because the U.S. government now sells sufficient gold into the open market to keep the price at $35.

THIS COPY FOR CUSTOMER

GOLD CERTIFICATE SALE

COMMERCIAL INVOICE

Invoice No. **A   171**

THE BANK OF NOVA SCOTIA
TORONTO 1, ONTARIO

DATE	October 19th, 1960
SOLD TO	Mr. Morton P. Shulman 376 Roncesvalles Ave. Toronto, Ont.
ACTING ON	☐ LETTER ☒ TELEPHONE CALL ☐ CABLE Mr. Robb, R.A. Daly & Co.
DATED	October 19, 1960

CERTIFICATE NO. TOR. 3527	2000 ozs. AT $ 35.68			$ 71,360.00
SAFEKEEPING CHARGES (PAYABLE IN ADVANCE) TO Sept. 25/61				
AT . . . . 1/4 % ON (MINIMUM $10.)	$ 57,616	$ 134.57		
1/8 % ON	13,744	16.85		
1/16 % ON				$ 150.62
				$ 71,510.62
INTEREST (PAYABLE IN ADVANCE) AT 5 % P.A. TO Jan. 17/61				
ON $ 67,900.				$ 837.12
TOTAL AMOUNT OWING				$ 72,347.74
AMOUNT OF LOAN INTEREST PAYABLE FROM DATE OF CONFIRMATION				$ 67,900.00
BALANCE OWING				$ 4,447.74
PAYMENT RECEIVED				$
BALANCE DUE				$ 4,447.74
			$4,356.01 Can	

But profits need not be delayed for years, for there is one sure way to make profits even if the price of gold is not raised. For the past decade, about once a year, usually just before the meeting of the International Monetary Fund, there is a renewed wave of speculation as to when the United States will raise the price of gold. Because the U.S. is now acting to stabilize the price of gold at $35, the bullion itself does not vary in price. But as so many Americans wish to participate somehow in the gold boom, there is always a pronounced upsurge

THIS COPY FOR CUSTOMER

INVOICE No. **A**   **27**

GOLD CERTIFICATE REPURCHASE

THE BANK OF NOVA SCOTIA
TORONTO 1, ONTARIO

COMMERCIAL INVOICE

DATE October 20th, 1960

BOUGHT FROM Dr. Shulman,
378 Roncesvalles Ave.,
Toronto, Ontario.

ACTING ON ☐ LETTER ☒ TELEPHONE CALL ☐ CABLE

DATED October 20, 1960 Mr. Robb, R.A. Daly & Co.

CERTIFICATE NO. TOR. 3560 _____ 800 ozs. AT $ 38.00 _____ $ 30,400.00

SAFEKEEPING CHARGES (CHARGE PER ANNUM): 9/12 refund of

AT . . . . . 1/4 % ON $ 14,800 $ 27.75

1/8 % ON 13,744.00 12.89

1/16 % ON _____ $ 40.64

$ 30,440.64

_____ INTEREST AT _____ % PER ANNUM

FROM _____ TO _____ ON $ _____ $ 0

TOTAL AMOUNT $ 30,440.64
27,160.00

DEDUCT AMOUNT OF LOAN $ ~~XXXXXXX~~

BALANCE, ~~BY CHEQUE ENCLOSED~~ $ 3,280.64 U.S.
applied on balance
owing to us Can amount 43,202.75

in the price of gold stocks, particularly Homestake and Dome.
In previous years after the meeting was over and the U.S. announced its determination (for a while anyway) not to devalue,
the price of these gold stocks has slipped back. This situation
produced large profits with no risks for a few astute speculators. Just before the I.M.F. meeting, while the papers were
anxiously writing up the possibility of a gold price rise, these
individuals bought gold bullion and simultaneously sold short
an equal amount of gold stock. Every year up until now they
have about broken even on their gold bullion (less interest
charges) but have made substantial profits by buying back their
gold stocks at much lower prices after the I.M.F. meeting was
over. Most important, they have been able to make these short

sales, which are usually highly risky, without any danger whatsoever.

What if the price of gold were to be raised during one of these meetings? Then these speculators would make even larger profits—for although they would lose a great deal of money on their short sales, they would make huge profits on the bullion they had purchased.

To take a specific example, last year Homestake was trading at $50 as the I.M.F. meeting began. Our gold arbitrager (arbitrage is the simultaneous purchase and sale of equivalent-valued securities with a sure profit because the sale price is higher than the purchase price) sold short a thousand shares of Homestake. Simultaneously he bought 1,300 ounces of gold on margin. Two weeks later he sold his gold, taking a loss of $190, and bought back the Homestake at $45½, making a $5,000 profit. If, on the other hand, gold had been increased in price to $100 per ounce, Homestake would have undoubtedly sold up to somewhere between $75 and $100 per share, resulting in a loss on this stock of between $25,000 and $50,000. However, the simultaneous profit on the 1,300 ounces of gold would be $84,500, thus producing an overall profit of between $35,000 and $60,000.

This is a certain profit situation, and it will repeat itself annually until the price of gold is finally raised. It should not be overlooked.

13

THE TAKEOVER

Since the late fifties there has been an increasing number of large companies buying out smaller ones. These "takeovers" often produce very unusual profit opportunities for the speculator. In some cases it means tying up funds for some time, but the returns can be spectacular.

In October, 1955, the Regent Oil Refining Co., a small Canadian and West Indies oil company, "went public", issuing stock in conjunction with a bond issue. The stock began trading at $10¼ and remained in the $10 to $11 range for about a year. This company was headed by an aggressive gentleman, a Mr. Reuben Rosefield, who had in a very few years expanded one single gas station into a twenty-million-dollar company. It was an attractive investment for two reasons. The oil business in Canada is constantly expanding and must continue to expand, because nowhere else in the world is sure, safe oil available to the United States. In addition the Canadian economy is growing more rapidly than those of most other countries in the world. This combination appeared unbeatable, and a considerable number of investors seeking growth stocks were happy to buy shares in Regent Oil Refining. Below are reproduced my purchases for that month.

IN ACCOUNT WITH

DOHERTY ROADHOUSE & CO.

255 BAY STREET
TORONTO

DR. M. SHULMAN
378 RONCESVALLES AVENUE
TORONTO ONTARIO.
109-8.

−1

DATE	NO. OF SHARES BOT. OR RECEIVED	SOLD OR DELIVERED	S T O C K	PRICE	DEBIT	CREDIT	BALANCE
1955 SEP. OCT.			BALANCE				4,653 47
3,	100.		REGENT OIL COMMON	10¾	1,095 00		
	100.		DO	11	1,120 00		
	200.		REGENT OIL COMM.	10½	2,090 00		51,497 32
6,	200.		DO	10½	2,100 00		
	300.		DO	10½	3,150 00		
	100.		DO	10½	1,050 00		
	100.		DO	10½	1,050 00		

Larger oil companies were aware of the promise provided by Regent, and just two years later huge McColl Frontenac Oil Company decided to increase their rate of growth by buying out Regent. They offered a share exchange which was equivalent to a price of $20 per Regent share. Practically all the shareholders were delighted to have doubled their money in two years and sold their stock to McColl. I was no exception and considered the price a very fair one.

However, I remembered that Reuben Rosefield had started his first gas station with one thousand dollars earned selling life insurance with my father, and as a sentimental gesture I put aside five shares to give to my son. The five shares gave me quite an education.

Because the oil business is growing so very rapidly in Canada, the huge oil companies were soon coveted by the giants. Just two years later, in 1959, McColl Frontenac disappeared when it was completely taken over by Texaco. McColl had not cared if there was a small minority interest in Regent. Texaco, however, wanted to integrate Regent into the Texaco Company, and so they determined to buy my five shares.

In 1964 their offers began to move upwards—to $75 per share, then $100, and finally $200. My protests that I didn't want to sell were brushed aside with, "How much do you really want?"

In early 1965 my friend and broker, Mr. Bev Burns, pointed out that I was seriously impeding the development of a billion dollar corporation. He said that, although I could probably hold them up for a huge sum, their offers were really very fair, and he suggested that I set a price and get out of their way. I sold my five Regent shares in June, 1965.

TEXACO CANADA LIMITED   FORM 5-37 (1-64)

STATEMENT ACCOMPANYING CHEQUE

No. 51855

To purchase price of 5 shares of Common Stock of Regent Refining
(Canada) Limited as per offer dated July 14th, 1965 from
Dr. Morton P. Shulman. $6,000.00

After all, $50 to $6,000 is pretty good, even for a ten-year investment.

This fantastic tale is unusual but not unique in the very remunerative takeovers now going on in the United States and Canada. It appears only common sense that, if a large corporation is willing to pay $20 for a share of a small company, the share is probably worth at least $20, for large corporations do not make many mistakes in valuations. On this basis there can be no possible danger in making small purchases of such takeover stocks to be put away for the long pull. Many of these purchases will be futile, but the occasional one will hit the jackpot. Even those that are futile will not produce a financial loss, though they may produce a temporary tie-up of capital with no return. In these cases some jurisdictions have a law which allows a corporation to call in all held-out shares if a minimum of 90% of outstanding stockholders have accepted an offer.

Another rare possibility is that the corporation taking over the smaller company may get so annoyed with the holdout shareholders that they will try to wait them out.

Such an example is Admiral Corporation. In 1952 this company made a one-for-two share exchange offer to the shareholders of its subsidiary, Canadian Admiral. This offer was worth about $9 a share, and after the offer had expired, Admiral Corporation owned over 99% of Canadian Admiral and attempted to take over the remaining few shares through court action under the Canada Companies Act. They were challenged by a few stubborn shareholders, who won their case through a technicality.

Now began a long war of attrition. Although the Canadian subsidiary did very well financially, its annual 15¢ dividend was soon cut off, and by 1965 the strange situation had arisen where the company had retained earnings of $10 million, equal to $33 per share. This cash holding plus the company's earnings gave the stock a value of about $70, yet no dividends had been paid for years, and the few stock trades took place between ten and fifteen dollars a share.

Canadian Admiral's dissident shareholders had certainly suffered, but so had the parent Admiral Corporation, for if Canadian Admiral's huge cash surplus had been paid out in dividends, over 99% of this would have gone to Admiral Corporation, putting many millions into their treasury. However, there was no outcry from the shareholders of the U.S. firm, who were probably unaware of the situation.

This situation has been a stalemate up till now. The resale value of the little independently held Canadian Admiral stock has remained very low, while a few Canadian Admiral shareholders have used the occasion of Canadian Admiral's annual

Code	A	AS PRINCIPAL WE HAVE SOLD TO YOU
	B	AS AGENT WE HAVE SOLD THROUGH YOU
	C	AS AGENT YOU HAVE SOLD FOR US*
	D	AS AGENT WE HAVE PURCHASED FOR YOU

R. A. DALY & COMPANY
MEMBERS
TORONTO STOCK EXCHANGE
THE INVESTMENT DEALERS' ASSOCIATION OF CANA

R. A. DALY & COMPANY LIMITED HAVE PLEASURE IN CONFIRMING THE FOLLOWING TRANSACTION EFFECTED WITH YOU SUBJECT TO THE RULES AND

CODE	ARRANGED BY	MARKET	DATE TRADE	SETTLEMENT	NO. OF SHARES OR PAR VALUE	DESCRIPTION OF SECURITY	PRICE	GROSS AMOUNT	ACCRUED INTEREST	CO
D	G.B.	OC	OCT 22 58	OCT 27	100	CDN ADMIRAL CORP	11.¼	1125 00		

E. & O. E.

PLEASE NOTE

1. IF FUNDS ARE NOT ALREADY IN OUR POSSESSION, PLEASE ARRANGE FOR PAYMENT DIRECT OR AGAINST DELIVERY. O
2. WHEN CARRYING SECURITIES FOR CLIENTS WE RESERVE THE RIGHT OF PLEDGING THE SECURITIES AND RAISING MO CONVENIENT TO US, CHARGING INTEREST ACCORDINGLY.
3. THIS CONTRACT SHOULD BE PRESERVED FOR TAX PURPOSES AS INTEREST PAID BY YOU MAY BE OFFSET AGAINST YC
4. WHEN ACTING AS AGENT WE WILL FURNISH THE NAME OF THE OTHER BROKER OR BROKERS INVOLVED IN THE TRA!

SETTLEMENT MAY BE EFFECTED AT THE BRANCH THROUGH WHICH YOU ARE DEALING, STREET ADDRESS OF WH

meeting to raise as much hell as possible. The first signs of a break appeared in late 1965, when Canadian Admiral suddenly voted a 35¢ dividend. Because of present pressures being exerted by the U.S. government on firms like Admiral to bring home loose foreign exchange, it would appear that the shareholders are likely to gain the final victory. An announcement of a $25 dividend per share would not be surprising.

The largest profits in takeovers, of course, occur if the takeover stock is purchased before the announcement is made. Selecting the right stock is not just a matter of blind luck and can often be forecast with reasonable accuracy. Some companies are obvious targets for takeovers. They fall into three groups.

1. Certain industries go through periods of widespread takeover, usually due to expansion and strong competition. The Canadian petroleum industry has been going through just such a period for the past fifteen years. One after another, each of the small integrated oil companies has been bought out, until finally only one remains.

In 1962 Shell decided to expand in Canada by taking over the Canadian Oil Company, a medium-size, well-diversified Canadian company. Just prior to Shell's move there were only two independents left in Canada, Canadian Oil and Supertest. Canadian Oil was then trading at around $25, and as is common in such takeovers, the offer was made for a much higher price, an astronomical $55. The shareholders of Canadian Oil were happy to receive this huge sum, and as in the story of the ten little Indians, "Then there was only one".

The one remaining Canadian independent is Supertest. Among oil men, the question is not *whether* one of the U.S. giants will take over Supertest, but rather *when* will it occur? Market- and oil-wise investors have been gradually buying this stock since 1962 ($19 at time of writing). The delightful part of such a speculation is that this is a highly regarded company which meanwhile pays a reasonable dividend. It is another "can't-lose" situation. Such likely takeovers appear periodically and should be included in every investment portfolio.

2. Small Canadian subsidiaries of U.S. and Canadian corporations have been expanded, taken over, and set up at a bewildering rate in recent years. One reason is a Canadian law brought in a few years ago which gives large tax advantages to such subsidiaries if 25% of the subsidiary stock is held by Canadians. This law puts the subsidiary whose stock is all held by the American parent company at a very severe competitive disadvantage and has encouraged many firms either to broaden their list of Canadian shareholders or in some cases to take over the subsidiary completely and integrate it with the parent company. In addition, large Canadian companies have been swallowing their subsidiaries. Outstanding in this field has been Noranda, who year by year have been making very generous offers to one after another of their small satellite companies. As these have disappeared, the ones remaining have become increasingly interesting to investors and speculators. Quemont and Placer Development are two obvious targets for takeover offers.

3. The best possible takeover target is the company droning quietly along, often in an old-time, family-established business, whose assets are considerably higher than its market price. These companies are surprisingly numerous, and every little while one of them falls victim to the takeover artist. The beauty of buying stock in such a company is that, because it

sells at a large discount from true value, there is very little risk involved. Once a takeover effort begins (or even a takeover rumour) it can move up very rapidly. It always seems best to sell if rumours of a takeover reach the newspapers, because the vast majority of these do not materialize.

Very rarely a broker will pass on to his clients advance information about a takeover. This should be a once-in-a-lifetime opportunity to make a large amount of money, but sometimes plain bad luck intervenes.

For years my wife's gynecologist has complained of his unbelievably bad luck in the stock market—as soon as he bought a stock its price would begin to sink. Al Capp created a character in Lil Abner called Joe Bflspk who was followed by a black cloud and disaster wherever he went. The gynecologist felt that he was the Joe Bflspk of the market, but I was determined to show him that by scientific stock purchasing, even he could make money. One day I learned that the Hancock Oil Company of California was to receive a $50 takeover offer the next morning. The stock was then only $43. With great excitement I phoned this doctor, explained the situation, and said "Buy." He bought. Two hours later Hancock Oil's major field caught fire and burnt up $17 million worth of oil. The takeover offer was temporarily withdrawn, and the stock opened the next morning at $38. Some people just shouldn't be in the market.

The classic example of making money by refusing a takeover offer is Seven Arts, a company listed on the American Stock Exchange, which is in the business of producing and distributing movie films. Few remember that in 1955 Seven Arts' business was confined to the tanning of leather and the sale of mouton fur.

The company was then called Donnell and Mudge, and for 35 years it had run a moderately successful tannery. After the war, however, competition had increased, and Donnell & Mudge had not kept up. Sales and earnings plummetted, and by the early fifties the company had dropped its dividends and was showing losses of over a quarter of a million dollars annually. The stock fell from a postwar high of $12½ to reach a low of 35¢ in 1955.

At this point bankruptcy appeared imminent, and when a group of apparently foolish financiers appeared on the scene and offered to pay $2 per share for all the outstanding stock, the directors of the company hastened to turn in their stock and advised all the shareholders to follow suit. Practically everyone did, but as I held only 100 shares I hesitated. My hopes of higher prices were confirmed when after only two weeks the new owners raised their offer to the few holdouts to $2.50 per share. The stock remained at this level for only a few days, then began to soar upwards. By March of 1956 it was trading at $23.50. A twenty-for-one stock split was now announced, and an underwriting and sale of debentures was arranged, while the company now declared that it was going into the business of distributing motion pictures to television.

In March, 1958, the company's name was changed to United Telefilm, and in 1960 a reverse split was announced whereby the company's name was again changed, this time to Creative Telefilm. Shareholders received one share of Creative Telefilm for every three shares they had of United Telefilm. The following year the company once again changed its name, to its current Seven Arts, and announced an expansion of its business to include the distribution to television of motion pictures, the production and distribution of motion pictures, the production of plays, the production and distribution of phonograph records, and incongruously, the development of land on Grand Bahama Island. They no longer, however, sell mouton fur, nor do they tan leather.

Seven Arts has done well. My $35 investment would now be worth $21,000, whereas if I had accepted the takeover offer I would have received only $200. Seven Arts once again proves that if you have only a small investment in a company receiving a takeover offer, there is no harm in waiting a while to see what developments may take place.

After all, a $1,000 investment in Donnell & Mudge in 1955 would be worth $600,000 today!

In summary the rules for sure profits in takeovers or potential takeovers are these:

1. Try to buy stock in companies which are likely to receive takeover offers. These should be chosen by the rules given previously.
2. When takeover offers are extended to U.S. or Canadian corporations in which you hold stock, hold back a few shares for good luck.
3. It never does any harm to purchase for speculation a little stock for which a takeover offer has already been made. If the takeover fails, much higher prices may result.

14

GLAMOUR STOCKS

Polaroid went from $3 to $500 in two years.
Fairchild went from $40 to $150 in six months.
Syntex went from $90 to $200 in one year.
Molybdenum went from $28 to $70 in less than one year.
Rollins went from $14 to $150 in one year.

A glamour stock is one which has a glamourous new invention or process associated with it and which has moved up many multiples in price as a result.

Every investor and speculator has heard of the glamour stocks' fantastic market moves during the past few years. In every case the stocks have been legitimate ones which have made a tremendous turnabout in their profit potential often due to a startling new discovery. Most of these companies were listed on the American Stock Exchange, but a few were on the New York Exchange.

How can the average speculator make money from these glamour stocks? The answer is that he can't. Unfortunately a glamour stock is about as hard to spot before it has moved up in price as it would be to decide which one of the million babies born this year will some day be president. Theoretically it appears very simple to buy into companies that have new discoveries and watch them grow, but the hidden pitfalls can be crippling. To take two examples, six years ago two companies developed new ideas. One was Syntex, who were pioneering a new pill that they believed women could take to control their fertility cycles; the other was Steadman Industries, who had developed and patented a clever system of directly unloading piggyback from trains to trucks. Both stocks were selling at $8. Any reasonable man could see that Steadman had an immediately usable, revolutionary, money-making invention that must bring it a rapid rise in earnings. Syntex's invention, if it worked, would certainly require a long educational campaign to persuade women to use it, and there might very well be dangerous side effects which would prevent it from ever going into practical use. Of the two there appeared little doubt that Steadmans was the better buy.

Today Syntex is $200 and Steadmans is $5.

Unfortunately it is only clear that a glamour stock is a glamour stock after it has become one. That is, unless you are an insider in a company, it will probably be too late to buy its stock once the glamour label is attached. Today the acknowledged glamour stocks are trading at ridiculous multiples of their current earnings—as high as 100 times earnings. These prices discount future earnings for many, many years and render these stocks very vulnerable to any stock market reaction. In fact it is likely that today's leading glamour stocks, which are now being widely distributed to the public, may very well lose half or more of their value in the next two or three years.

One has only to look at the past history of other glamour stocks to see the same depressing picture. Five years ago the public latched on to the vending machine companies in the belief that everything would soon be sold by vending machines. New machines were described that could recognize and give change for paper money, and vending stocks soared to unbelievable heights. One example was Universal Match, which rushed all the way from $6 up to $70 on the basis of huge projected future earnings. As always happens in such bubbles, common sense finally reasserted itself, and the stock plunged back to $12, producing huge losses for those foolish individuals who bought on the way up or the way back down.

There is little doubt that the same fate awaits today's glamour stock purchasers. Many of these stocks cannot justify their current price on any basis, and this bubble too must finally burst.

An interesting side effect of the current glamour stock boom is the emergence of "hot" customer's men. These are salesmen who were fortunate enough to have good inside information on one or more glamour stocks at an early stage in their rise. They recommended purchase of the stocks at relatively low prices and were then able to go back and say, "If you had followed my advice and bought and held on, you would have quintupled your money in six months." Some of these salesmen cashed in on their enhanced reputation by recommending other potential glamour stocks. Sooner or later disaster struck their clients.

One very "hot" customer's man was well connected with directors of three New York Exchange listed companies and always knew of their earnings and announcements one or two days before the public were informed. He used this information to very good advantage, and his clients did very well. Unfortunately he did not restrict himself to these companies and soon involved his customers in a variety of potential glamour stocks in such diversified fields as computers and clothing. Within a few weeks several of these stocks lost up to 50% of their value, and another hot customer's man cooled off very rapidly.

In summary, for the average investor to seek or buy so-called glamour stocks is foolishness of the highest degree. The glamour can wear off very quickly and this type of speculation is more likely to yield headaches than profits. To buy these stocks is truly idiotic when there are so many other opportunities for large capital gains with no risks.

15

COMMODITY FUTURES— THE IDEAL GAMBLE

"Mrs. Jordan, your husband bought 30,000 pounds of sugar futures six months ago. Apparently he went on his vacation without arranging its sale. Where do you want it delivered?"

Everyone has heard this old chestnut, and it still frightens the novice "future" buyer. Actually it is just a myth, and no one has ever had 30,000 pounds of anything dumped in his backyard. Like everything else in future trading, even the stories are magnified tenfold.

Commodity futures represent the quickest possible way to get rich or go bankrupt amongst all forms of market trading. They are exceeded only by puts and calls in their volatility and are exceeded by nothing in their low margin requirements. Comparatively few speculators participate in this form of gambling because of a mistaken belief in the complications of commodity trading and because the books available read with such great difficulty. This is a pity, because here is probably the only completely honest form of pure gambling in the market. Commodity futures are neither investments nor speculations and should not be purchased for either purpose. But as an exciting form of gambling from which small amounts of money can turn into huge fortunes, futures can be recommended for risk capital. Only moneys which can afford to be lost should be used in such ventures for the entire capital can disappear with disquieting rapidity.

What are commodity futures?

Commodities are articles produced for trade. They include things that are grown, such as wheat and animals, and things that are dug up, such as copper and silver. All commodities are bought and sold or traded.

Futures are titles of ownership of specified commodities at some future date. For example, one contract of December cocoa represents title to 30,000 pounds of cocoa that will be ready for delivery in December. All commodities do not have future trading, for in order to be so traded they must be storable, have a fluctuating price, and be widely traded. Practically speaking, the commodities that are traded in futures are copper, tin, lead, zinc, platinum, silver, and aluminum; plus cottonseed oil, silk, potatoes, rice, eggs, cotton, cattle, pork, hides, and wool; and also rubber, cocoa, coffee, and sugar. For the speculator's purposes, this list can be drastically shortened.

There are two groups who trade in futures: those who produce and use the commodities and who are future trading to avoid risks; and speculators who seek the risks because of the great rewards possible. Originally commodity future trading served two purposes:

1. To enable producers of commodities to be certain of receiving a fair price for their commodity. For example, if a planter is producing sugar there are many months between the time of planting and the time that actual physical delivery of the sugar can be made. If during this interval the wholesale price of sugar were to fall from say 4¢ a pound down to 2¢, the planter might discover that all his labour produced no profit. On the other hand, sugar might have climbed to 6¢, but planters cannot afford to gamble with their crops, and so they seek some way to ensure a fair profit for themselves. They accomplish this by selling their crop, or at least a portion of it, through a future trade. Thus if the sugar were trading at 4¢ a pound for immediate delivery, there should be little difficulty in selling futures on sugar at 4¢ a pound (possibly a little more or less; this will be explained later) for delivery six months hence. In this way the planter has ensured a successful sale of his crop at a good price.

2. To enable users of commodities to be certain of obtaining supplies of their needed commodities at a reasonable price. For example, a manufacturer of candy bars must contract in advance to deliver the candy to his wholesalers. If while his contract is still in force he finds that the price of sugar has considerably increased, he may be put in the difficult position of having to produce his candy and sell it at a loss. It is not possible for him to store his sugar supplies very far in advance because of the costs and capital involved, so he protects himself by purchasing a sugar future at 4¢ a pound. Regardless of any price fluctuations, the manufacturer is now sure that he can manufacture and sell his candy bars at a profit.

Who runs the risks that these producers and consumers are seeking to avoid? Unfortunately the times when producers wish to sell futures rarely coincide with those when consumers wish to buy, and so a third party is welcomed to commodity trading —the speculator. Because producers and consumers *must* buy and sell at certain times (or *hedge*, which is the technical term) there are tremendous profit opportunities for the speculator who can buy or sell when and if he chooses.

Because the speculator has become essential to the smooth running of the futures markets, a huge industry has developed to service and inform him. Numerous firms specialize in handling speculators' accounts and in rushing information about commodities to them. Newspapers carry crop and weather reports, and even the United States government co-operates by simultaneously releasing crop forecasts to all interested parties. Because weather changes or large sales or purchases can rapidly affect commodity prices, the brokerage firm with whom each speculator deals will send him a daily letter, reporting all such changes and giving that firm's opinion as to future changes. Thus it is very easy for the speculator to keep well informed about the current national and world factors which may affect any commodity in which he is interested. In fact it is not uncommon for a speculator in a certain commodity to be far better informed about that commodity's current and prospective market than are the actual producers of the commodity. Certainly it is easier for a sugar speculator in New York City who is reading Merrill Lynch's daily sugar bulletin to be more up to date on the world sugar situation than can be any sugar beet grower in Louisiana or Haiti.

How are these futures traded? The mechanism is very simple.

Each commodity has a specific trading unit which represents the quantity of the commodity covered by one future contract. For cocoa, for example, the trading unit is 30,000 pounds. (Although it is possible to trade in fractions of a contract, it is unwise because it may be difficult to dispose of such a purchase.) When one buys or sells one cocoa contract, one is automatically buying or selling 30,000 pounds of cocoa. The orders to buy or sell these contracts can be placed with any member of the various commodity exchanges who are listed in every city's telephone book. Many of them are also prominent stockbrokers.

Primarily because it is essential that there be a large volume

MERRILL LYNCH, PIERCE, FENNER & SMITH INC

UNDERWRITERS AND DISTRIBUTORS OF INVESTMENT SECURITIES, BROKERS IN SECURITIES AND COMMODITIES

REPRODUCED FROM M. L. P. F. & S. NEWS WIRE

DAILY SUGAR LETTER 1/19/66

NBR 3

LDN SPOT RAISED TO 23.75 BELIEVED BASED ON EQUIV YESTY SALE AT 2555
OUR BASIS . FUTURES CLSD SLITELY LWR ON 966 LOTS . PARIS CLSD SLITELY
LWR ' SPOT INCREASED TO 2.85. N Y CLSD 1 TO 6 PTS DECLINE ON 1469 LOTS .
IRAN HOLDING TENDER 1/22 FOR 30'000 TONS WHITES APR /MAY /JUNE SHIP
SELLERS OPTION . BZL REJECTED ALL FOUR BIDS RANGING $54.23 TO $52.67
HIGHEST EQUIV ABOUT 2.46/47. EVEN WHEN BIDS WERE LWR REJECTION BY BZL
AND THE WILLINGNESS OF MORE TRADING HOUSES BIDDING NEAR FUTURES PXS
WAS CONSIDERED CONSTRUCTIVE . NEXT TENDER FRI AS TMW HOLIDAY IN BZL .
CMN HSES SELLG NEARBYS WAS WELL ABSORBED BY TDE SHORT COVERING . THR
WERE 197 LOTS MAY POSTED AGAINST ACTUALS . SPOT SAME 255.

NBR 7

LATE YESTY REVERE BOT 5500 TONS DOMINGOS AND COLONIAL 6500 TONS
COSTA RICAN BOTH DUE LATE FEB AND EQUIV 690 NORTH HATTERAS . FUTS
CLSD 2 PT DECLINE TO 1 PT ADVANCE ON 306 LOTS ' SPOT AGN 690. USDA
ANNCD THE SET A SIDES FOR SECOND QUARTER .

Commodities

* * *   *** * ***

Price Trends of Tomorrow's Meals and Manufactures

Futures prices of feed grains, soybeans and soybean oil were strong.

When markets closed, corn had a top gain of 1⅜ cents a bushel, oats ⅝ cent a bushel, soybeans 3⅜ cents a bushel and soybean meal $1.80 a ton.

Higher quotations were also posted for world sugar and cocoa as well as for pork belly futures.

Prices of live hogs fell as much as 50 cents a hundred pounds.

Heavy demand from speculators, exporters and processors for feed grains and soybeans uncovered only light selling. In the soybean market, prices of all contracts rose to highs. So far this week, prices of active soybean contracts advanced as much as 6½ cents a bushel. In addition to large export sales, the soybean futures market continued to be influenced by the smaller-than-expected supply of soybeans on farms Jan. 1. The Government estimated this supply at 284.4 million bushels on Monday. Because of last year's large production, traders expected officials to place stocks at more than 325 million.

Exporters sold Norway 523,000 bushels of U.S. soybeans, and grain dealers said further business was pending. The grain men also sold 3.2 million bushels of corn to several European nations. Yugoslavia bought 560,000 bushels of U.S. wheat, bringing its purchases since Monday to 6.5 million bushels; it has an additional 5.7 million bushels to buy. Orders for the rest are expected to be placed soon.

Additional Exports

Additional export business included 1,080,000 bushels of sorghums to Great Britain and Japan.

Grain dealers expect foreign orders, especially from Europe, for large quantities of U.S. feed grains. Bad weather hurt production in these countries last year. Some traditional exporters also had crop reverses.

South Africa, normally an exporter of corn, will require imports of around 6 million bush-

Markets at a Glance

COMMODITY INDEXES

Dow-Jones Futures — 140.92, up 0.16; last year, 136.51.

Dow-Jones Spot — 144.57, up 0.42; last year, 143.46.

Reuters United Kingdom — 467.9, off 1.5; last year, 459.8.

FUTURES PRICES

Higher — World sugar, coffee, cocoa, eggs, frozen pork bellies, cattle, corn, oats, rye, soybeans, soybean meal, flaxseed, lead and zinc.

Irregular — Domestic sugar, soybean oil, cottonseed oil, hides, wool, cotton, silver, Chicago and Kansas City wheat.

Lower — Copper, platinum, rubber, potatoes and Minneapolis wheat.

---

pound, selling subsided and prices moved higher. In the marketing week ended yesterday, the board bought 21,971 tons of cocoa, up from 20,385 a week earlier.

In the world export market, Libya bought 15,000 tons of refined sugar. Brazil was scheduled to sell 60,000 tons of raw sugar to the world market but postponed accepting orders until today.

Prices of raw sugar in the domestic market were firm. An Eastern refiner bought 10,200 tons of raw sugar due to arrive next month at $6.90 a hundred pounds delivered in New York. This price was 5 cents above last transactions.

Business in the New York copper futures market was slow, reflecting quiet conditions in the U.S. scrap copper market. In London, copper prices were ⅛ cent a pound higher to ⅜ cent lower. Dealers in the British market said profit-taking depressed prices of copper contracts for forward delivery.

After early weakness, pork belly futures rallied to close unchanged to $1.25 a hundred pounds higher; deferred contracts were in de-of trading if futures are to be easily bought and sold, each commodity is normally traded for delivery in certain specified months. Cocoa, for example, is traded for delivery in March, May, July, September, and December. This increases the number of contracts for these months to a level where individual large buy or sell orders do not unduly raise or depress the market.

This is very important, because if a trader wishes to sell 10 contracts of December cocoa and the total daily trades in December cocoa number only 20, it is obvious that such a sale will seriously depress the market and restrict trading. If, on the other hand, the total daily volume is 200 contracts, then a sale of 10 or 20 contracts can easily take place.

Once a future contract has been purchased, it can just as easily be sold. It is different from a put or call, which has little liquidity; it can be compared with a common stock, except that it has a limited life. A future contract is neither a warrant nor a call, which represent only options to buy; a future represents actual ownership, even though only a small amount of the purchase price has been paid as a down payment.

Before proceeding further, one should understand certain terms used in commodity trading.

Hedge: The sale of a future in a commodity by a producer of the commodity or the purchase of a future in a commodity by a consumer of that commodity.

Last trading day: The last day in which a commodity may be sold before actual physical delivery occurs (physical delivery means delivery to a warehouse).

Limit: The maximum daily price move permitted in a commodity by the exchange on which it is traded.

Long: The owner of a future.

Short: The seller of a future in a commodity that he has sold without any offsetting ownership of production in that commodity.

Margin: Money put up by the speculator when purchasing

(or selling short) a futures contract. It will vary between 5% and 15% of the value of the contract.

Margin call: A request for more margin from a broker if a loss is occurring on a futures contract.

Stop loss order: An order to automatically sell a contract if the price of that contract falls to a predesignated figure.

Option, call, spread, straddle: It is not necessary for the speculator to understand these terms, but he *should* understand that their meanings are quite different from the same terms when applied to puts and calls as described in Chapter 6.

Pyramid: To automatically increase one's holdings in a specific future as its price rises. This is without a doubt the most important tool that a speculator in futures can use to increase his profits. It is based on the fact that trends often develop in certain futures, and a price movement in a future is often sustained for long periods of time. It will be fully explained later in this chapter.

Now, what are the financial advantages to the speculator in buying commodity futures?

1. The commission is very low—only a fraction of that compared to stock purchases. This is very important to the trader who is doing a lot of buying and selling. When, for example, world sugar is trading at 3¢ a pound, one contract is worth $3,360, and the commission on such a purchase is only $12.50. The commission on a stock purchase of equal value on the stock exchange may be up to five times as high.

2. Margin requirements are very low. In the stock exchange these requirements are never under 50%, but in the purchase of commodity futures they may be as low as 5%. This can produce tremendous percentage profits on the small amount of money put up. Very important is the fact that no interest is payable on the balance, unlike stocks purchased on margin, where interest payments can materially raise the cost of the

stocks purchased. As an example of how this low margin requirement can produce spectacular profits, examine the situation if one had bought sugar futures just before the Cuban crop failure a few years ago. At that time sugar prices jumped all the way from 2¢ a pound up to 12¢. Each contract which had been worth $2,200 zoomed all the way up to $13,200. If $200 had been deposited as initial margin, it would have grown to be worth $11,200—an increase of over 5,000%. Furthermore, if pyramiding of the original $200 investment had been fully followed, the $200 would have grown within six months to $5,000,000! That is why this type of gambling speculation should be carefully examined. An example of a simple trade is shown below. One July sugar contract was purchased in March. The deposit requested was $600.

The contract was resold one month later.

Although sugar had moved up only one-sixth of a cent during this time, the profit was $185 less $30 commission, or a net profit of 25% in one month.

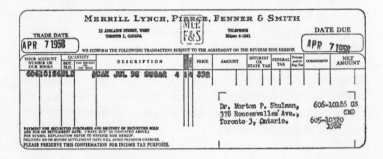

What are the disadvantages and dangers in commodity trading? There are two.

1. Because of the small amount of margin which is deposited in purchase of a futures contract, a very small fluctuation can completely wipe out an investment. For example, if a world sugar future contract is purchased when sugar is trading at 3¢ a pound, the deposit may be $500 on the $3,300 contract. A decline of only ½¢ in the price of sugar would produce a total loss of the $500 put down as margin. One must be prepared to lose his initial margin time and time again in order to await and follow a trend.

2. In order to protect commodity prices from very severe price fluctuations on the receipt of good or bad news, every commodity has a daily price limit beyond which it may not move. For example, sugar may not move more than ½¢ per pound per day. There is no more unnerving experience in the whole financial world than to be attempting to sell a position held in some commodity, and to be unable to do so at any price because there are no bids at the price level within which the

commodity may legally be sold that day. When a situation of this type is prolonged for several days and the speculator sees his profits or capital melting away without his being able to do anything about it, even the most strong-minded may have difficulty sleeping. Fortunately this type of situation is not common, although when it does occur it may persist for several consecutive days.

In commodity trading one must have strong nerves!

Now what should the speculator do to make money in commodity trading? First he must understand volume, open interest, short sales, and charting. Volume refers to the amount of trading taking place in each commodity daily and is broken up into the various trading months. It is unwise to speculate in commodities or in months in which the volume is small. This is because it may be difficult to liquidate a commodity at a fair price if there is little interest. The daily future volumes are listed in the *Wall Street Journal* and other newspapers. Two such lists are reproduced on the next page.

Note that some of the commodities had very few sales; some, none at all. Aluminum, for example, declined ½¢ per pound on only one sale. Commodities that are inactive should not be purchased.

Open interest refers to the number of contracts currently outstanding in each commodity, divided up into the various delivery months. These are also listed every day in the press, and the same rule applies here as in volume: Don't buy commodities for delivery at a time when there is a small open interest. The larger the open interest, the easier to liquidate your purchases.

Short selling is the sale of a commodity which the seller does not own, but which he believes will decline in price so that he will be able to repurchase his commodity more cheaply and thus make a profit. This stratagem is mentally difficult for the average speculator, who is never quite comfortable making such a sale. In the stock market it is very inadvisable for non-professionals to participate in short selling, because certain un-

COMMODITY FUTURES

COMMODITY FUTURES INDEX
NEW YORK — The Dow Jones commodity futures index closed at 140.61 yesterday, off 0.31 from the previous day.

SPOT INDEX
NEW YORK — The Associated Press weighted wholesale price index of 35 commodities yesterday advanced to 177.33.
Previous day 176.53, week ago 176.14, month ago 176.59, year ago 166.45.

	1965-66	1964	1963	196
High	177.73	166.99	162.77	166
Low	166.20	160.56	157.51	15

(1926 average equals 100.)

LONDON METALS
LONDON (AP) — Closing me (in pounds sterling a long ton): per spot bid 594 asked 596; for bid 570½ asked 571. Tin spot 1417½ asked 1420; forward bid asked 1410. Lead spot bid 110 110¼; forward bid 106½ asked Zinc spot bit 110½ asked 111½ ward bid, 107 asked 107¼.

PLATINUM
NEW YORK (CP) — Platin tures closed unchanged to .50 Jan. 1966 145.50; April 142.0 140.50; Oct. 135.00; Jan. 1967 April 132.50; sales 12 contracts

COTTONSEED OIL
NEW YORK (AP) — B1 cottonseed oil futures closed lower. Sales 56 contracts.

	High	Low
March	14.35	14.
May	14.35	14
July	14.40	14.
Oct.	13.78	13

Closing bids: Sept. 13.95.
Mississippi Valley crude oil was quoted at 14.00A ce

SILK
NEW YORK (AP) — Snof

WOOL GREAS
NEW YORK (AP) — '
closed .6 to .9 of a cent lc

	High
March	133.1
May	135.8
July	135.8
Oct.	136.8
Dec.	136.9
March	136.7
May	136.

Certificated wool spo Wool tops futures c sales.
Certificated spot woo

SILVER
NEW YORK (AP) — Silver futures |

ALUMINUM
NEW YORK (AP) — Aluminum futures closed 50 lower. Sales one contract.

	High	Low	Close
Jan	21.50	21.50	21.50

POTATOES
NEW YORK (AP) — Potato fu closed 1 to 6 cents high-

Volume and Open Interest

The Commodity Exchange Authority reports grain futures trading on the Chicago Board of Trade as of the close of business Tuesday, Jan. 11 (in thousands of bushels):

	March	May	July	Sept.	Dec.	Total
Wheat	6,843	4,757	3,218	1,706	296	16,820
Corn	9,796	5,694	2,224	572	622	18,908
Oats	844	1,268	304	35	45	2,496
Rye	473	1,116	215	95	85	1,984

Soybeans: January, 11,822; March, 28,362; May, 40,363; July, 20,440; August, 5,873; September, 6,243; November, 5,031; Total, 118,134.
Soybean oil trading (in tank cars of 60,000 pounds) totaled 3,003. Soybean meal trading (in hundreds of tons) totaled 1,760.

Open Interest (in thousands of bushels):

	Wheat	Corn	Oats	Rye
March	48,647	59,751	8,489	3,484
May	49,943	50,431	7,622	6,119
July	36,635	37,539	1,401	2,421
September	14,595	6,740	259	1,057
December	1,156	2,849	45	336
Total	150,976	157,310	17,816	13,417

	Soybeans	r-Soybean Meal	s-Soybean Oil
January	24,775	1,277	1,534
March	62,371	3,241	3,857
May	77,256	3,655	4,950
July	53,396	3,246	4,543
August	10,677	1,359	1,223
September	10,099	239	972
October		82	472
November	10,948		
December			
Total	249,522	13,116	17,827

r-In hundreds of tons. s-In tank cars of 60,000 pounds.
Open contracts for Tuesday and changes from Monday were as follows: Copper (50,000 pounds each), March 540, May 654, July 491, Sept. 795, Oct. 714, Dec. 184, Jan. 43, Total, 3,825, up 29. World Sugar (112,000 pounds each), March 3,825, up 29. World Sugar (112,000 pounds each), March 4,105, May 3,695, July 3,530, Sept. 2,342, Oct. 1,133, Nov. 269, March 343, May 101. Total, 15,518, up 352. Cocoa (30,000 pounds each), March 3,626, May 5,966, July 6,790, Sept. 3,382, March 876, May 82. Total, 24,146, up 29. Frozen Pork Bellies (30,000 pounds each), Feb. 3,239, March 3,422, May 2,588, June 9, July 1,922, Aug. 2,475, Total, 12,813, down 106. Shell Eggs (500 cases each), Jan. 1,145. Sept. 170, Oct. 15. Total, 1,330, down 35.

pleasant circumstances occasionally develop, such as a "short squeeze", in which the promoter of the stock buys up all the floating supply of the stock, temporarily forces the stock price up, then demands delivery of his stock. In the commodity market, however, such a corner of the market cannot occur, because there is a regulating body for commodities which strictly limits the amount of any commodity that may be held by any single speculator.

In addition the seller of a commodity cannot be requested to make delivery "on demand" but only when his futures contract has expired. For these reasons short selling in commodities is not so dangerous as short selling in stocks. Because there will be circumstances when certain commodities are obviously overpriced, speculators should overcome their prejudices against short selling. Short sales represent 50% of all profit possibilities in the commodity market and can be made as easily as a purchase.

An essential for the speculator in a commodity is to understand his commodity. He may never see the actual product, but he should know everything about it. No one can hope to keep track of all the commodities, and at least initially it is wise to restrict oneself to one or at the most two commodities. The daily market letter from a firm such as Merrill Lynch should be carefully read for some weeks before an initial trade is made. This diligence will take only ten minutes a day and will be amply repaid. It will not be long before the reader thinks that a commodity shows a possibility of price improvement. At that time he should buy one contract.

In order to make large profits, the speculator must determine to ride with the market but never to fight it. In purchasing a stock at a certain price, the intelligent speculator or investor will have carefully analyzed the company's value and prospects. If after such a purchase the price of the stock declines, it is often wise to buy more and average down the overall cost. After all, if Newconex stock appeared a good buy at

$5.25, it was an even better one at $4.75. This logic definitely does not apply to commodity futures, and the smart speculator *never* averages down. The reason is that it is impossible to analyze the value of a commodity as one can do with many stocks, and sugar that appears cheap at 3½¢ a pound may sell at only half of that figure in a few weeks. If a downward price trend develops in a commodity, it may go a very long way further than logic would suggest, and the speculator who continues to buy as it falls will soon have his capital wiped out.

Thus the primary rule for making money in futures is to sell if there is a small price decline after purchase, but hold on and buy more if the price goes up. An example is shown below.

MORTON P. SHULMAN
378 RONCESVALLES AV
TORONTO 3 ONTARIO　1962　606 10186

C

MERRILL LYNCH,
PIERCE, FENNER & SMITH

4-14-58.

THE MARKETS ON WHICH THESE TRANSACTIONS WERE MADE ARE INDICATED BY SYMBOLS WHICH ARE LISTED ON THE REVERSE SIDE.

ACCOUNT PURCHASE AND SALE OF ITEMS DESCRIBED, FOR YOUR ACCOUNT AND RISK.

| DATE | | | QUANTITY PURCHASED | QUANTITY SOLD | DESCRIPTION | MKT. | PRICE | COST OR PROCEEDS | DIFFERENCE | FEE AND/OR TAX | COMMISSION |
MO.	DAY	YR.									
4	8	58	1		CAK JUL 58 SUGAR 4	14	343	384160			
4	14	58		1	CAK JUL 58 SUGAR 4	14	339	379680	4480DR		3000

This way the speculator ends up with many small losses and a few huge profits. He need only detect and buy with one trend in order to make a fortune from a small investment.

Understanding charts and chartists is essential to the speculator in commodity futures. I have briefly discussed charts in an earlier chapter. Everything that has been said about them in reference to stocks applies twice as strongly in the commodity field, because chart followers are so very much more numerous here. Chart followers comprise the vast majority of speculators dealing in commodity futures. This produces tremendous opportunities for more sensible speculators.

The chartist pays little or no attention to news regarding supply and demand in his commodity; he ignores weather data and world crises but makes his sales and purchases according to records of the daily price range and volume fluctuations of each commodity. He believes that future price fluctuations can be predicted by studying recent, past, and current market action. The chartist explains his theories by saying that all news and facts are subject to different interpretations and that it is impossible for any individual to forecast price changes, because in addition to misinterpreting the significance of some facts, he is unaware of others. Furthermore, he believes that by the time pertinent events reach the newspapers, many individuals who have had prior knowledge have already made their own purchases or sales. The market, however, cannot be fooled (he believes), because all events and news are reflected in buying and selling in the market, and so by carefully studying market action one can predict future prices. The market action is studied by producing pictures or charts of daily price volumes and ranges in individual commodities. He believes that certain pictures forecast higher prices and other pictures lower prices.

To add to the confusion, chartists produce their charts in several different ways. Some use the daily price range and close; some also study the volume at each individual price; while others use price averages over longer periods of time.

Perhaps the market cannot be fooled, but unfortunately most chartists have a little problem in that they cannot understand their own charts. There is not a commodity salesman who has not heard the plaintive complaint, "My chart was right, but I read it wrong." Another important factor is that even when the chartist makes a correct guess of what he believes the chart says, he is often buying well after a trend has been established.

Despite all this scoffing, there is no question that when there are many chartists trading in commodities (or anything else), and when certain well-recognized "signals" appear in trading charts, indicating an upward or downward move in prices, usually such a move immediately follows. The reason is obvious. When thousands of chart followers expect an upward move in price, they buy—and of course there then occurs an upward price movement. Similarly, when thousands of chart followers expect a price fall, they sell, and prices must fall. Fantastic as this sounds, it is undoubtedly true; the chartists are producing their own price changes—and thus proving the merit of charting!

Because of the large number of chartists in the future market and because of the tremendous impact they can have on commodity prices, there will develop irrational price moves from time to time, based purely on widespread buying and selling by chart followers.

Because of the combination on the one hand of hedgers who must buy and sell regardless of price and on the other hand of chartists who follow present and past price and volume performance, an intelligent speculator has a greater chance of making huge profits in commodity futures than in any other gambling activity.

Briefly the pictures which chartists look for as guides are trend lines, double bottoms, double tops, head and shoulders tops, head and shoulders bottoms, congestion areas, triangles, flags, round tops and bottoms and gaps. These are illustrated on the following pages.

There does not appear to be any point in the speculator preparing his own charts. They are of value only to keep him informed of whether the thousands of chartists are buying or selling. His broker will be glad to inform him when the charts are clear cut, or he can subscribe to an excellent, reasonable service supplied by the Commodity Research Bureau, Inc., 82 Beaver St., New York.

In what commodity or commodities should a speculator seek to make his fortune?

Of the many that were listed earlier, the vast majority are unsuitable because of low volume or minimal price changes. For example, the low volume of aluminum rules it out; the protected market in domestic sugar makes a price rise rare and a price fall impossible. Out of the entire list, the six with the best possibilities of large price fluctuations are world sugar,

DAILY HIGH, LOW & CLOSE EGGS OCT. 1932 CHICAGO MERCANTILE EXCHANGE

DAILY HIGH, LOW & CLOSE ONIONS NOV. 1951 CHICAGO MERCANTILE EXCHANGE

Reprinted from
GUIDE TO COMMODITY PRICE FORECASTING
Published by
Commodity Research Bureau, Inc.
82 Beaver St.
New York, N.Y. 10005

DAILY HIGH, LOW & CLOSE HIDES DEC. 1948 COMMODITY EXCHANGE, INC. — N.Y.

DOUBLE TOP

UPTREND LINE

HEAD & SHOULDER BOTTOM

DOUBLE BOTTOM

Prepared by
COMMODITY RESEARCH BUREAU
82 Beaver St., New York 5, N.Y.

JAN. FEB. MAR. APR. MAY JUNE JULY AUG. SEPT OCT. NOV. DEC.

1948

DAILY HIGH, LOW & CLOSE CORN MAY 1925 CHICAGO BOARD OF TRADE

Prepared by
COMMODITY RESEARCH BUREAU
82 Beaver St., New York 5, N.Y.

COMPLEX HEAD & SHOULDER TOP

DOUBLE HEAD

DOUBLE SHOULDER

SHOULDER

BREAKAWAY GAP

PENNANT

FALSE BREAKOUT

EXHAUSTION GAP

PENNANT

PENNANT

DOWN PENNANT

PENNANT

FLAG

TRIPLE BOTTOM

PENNANT

FLAG

EXHAUSTION GAP

ISLAND REVERSAL

JUNE JULY AUG. SEPT OCT. NOV. DEC. JAN. FEB. MAR. APR. MAY

1924 1925

coffee, cocoa, soybeans, silver, and copper. This list will vary from time to time depending on world news and market conditions; when war threatens, for example, rubber futures soar. But four commodities that are always volatile are world sugar, cocoa, soybeans, and copper.

The single factor that produces volatility in the price of a commodity is a varying supply and/or demand. Inasmuch as demand usually remains fairly constant, showing a steady growth or decline, supply is the big factor. In some commodities, such as nickel or aluminum, supply is usually closely attuned to the demand, but in others, such as copper, supply is often outstripped by demand, resulting in much higher prices. This in turn stimulates more production, which finally results in prices falling. This is the ideal situation for a commodity speculator. Commodities that show the widest price swings invariably are produced in many countries and consumed in many other countries. The constant competition prevents price stabilization.

Occasionally a special situation develops in a normally stable commodity due to static supply but suddenly or gradually increased demand. This occurred in the silver market in 1964. For many years the price of silver had been stabilized at 92¢ by the U.S. government's freely selling silver at that price. A price rise had been forecast for two years by numerous authorities, because consumption was greater than production and the United States would certainly not be willing to sell their whole stockpile just to maintain silver's price at an artificially low level. Sure enough, the U.S. government stopped selling their silver, and the price soared to $1.29. Six-month and one-year futures had been available at prices ranging between 95¢ and 99¢ with only a 10¢ deposit. Thus speculators who had run practically no risk turned every $1,000 put up into $3,000 within a very few weeks. These advertised special situations appear every few years in the commodity market and the speculator should take advantage of them.

When making his initial investment the speculator should pick a "hot" commodity, one that is receiving a heavy trading volume and has a large open interest. It should show a large price range over the previous year and should be currently the subject of newspaper comment either as to its large price fall or its current short supply associated with a price rise.

The speculator must then decide whether he thinks this commodity will increase or fall in price in coming weeks. Strangely enough, it doesn't really matter what conclusion is arrived at, because half the time the "guess" will be right and half the time wrong. The speculator who pyramids his right guesses can afford to be wrong nine times out of ten and still end up a winner. The reason is that the wrong guesses should each end up with a small loss, whereas the right guesses should produce very large profits. This is where the stop loss comes in.

In an earlier chapter about stop loss selling, I condemned it as a practically useless tool in the stock market. The situation is quite different in the commodity market, because much more often trends will develop, producing a steady upward or downward price swing which goes far past true value levels. Because of this, it is essential that a speculator not attempt to fight a trend. Once a purchase has been made of a commodity future, a stop loss sell order should be entered at a level 5% below the purchase price. If there has been a short sale, a stop loss buy order should be entered 5% above the sale price. This 5% will actually represent 50% or more of your initial margin, and no loss on any contract should ever exceed 50% of the original margin. As an alternative to entering a stop loss order, one can follow the blanket rule of never putting up more margin.

Once a futures commodity has moved in price sufficiently to lose 25% of an initial margin deposit, the commodity broker will phone his client requesting more margin. On such occasions the astute speculator will not put up more money but will sell out his contract and take his loss.

This rule is basic to commodity trading—the man who becomes stubborn and sticks with a commodity that is going against him will soon be bankrupt. If a person cannot admit making a mistake, he should not buy commodities. The speculator who makes money in commodities is willing to accept loss after loss until he finds a commodity future that goes as he had expected. Such a future will quickly make up his losses.

The numerous losses are all quickly forgotten when one has a winner. The essential with a winner is to take full advantage of it and to make the largest possible profit. This is done by pyramiding. Pyramiding can be carried out in two ways.

The first is by simply instructing the broker to keep you within 10% of being fully margined. That is, if a commodity future which has been purchased goes up, the broker will buy another contract on the same future as soon as he can do so without any further investment of capital. If a November sugar contract has been purchased at a price of 3¢ per pound with a $500 down payment, once the sugar price climbs to 3½¢ and there has been a $500 paper profit, the broker uses the paper profit as margin to purchase a second contract in November sugar. Each contract represents 112,000 pounds of sugar, and so now the speculator owns 224,000 pounds of sugar. Now if sugar goes to 3¾¢, the broker buys another contract, using the additional $500 paper profit from the first two contracts as margin. Now the speculator owns 3 contracts, and sugar has only to go up one-sixth of a cent to 3.91¢ per pound to produce another $500 paper profit, allowing the purchase of still another contract. Following along on the same system, by the time sugar reaches 5¢ a pound, the speculator would own 33 contracts and would show a profit of $16,500 on his original $500 investment.

The reason that the broker is not instructed to keep you fully margined, but only 90% so, is to act as a protection in case of minor dips in the upward movement, which otherwise would result in a call for more margin.

The second type of pyramiding is usually the more profitable one, but it requires more margin and thus more risk. This involves purchasing more contracts at stated intervals as the price goes up. Thus the initial contract is purchased at a price of 3¢

per pound, and instructions are given to purchase additional contracts as quickly as they can be purchased from profits but with the difference that they must be purchased at intervals of no more than one-tenth of a cent. Thus when the sugar price reaches 3.1¢, a second contract will be purchased. At this point the profit is only $100, so an additional $400 margin must be deposited. At 3.2¢ a third contract is purchased which requires another $300 margin. At 3.3¢ a fourth contract is purchased which requires $200 margin, and at 3.4¢ a fifth contract, which will require $100 margin. From this point on no further margin is required and the total margin remains at $1,500.

If this procedure is continued and sugar continues to rise in price, by the time it reaches only 4½¢ a pound the speculator will own 38 contracts and will have made a profit of $38,000.

Admittedly this type of fantastic run is unusual without intermediate corrections, but it illustrates in a dramatic way the large profits possible in commodities, if one pyramids one's winning purchases and cuts losses to a minimum. It is very important that, if an upward move should be broken and more margin called for, the account be sold out and profits taken. There is always another commodity that can be purchased.

Exactly the same rules should be followed in selling a commodity short. If it then goes up, buy it back and take a small loss. If it goes down, sell more and pyramid the profits.

In all commodity trading there is one basic rule, which is exactly opposite to that in stock market trading: cut your losses and let your profits ride. Never average down.

One point which has not been discussed is which trading month should be bought or sold. Commodity brokers will usually recommend the earlier months and the shorter contracts, which automatically produce more frequent commissions, rationalizing this by saying that these months show the widest price swings and one can always trade the position for a later month if the contract becomes due. This is bad advice. It is wisest to purchase contracts for the most distant months except when there is a very wide price differential between the near and far months. (The price differential between near and far months should never exceed storage charges, because a commodity can always be purchased and stored for later delivery.) Buying distant contracts avoids the necessity of trading of contracts, thus reducing commissions.

In summary the rules for commodity trading are:

1. Pick an active commodity with a large open interest that is vulnerable to wide price swings. Soybeans, cocoa, world sugar, and copper are four perennial favourites.

2. Restrict your trades to one or, at the most, two different commodities.

3. Take an initial small position of one or two contracts in a distant month. Put in a stop loss order 5% below the market price in purchases and 5% above the market price in short sales.

4. Never put up additional margin.

5. Pyramid profits to within 90% of the maximum possible.

16

THE MONEY MARKET

This is also a future market—only instead of buying and selling commodities it involves the buying and selling of currency. This can be a very profitable undertaking and carries very little risk. Even more remarkable is the fact that no margin need be put up, and on occasion millions of dollars have been made with absolutely no investment.

The buying and selling of foreign currency is done constantly by importers. If an importer has ordered from another country a shipment of goods that he will have to pay for in some months, he may purchase a future for that amount of foreign currency, thus protecting himself against any price fluctuations. He wants to be sure to get his goods at the pre-arranged price and does not wish to gamble on the chance that the foreign currency might cost him more some months hence. It could, of course, also cost him less, but an importer knows that he can make money sticking to importing, and few of them wish to gamble in other matters. An exporter, on the other hand, may have sold to another country manufactured goods that are to be paid for in that country's currency. He cannot afford to take the chance that the foreign currency may have been devalued by the time he is paid, so he sells the equivalent amount of foreign currency in a future.

The mechanism of such a sale is very simple. The person wishing to buy or sell the future goes to his local bank and tells the accountant that he wishes to buy or sell the amount of the foreign currency for delivery on a predesignated date. For example, he may say, "I wish to sell 10,000 English pounds for delivery next July." The accountant will then say, "The rate is $2.99^{15}\!/_{16}$ per pound for next July delivery." The bank will require a form to be signed, a copy of which is given to the seller.

The exporter or importer has now protected himself completely and can forget all about the foreign currency. When the goods are ready, they will be paid for and delivered and the matter is finished.

The speculator has a different interest but his transactions are handled in the same way. When the speculator believes that a currency is about to be revalued, he will go to his bank and purchase or sell a future in that currency. When the future's time is up, or before if he wishes, he liquidates the transaction by buying or selling back the foreign currency.

This type of speculation is a relatively safe one, in that the risk is very small while the potential profit can be very large, because currency changes are rarely deep, dark secrets but are almost always predicted in the public press. The reason for this is that in the past thirty years all currency changes have been devaluations (with the single exception of a minor upward change in the Deutschmark), and devaluations only occur as a result of pressure upon a country's finances; these pressures build up gradually until the affected country finds it easier to

FORM 365 (REV. 4-50)

THE TORONTO-DOMINION BANK

June 10, 1966
DATE

We confirm having bought from/ sold to you today exchange
as detailed below:

TO ⌈   ⌉

   ⌊   ⌋

RATE — 2.99 15/16	AMOUNT AND KIND OF CURRENCY —	
DELIVERY Your Option — spot 30 days July 10th, 1966	£10,000.	
REMARKS —		

_____ Accountant   _____ Manager

NOTE—Please sign duplicate officially
and return promptly.

devalue than to continue to fight. For months before each devaluation, rumours and hints of the coming event are discussed in the financial pages.

In every such case the speculator cannot go very wrong by selling the threatened currency via a future. Even if the suggested devaluation does not ensue, the speculator loses very little. For example, in the fall of 1965 there were widespread rumours of a devaluation of the English pound. The English government was able to stave off this change and succeeded in maintaining the price of the pound at $2.73 U.S. Even at the height of the pressures against the pound, futures never sold at more than a few pennies below its spot conversion price, and so speculators who were proven wrong had very limited losses. On the other hand, those who sold the pound short after the war, when it was last devalued, made huge fortunes.

At that time the value of the pound was lowered from $5 to $2.75, and a speculator selling 100,000 pounds short would have made a profit of almost a quarter of a million dollars.

Sometimes governments publicly proclaim their intention to devalue. In 1962 Donald Fleming, the Canadian Minister of Finance, announced in a public speech that he felt the Canadian dollar was at too high a level and that it was his governments' intention to force it lower. On that date the Canadian dollar was at par with the U.S. dollar. Any Canadian who wished to make money merely had to go to his bank and buy a future on the U.S. dollar. Any American who wished to make money sold a future in Canadian dollars. The banks asked for no down payment or margin as long as they knew you and your credit rating was satisfactory. The $500,000 purchase shown below was made without putting up a penny.

FORM 565 (Rev. 4-54)

THE TORONTO - DOMINION BANK

July 19/63
DATE

We confirm having bought from/ sold to   you today exchange
as detailed below:

TO ⌈   ⌉

L   ⌟

RATE   — 8 1/8%

AMOUNT AND KIND OF CURRENCY —	
$500,000	U.S. Currency

DELIVERY
Your Option —

REMARKS —

Accountant

Manager

NOTE — Please sign duplicate officially and return promptly.

Six months after Mr. Fleming's speech, the Canadian dollar was reduced to 92½ U.S. cents, giving a clear profit on such a trade of $37,000.

Such devaluations are not always predicted as definitely as Mr. Fleming announced the Canadian one, but they are almost all announced in one way or another. Since the war one country after another has solved its balance of payments problem by devaluation. Some countries, like Canada, have done this twice. Only the United States has never devalued (see chapter on Gold).

About once a year such opportunities arise in the currency market. Once again it represents the opportunity for huge gains with very little risk.

17

INVESTMENT CLUBS

An investment club consists of a group of people who have joined together to pool funds, which are then invested in securities.

In the 1950's there was a rapid proliferation of these clubs, and many thousands were formed in the United States and Canada. In the boom markets which have since generally prevailed, many of these clubs have done fairly well, a few have foundered disastrously, and the vast majority have bumbled along with their investments doing slightly worse than the stock market averages. The reasons for this are not difficult to find.

Most clubs have anywhere from 6 to 20 members who make

a monthly contribution to the general kitty. At the regular meetings (usually monthly) the portfolio of the club is discussed and sales or new purchases are voted upon. Various members will discuss stocks they have heard about or read about and they will recommend these stocks for purchase by the group. Occasionally one member is assigned to study a specific stock and report back at the next meeting. Sometimes individual stockbrokers are invited to the meetings to give advice on the current portfolio. It has been my experience that impatience, inconsistency, a desire to take profits, and plain greed are the basic causes of the problems of investment clubs.

When a group forms an investment club, presumably it should be for the purpose of making their dollars grow while at the same time having the pleasure of monthly get-togethers. Capital gains should be the primary interest, and dividends should be of little account. Thus every stock purchase should be made with growth in mind, and each security should be analyzed as to its growth possibilities and its safety. Once a stock has been bought for these reasons, it should be held indefinitely.

Unfortunately impatience is the keynote of too many investment clubs. All too often I have heard, "We've held it for a year, and it's done nothing. Let's sell it and switch the money into something that's moving." Six years ago those words persuaded one group to sell Simpson's stock at $23 and Bank of Montreal stock at $40. Both more than doubled during the following months.

An investment club is constantly hearing new suggestions of stocks in which to invest. The temptation to sell part of their holdings in order to buy something new succeeds only in giving commissions to the brokers. This urge to buy every stock suggested leads some groups to trade the market so as to catch the price swings. It is absolutely impossible to be successful in such a venture, and it invariably leads to a serious loss of capital.

Inconsistency is a very serious problem in some investment

clubs. Because of the number of people involved in the investing, some of whom will present their arguments more force-
fully from time to time, and some of whom may not be present
at subsequent meetings, the club may change its investment
policy many times in a year. One club swung from buying convertible bonds, to selling calls, to buying mining stocks, and
finally to buying American exchange glamour stocks. Every
time they changed their policy, they lost money because of the
switch in securities with consequent necessity to pay extra commissions. There does not appear to be any way to prevent these
inconsistencies. One club had written into its constitution the
rule that it must not buy on margin, and yet within a year it
was persuaded to do just that.

The desire to realize profits often is overwhelming: "All
right, this has gone up from $50 to $55. That's a pretty good
profit for a three-month hold; let's sell it and switch into something that's still down." Two years ago I persuaded an investment club, of which I am a member, to buy several hundred
shares of Federal Pacific Pioneer Electric convertible preferred
at $53 a share. It has moved up steadily since that time to its
current $70, but there has not been a meeting since when some
well-meaning soul has not suggested selling "at least half" before it goes back down again.

The club has one member who has a new "hot tip" for every
meeting: "My customer's man says Fairchild (or Syntex or
Moly) is going to $200 a share this year. Let's sell everything
and buy it. It earned 20¢ last year and next year he says earnings will be over $10." The fact that the stock may be selling
at 100 times its current earnings does not faze this gullible investor, and he is quite willing to accept fantastic estimates of
future earnings as definite fact. I missed one meeting and he
triumphantly persuaded the members of the investment group
to sell part of their Federal Pacific Electric and buy Sharon
Steel at $25 a share. "It'll earn $3 a share next year." The group
sold the Sharon at $22 one month later.

Greed is the final drawback to investment clubs. We are all greedy in that we want to make money either for its own sake (a very common illness today) or else for the material comforts and ease that the money can buy, or perhaps for the good that we think we will be able to perform with money. Unfortunately greed in a group often will cause the group to toss aside prudent restraints as no individual in that group would on his own.

Thus we find investment groups purchasing wild promotional stock which may very easily lose its entire value before the investment group's next meeting. They find it hard to resist the lure of, "It could easily go from $2 to $200. They have a patent on a new invention that will revolutionize the industry." It is amazing how much worthless stock is sold in this way.

Despite the foregoing, investment clubs are not all bad. They have two great virtues.

1. They enable the novice investor to learn many of the market rules at very little cost to himself. If a stock costs $1,000 to buy and it goes down to $100, each individual member of an average size club will have lost only $50, which is a pretty cheap lesson of this sort. Membership in a club gives a beginner the chance to participate in discussions leading to purchase of many securities. In this way an investment club is better than a mutual fund, in which the investor may make money but will learn nothing. Besides which it is much more fun.

2. I am afraid that the major advantage of investment clubs is social. Many of these organizations have a brief half-hour meeting, which is followed by a poker game. In many clubs the card game has become the major attraction, to the point where it attracts many ex-members or non-members of the club. And it's a lot easier to tell your wife that you are going to an investment meeting than to a poker game.

In summary, investment clubs can be a lot of fun for social

and educational reasons. Individual investments should be kept to a very small sum, and under these circumstances the fun cannot be seriously marred by financial loss. Large investments should not be made in this way.

18

LIFE INSURANCE

The single most common investment for the individual in North America today is life insurance. In addition to being the most common investment it is also the least productive; in fact, insurance should not be considered an investment at all.

Life insurance is bought for two reasons—protection and savings. As pure survivor protection there can be no quarrel with insurance. By paying small premiums each individual helps alleviate the risk of untimely death of many other individuals. This is term insurance; its cost is very low, and it allows the family's breadwinner to be sure that his wife and children will have an adequate income should he die unexpectedly. The man who buys term insurance is proving his love for his family.

Unfortunately most insurance that is sold is not term insurance. All other insurance plans contain a combination of protection and savings and cost much more than term insurance plans. The names of the various policies may be ordinary life, 20-year pay or endowment, or whole life, but these terms refer only to the varying percentages of protection and savings in each policy.

Millions of dollars have been spent in advertising the merits of ordinary insurance and the virtues of investing in life insurance. The protection aspect of insurance is often played down and the excellent investment aspect is emphasized. Who has not seen an ad in which the happy 65-year-old has completely paid up his policy and now begins to draw monthly annuity cheques? Unfortunately when we consider the three basics of any investment—yield, safety, and possible capital appreciation—it soon becomes clear that insurance is probably the worst investment of any described in this book.

Most insurance companies sell term insurance only when requested. They strongly advise their agents to recommend the other types of insurance, and as a financial inducement to the agents have made the commission on term insurance only a small fraction of that paid when other life insurance is sold. The companies even go so far as to accuse an agent of "twisting" if he advises any insured person, whether or not he is that company's client, to change from higher cost insurance to term. A twister will be quickly fired by many insurance companies. When an individual has purchased term insurance, the company will periodically go to great efforts in an attempt to persuade him to convert his policy to a more expensive insurance.

Why do insurance companies prefer not to sell term insurance? Their salesmen give 6 reasons:

1. Regular insurance gives permanent protection. Term insurance runs out at age 65.

True; but if the purpose of insurance is to protect one's family from financial loss in case of death of the breadwinner, this reason is foolish. How many men of 65 have children still going to school? How many dying with insurance at that age do not already have adequate investments elsewhere to look after their widows?

    2. The cost of term insurance rises yearly until it becomes prohibitively expensive in one's late fifties.

This is only true if the term insurance is so-called one-year renewable term, which is usually purchased by the man investing elsewhere who wants temporary protection. He buys this insurance because it is very cheap and he has no intention of keeping it for more than a very few years. The individual wanting permanent protection should buy flat-rate term insurance. The premium on this type of policy remains constant and does not rise as the owner gets older.

    3. Regular insurance compels people to save who would otherwise spend their money on frivolities.

I have wondered for some years whether this might not be the only valid reason to recommend ordinary insurance. However, I have concluded that any individual who has the will power to meet the regular insurance payments would also have enough will power to save in any other scheme. In any case if there are a few persons to whom this forced saving would be of value, they are unlikely to be among those who have invested several dollars to buy this book.

    4. With regular insurance there is always a backlog of savings which can be borrowed if necessary. This is not possible with term insurance.

Very true, but what the insurance companies do not point out is that the amount that can be borrowed is equivalent to the overpayments that have been made on the policy in excess of the cost of term insurance. What is much worse is the fact that the insurance company will charge you 5% for the privilege of borrowing your own money! Furthermore if there should be such a loan outstanding at the time of your death, the amount of the loan will be deducted from the face value of the policy, even though it represented an earlier overpayment of premium.

  5. Ordinary insurance has a cash surrender value in case of emergency. The policy can be turned in, and the policy holder will receive a sum of money equal to the size of the savings portion of the policy.

Also very true, but the flaw is that in order to get his cash surrender value, the policy holder must give up his insurance protection. If the savings had been in some other form than insurance and the same emergency arose, the policy holder could have used his savings without losing his insurance.

  6. The lapse rate of term insurance is much higher than that of ordinary insurance.

This is very true, and the reason is very obvious. Term insurance is like fire insurance in that it is purchased for a specific purpose, in this case to insure a specific life. Once that need for protection is gone—if, for example, children have grown up and gone to work or the owner of the insurance has made a great deal of money—then the insurance will often be deliberately cancelled. Ordinary insurance on the other hand, has involved the owner in a long-term savings program which will be lost if the insurance is lapsed.

What is wrong with ordinary insurance as an investment? Let us consider the three basics—yield, safety, and possibilities of capital appreciation.

First it must be understood that the premium in an ordinary insurance policy consists of two parts: one for protection, which is the term insurance part, and one for savings. When considering the yield, one must disregard the part of the premium that goes for protection, because this money would have to be spent for protection anyway and so no yield should be expected upon it. Let us suppose that the owner of an ordinary policy has the good fortune to live out his policy term, say twenty years, and receives a capital sum. He will find that he will have received back his complete overpayment plus interest at the rate of about 6% compounded annually. Not bad, except for one flaw. If he makes the mistake of dying before the twenty years is up, the entire "savings" portion of the policy is forfeited to the insurance company. Therefore, in order to make certain that his capital is safe and that he will get his 6%, the policy holder must be sure to outlive his policy. If he does not do so, both capital and interest are completely lost to his surviving family.

But won't they get the insurance? Certainly it will be paid, but the total overpayment of premiums which went into the savings part of the policy is lost.

The third factor is appreciation of capital. There is no argument on this point. There is no possibility of capital appreciation in the savings portion of a life insurance policy. The best that can be hoped for is a return of capital plus interest.

Now we find a seventh reason why insurance companies prefer to sell ordinary insurance, but their salesmen don't tell you this one: They must make money from such sales. When they sell term insurance, the insurance company ends up making less than 10% of the total premiums as a profit after paying all claims and expenses. This percentage is arrived at by continually adjusting insurance premiums downwards as human longevity increases so as to maintain a reasonable profit margin.

In ordinary insurance, even if the same profit percentage were to be maintained, the company would make much larger profits because it would be making the same percentage on double or triple the premiums. In fact, their actual percentage profit is much higher because a little thought will show that the customer cannot win.

Everyone who buys a policy must either live for the lifetime of that policy or die before it has come due. If he dies before the policy has come due, the protection portion of the policy is paid to the family, but the savings portion is forfeited to the company. If, on the other hand, the policy holder outlives his policy, then he receives back his savings plus interest, but he has obliged the insurance company by not forcing them to pay a death claim, so that they gained all his premiums at no cost to themselves.

In other words, heads the policy holder loses, tails the insurance company wins! Small wonder that insurance company stocks have soared by thousands of per cent in the past decade.

What then is the proper course for the individual to follow? It is a very simple one. He should buy the insurance necessary to protect his family in case of an untimely death. He should buy the cheapest form of insurance, which is term, and he should drop it just as soon as the need for protection has passed. This point will come either when the family are independently on their own or when the policy holder's assets have reached the point that they are sufficiently large to look after his family in case of his death. The extra money that is left over, and which can represent as much as 90% of the premiums on certain endowment policies, should be invested in convertible bonds, mutual funds, or certain of the other investment suggestions described in this book.

These facts are not new. Thousands of insurance men know their truth, and a book was first published 'way back in 1936 exposing the truth. Yet every time some brave insurance agent or investment counselor attempts to show these facts to the public, there is an outraged cry of heresy from the insurance companies, and long, learned treatises are published pointing out the virtues of buying insurance.

I can't blame the insurance companies very much or their agents at all. After all, it is a multibillion dollar industry upon which now depends thousands of jobs. However, it is not necessary for the life insurance industry to survive by using these methods. The fire insurance companies make money every year by selling fire insurance protection, and they don't insist on their policy holders making a savings deposit with every fire insurance premium; nor should the life insurance companies.

What should the investor do who has been carrying insurance for some years and now finds that due to his over payments his policies now have a large cash surrender value? Regardless of his age he will find that he is better off to cash in these policies and purchase whatever insurance protection is needed in the form of term insurance. Caution must be followed here, however. The policy holder was physically fit when he originally bought his insurance, but today it may not be possible for him to pass the physical examination. Therefore, he should buy whatever term insurance he needs first before surrendering his other life insurance. The capital received back should be carefully invested.

Many holders of insurance have not given real consideration to their true insurance protection needs for many years. They have just automatically paid their annual premiums. A lot of these people will discover that they no longer need any protection at all and can cash in their policies without buying any term insurance. After all, the purpose of insurance is to leave sufficient money to allow the surviving family to continue to maintain the same standard of living. There is no need to leave survivors moneys beyond this necessity. The premiums going for unnecessary insurance would be better used to give more leisure from work, to travel, to enjoy, or for charity.

What kind of term insurance should the individual purchase? There are 3 basic types:

1. Renewable term
2. Flat-rate term
3. Decreasing term

Renewable term should be purchased by the individual seeking temporary protection. This is initially the cheapest possible type of insurance, but the premium gradually rises over the life of the policy. A professional man just starting his practice could buy this type of insurance with the intention of dropping it after he has built up a reasonable estate.

Flat-rate term is the cheapest long-term form of life insurance. It is recommended for the person who is probably always going to need protection insurance. Initially it will cost more than double the price of renewable term, but the premium remains constant at about one-half or less that of regular insurance.

Decreasing term is a special type of term insurance in which the premium remains constant but the face value of the policy gradually decreases. This is the best type of insurance for the person who is building up an estate and whose requirements for insurance are gradually decreasing.

In summary:

1. Life insurance is the worst possible form of investment. A young man in his twenties can buy $100,000 worth of term insurance for as little as $350 a year. He is foolish indeed if he pays $1,000 or $3,000 for the same protection, the savings feature of which disappears on death.

2. Buy enough term insurance necessary to protect your family.

3. When the need for protection ceases drop the insurance.

4. Invest the extra funds in convertible bonds or preferreds or in a mutual fund.

5. Do not continue to maintain ordinary insurance policies just because they have been held for some years. It is better to buy term insurance and cash the older policies.

6. When buying any insurance get the advice of a lawyer or trust company. It is very difficult for an insurance agent to give unbiased advice when one firm's term insurance policy pays him a commission of $12.50 while by selling an endowment policy with the same face value he will receive $190.00. It is asking too much of human nature for him to be unbiased.

7. Buy one year renewable term or flat-rate term or reducing term, depending on your individual needs as described earlier.

8. Never convert term insurance to regular insurance.

9. Finally, don't buy insurance as an investment. It is an excellent protection; buy it for that reason only.

19

REAL ESTATE

Real estate is second only to life insurance in the numbers of those who invest in it. Every worker in every factory in the country has the ambition to own his own home. Today more than ever he is succeeding in his ambition. For most North Americans, purchase of a home will be the largest investment they will ever make. How good is real estate as an investment? How does it compare with the stock market, with mutual funds, or with convertible bonds?

First, real estate must be defined. It includes raw land, homes, apartments, and commercial properties. It does not include mortgages. Mortgages are loans given to individuals by lenders at a fixed rate of interest with real estate deposited as security for the loan. If the value of the real estate is many times that of the loan, the risk is very small. The interest rate will then be lower than if the loan is very close to the value of the real estate, in which case the risk is much larger. A first mortgage represents a primary debt; in the event of default of the loan, the real estate must be sold to pay this debt. A second mortgage in such a case will be paid only if there are funds available after the first mortgage has been paid. Interest rates are, therefore, much higher on second mortgages. On a first mortgage rates vary between 4¾ and 8 per cent, depending on current money costs. On a second mortgage the rate may go as high as 15% per year.

Most homes that are bought today are largely paid for by placing a mortgage on the home. This will normally supply three-quarters of the cost of acquiring the home. If the new homeowner does not have enough money to pay the remaining portion, he must place a second mortgage on his house, greatly increasing the interest and payment burden he must meet.

Mortgages are, therefore, loans. They are directly comparable with bonds, which were discussed previously, and most mortgages are given out by large corporations, trust and insurance companies, etc., who make their profits by collecting the interest. Some individuals also give mortgages in real estate, often at the suggestion of their lawyer, who will also have clients buying homes who need such mortgages. These individuals are making a serious error. Some investments are excellent in good times and dangerous in bad, while others flourish in bad times and are not so good in inflationary days. Mortgages, on the other hand, can be bad in bad times and bad in good times. It is best to leave them to the insurance companies.

The problem of the mortgage in times of inflation such as we are now experiencing is that the dollar can lose its buying value faster than it earns interest. Thus a ten-year mortgage paying 6% interest may very well have a buying power of only

60% of its face value when it comes due ten years hence. This is the same problem that bondholders face—no possibility of capital appreciation and no protection against inflation. In the real rip-roaring inflation some European countries suffered in the late twenties and early thirties, mortgage holders lost everything, for their mortgages were finally paid off with worthless money.

The problems of the mortgage holder in periods of severe deflation or depression can be just as bad. In the 1930's in the United States and Canada, thousands of homeowners could not meet their mortgage payments, and in many cases the homes were not worth in 1930 dollars anywhere near the face value of the mortgage. Not only the homeowner, but in many cases the mortgage owner as well, lost everything. To add to the woes of mortgage owners, many governments declared a "moratorium" which removed any requirement for payments on mortgages during the years that the moratorium was in force.

On top of everything else, there is one further serious disadvantage to ownership of mortgages even in normal times, and this is the complete lack of liquidity. Most of the disadvantages of mortgages apply to bonds, but at least a bond can always be sold even though sometimes at a loss. A mortgage, however, can only be sold by finding an individual buyer, and there is no exchange where buyers are always waiting. Practically speaking, because of the difficulty and expense involved, mortgages are rarely resold but must be held until maturity.

In brief, mortgages are poor investments for individuals. They should be avoided.

Now back to real estate. This can be arbitrarily divided between land and structures built upon the land. If there are structures on the land, a purchase can give income in the form of rent or it can give shelter if the owner lives in the building —or it can give both, as with a duplex. The purchaser of bare land, on the other hand, can usually get neither income nor security; if he is astute and lucky, however, he may make sizable capital gains.

Since purchase of a home is the American's commonest and largest investment, let us discuss it first. What should be paid, what should one look for, should one buy or rent, how does a home purchase compare with other investments?

On a purely financial basis, purchase of a home by the average person is bad economics. It is cheaper to live in an apartment close to the centre of the city both as to actual cost of living and time and expense saved in commuting. However, psychological and other factors are perhaps more important than finance in this particular investment. Wives want "a house of their own with a patch of grass", while there is no doubt that a husband gets more satisfaction and sheer pleasure from a home than he will get from any pile of stock and bond certificates. So on this particular subject I will plead "Nolo Contendere" and confine my remarks to what should be paid for a house.

The maximum total price should be three times the husband's annual income. Couples who use their combined incomes in calculating this figure may come to regret it, for all too often the wife's income soon ceases. In addition, the couple should be able to make a cash down payment of 25% of the purchase price, while the balance should be financed with one long-term mortgage, and provision should be made for unexpected house expenses.

Purchase of a house or houses for the purpose of renting is economically unproductive when compared with other investments. This is not true in reference to apartment houses. A fully rented apartment house today (and in most areas they are fully rented) can easily give an annual return of 15 to 20% after all expenses and mortgage payments are met. This high return has allowed a number of individuals to make very profitable investments in this field in recent years. The disadvantages are two. Lack of liquidity is one, although this is probably not so bad as with mortgages. The more serious one is the very grave financial setbacks that can occur in times of recession. That 20% return will rapidly diminish with a few vacant apartments. If a situation ensues as it did thirty years ago where apartments are half or more empty, financial disaster can supervene. The great disadvantage of this type of investment as compared with stocks or bonds is that while all of them will go down in price in depression times, the stocks and bonds may stop bringing an income, but they do not produce a drain. Apartment owners, however, may find that their steady income has turned into a steady outlay, because the apartment must still be serviced; it must be heated and tax and mortgage payments must continue.

Despite the return possible on this investment, it should be reserved strictly for the wealthy businessman or investor with large assets who can afford the potential risks involved. Apartment owning is not for the investor with limited means and is definitely not for the widow or orphan.

Now we come to land. This is the primary and ultimate wealth. All other assets and valuables can be increased or more can be found. Not so with land; there is only so much and it is all highly coveted. As our population continues to increase, the amount of land available per person must fall and its value must rise. Over the long-term picture, land is an investment that must increase in value. Unfortunately, long term is not too important to us, because we humans are short term. It really doesn't matter much to the individual if land goes up ten times in value over a fifty-year period. The original owner will not be there to enjoy his investment, and practically speaking no investment should be bought whose prospective rewards may take longer than five years to come to fruition.

Short-term land holding may be profitable, but it can be exactly the opposite. When we consider the three basics, income, safety, and capital gain, plus the problem of liquidity, it becomes clear that land speculation is very chancy indeed.

Raw land usually brings no income. In fact there is a constant outlay, because all potentially valuable land requires the annual payment of a land tax to the local municipality. This can range up to $200 an acre or much higher in highly developed areas. Occasionally the land can be rented for farming, but this brings very little income.

Raw land is much more liquid than other forms of real estate, with the exception of the single family home. It can always be sold. There is always someone willing to buy land, but the price may be disappointing.

There is certainly no safety of capital in owning raw land. In fact prices can fluctuate downwards by 50% or more in a few weeks. During the tremendous building boom in the fifties, raw land around Toronto surged from $20 an acre up as high as $10,000 an acre in a few areas. There was then a tightening of moneys available for mortgages and building, and this undeveloped land in many cases was dumped for whatever it would bring. In one case I know of, a 40-acre site was bought for $55,000 and the $10,000 down payment was completely abandoned in only ten weeks when the initial mortgage payment came due.

Capital gains are certainly possible in the purchase of land. In fact this is the only one of the three requirements for an investment that applies to the purchase of land (unless it is intended to develop it). Since the war huge fortunes have been made around every city in North America by land speculators. The technique that is used often will see $1,000 turn into $100,000 or even $1,000,000, even though the land only goes up perhaps two or three times in price. This is done through options or else through the small down payment-huge mortgage system.

Ideally a land speculator will attempt to buy a tract of land near a city by offering the farmer or original holder perhaps 20% more than the land is worth. After dazzling him with this relatively high figure, however, he then gives him perhaps

1% of the named price for a one-year option on the land. If the boom continues the speculator can make a huge capital gain. If it does not, he just drops his option. For example, a large farm twelve miles from Toronto might be worth on an immediate sale perhaps $500,000. The speculator will offer to pay the farmer $600,000 on an option basis. If the farmer bites, he will actually be given $7,500 cash for a one-year option on his land at the $600,000 price.

One year later, if the boom has continued, that same land might be worth $1,000,000. The speculator now exercises his option and resells the land, receiving $400,000 for a one-year $7,500 speculation. If, on the other hand, the land boom falters, the speculator will drop his option and lose his $7,500.

The alternative method of land speculation is the actual purchase of the land but with a small down payment and no sizable payments for some time. For example, the speculator might offer $550,000 for that same farm that was worth $500,000, but the down payment will only be $10,000 with no further payments for one year. The actual purchaser will be a limited company, and if land prices falter no second payment will be made and the mortgage will be defaulted.

Although land speculators can make huge profits, there is one additional overriding drawback to this type of speculation. Presumably most speculators and investors have their own jobs or businesses to which they devote most of their working hours. They find it quite possible to intelligently invest in convertible bonds or even in stocks or warrants by giving up only a few minutes per day. This is not true of land speculation or indeed of any aspect of real estate investment. This type of speculation is extremely demanding of time if it is to be successful, because each individual transaction requires days to properly investigate and consummate. Land speculation, therefore, cannot be successfully carried on by the dabbler. All drawbacks considered, it is best left to the full-time expert in this field.

In summary, although the rewards in real estate can be staggering in size, the costs, the time, the dangers and the lack of liquidity completely offset them. With the exception of purchase of a home, the ordinary investor or speculator is well advised to keep away from real estate.

20

CASH IN THE BANK—
AND OTHER ODDS AND ENDS

How much money should be kept as a cash reserve? Most financial advisors recommend that 25% of one's capital should be kept liquid in case of emergency. I do not agree with this, and in fact I have never had more than two or three hundred dollars in the bank for longer than a few days. It is my belief that investment money should be kept working all the time, and when it is in a bank earning 2% interest per year it is working for only a very small part of the day. Far better to invest your money in a mutual fund or convertible bond and draw 5% or 6% interest with the excellent possibility of large capital gains.

The bogie of financial emergencies has been greatly overdone. Mutual funds or bonds can be sold and the cash received within three days. It is hard to imagine an emergency in which the money must be produced in less than that time. If such a disaster should occur, it should be remembered that brokers will be happy to margin securities, lending 50% of the value on stocks and up to 90% on bonds. This cash loan can be arranged and picked up within minutes.

There is, therefore, no need for the average investor to have large sums of cash lying idle in bank accounts. However, for those investing largely in common stocks, funds are necessary in case the stock moves down in price so that the investor can average down. Those persons buying stocks on margin also must have a cash reserve; otherwise they may be forcibly sold out if their stocks move down in value and they are unable to put up more margin.

With these two exceptions there are better places for money than in bank accounts. This is not to suggest that investors should rush to buy securities just for the sake of having all their money invested. There will be occasions when securities have been sold and there does not appear to be a good buying opportunity currently available. It is far better to wait for a good investment rather than rush to buy one which may be only so-so. What should be done with the cash in the meantime?

Guaranteed trust certificates are now available whereby cash can be deposited with a trust company for periods varying anywhere from thirty days to five years, with a guaranteed return of anywhere from 5% to 7%, depending on the length of the deposit. For the speculator or investor with temporary cash, the thirty-days deposit is perfect. At the present time such deposits will give a yield of 6⅛%, and the money is soon available if during the thirty days a good investment opportunity arises. If at the end of that time there is no need for the cash, it can be redeposited for another thirty days. Furthermore, the risk to the invested capital is practically nil.

Long-term trust certificates should not be purchased. They

are equivalent to bonds in all of their characteristics, except
that they are less liquid. They are quite safe and the yield is
very reasonable, but there is no possibility of capital appreciation and there is no protection against inflation.

Some speculators hold on to their cash in an effort to buy
stocks in market depressions with the intention of selling when
the market moves back up.

How well can the market action be predicted? Everyone
wants to buy low and sell high. But the trouble is that no one
agrees on when the market is low or high. It is useless to try
and follow the experts' advice, for they seem to be consistently
wrong. The Securities Exchange Commission made a detailed
study of the 900 pieces of advice sent out by 166 investment
advisers and brokers before the 1946 market break. Only 4%
of these forecast the market fall. Going back to 1929, Alfred
Cowles III made a study of some 7,500 specific recommendations. He found that, over all, the recommendations behaved
slightly worse than the average behaviour of all common stocks.

Since the experts are consistently wrong, how can the ordinary investor hope to predict the market's moves. Of course
he can't. The point was well answered by Bernard Baruch who
replied to the question of whether the market was too high,
"I have never answered that question, because I do not think
anyone is smart enough to know and I certainly would not want
to put myself in that class of demigod." Baruch's must be the
final word in forecasting the market, and anyone who is foolish
enough to attempt to trade the market swings must end up
losing his capital. The market does not follow patterns of the
past, and its future cannot be predicted.

As a final note on the difficult art of predicting the future,
the experience of a friend corroborated my belief. The man is
a psychologist and statistics expert who has done very well in
numerous financial enterprises. He has rented from I.B.M. a
complicated computer into which he has fed thousands of facts
about the market's past performances. He is convinced that
this mighty machine, which is wiser and more knowledgable

than any human mind, has now solved the prediction problem. As proof some months ago he handed me the computer's prediction of an immediate rise in market prices. Since then stock prices have moved steadily downwards to reach a two-year low . . . and there goes another theory.

Although market action cannot be predicted, the action of individual securities often can. If they are purchased for reasons of basic value, as previously explained, the investment must be a profitable one. If the investor has erred in his analysis, he will at least be protected against large loss if he has been sufficiently prudent to purchase one of the convertible securities.

The subject of margin has not been discussed earlier. Whether to margin or not cannot be answered with a straight yes or no. Margin involves only putting up a portion of the purchase price of a security and borrowing the balance from the broker and paying interest on it. Buying on margin greatly increases both the profit possibilities and the risks. For that reason widows and orphans or anyone who cannot afford to lose should never use margin. For the speculating businessman there are occasions when he would be foolish not to margin.

To take an example, when Federal Pacific Electric issued their 5½% convertible preferred at $50 a share, it was the perfect time to margin. It was obvious to anyone examining the company and the stock that there was no risk of the stock's collapsing, and so there was no increased danger through margining. Also the 5½% yield of this preferred stock would more than cover the interest charges payable to the broker for the borrowed money. If the investor had $5,000 to invest, he could have either bought 100 shares of F.P.E. preferred outright or 200 shares on margin. When the stock rose the next year to $80, he would have made $3,000 without the margin, or $6,000 if he had margined—in either case there was the same $5,000 investment. Thus here was an example of how margining could double profits without either risk or cost.

In cases of convertible bonds the difference in profit through margining can range up to 1,000 per cent. For example, when Canadian Utilities issued their convertible bond, the downside risk was nil due to the high interest rate of 5½% on the bond plus the convertible factor. These bonds could be margined by putting up only 10% of the purchase price, so that an investor with $1,000 could buy one bond outright or 10 bonds on margin. Two years later when the bonds reached $1,600, the outright purchaser had made $600 while the man who margined made $6,000.

Margin properly used will greatly increase profits without undue risk. Improperly used it will increase risks beyond the potential profits. Each case must be decided on its individual merits. If the downside risk, as in a convertible security with a good yield, is minimal it is smart to margin.

Rights, Splits, and Shorts

Often a corporation will decide to raise fresh capital through the issue of more common stock. In order to successfully sell this stock, the corporation must offer it at a price below the current market price of the stock. In order (a) not to force down the market for the company's stock and (b) to be fair to the stockholders, the corporation will usually issue transferrable options to its shareholders to purchase the new shares. These options differ from warrants in that they have a much shorter life, usually running for only three or four weeks. This is because the corporation wishes to have the money immediately, and issuance of a long-term option or warrant would not bring in any cash for some time.

These options are called rights. Because of their short life, they also differ from warrants in that they usually carry no premium over their true value. Thus if Newconex is trading at $6 and has a warrant outstanding good to buy stock at $5 for two years, it will trade at about $2. However, a right to buy Newconex at $5 which is good for one month will trade at only $1. Because these rights do not trade at a premium, they often will have tremendous leverage (explained in chapter on warrants), and sometimes in a few days they can move up or down spectacularly. For example, the Bell Telephone Company issues very few bonds and instead every year or so will give its shareholders rights to buy more stock at a price below the market. A typical issue might see Bell stock trading at $55 and rights issued to buy more stock at $50, with 20 rights required to buy one share. Each right is therefore worth 25¢ and would trade at 25¢. The leverage factor is very high; the actual figure is 12:1, and in order for the rights to double in value the Bell stock need only move up 10%. Unfortunately Bell stock is very stable, and price moves tend to be very slow.

Thus in order for the speculator to make money in rights, leverage is not enough, and because of the short time available, the stock involved must be a very volatile one. An example of such an issue was made in March, 1963, by the Trans Canada Pipeline Company. At this time the company needed further capital to complete its expansion program and issued free rights to its shareholders at the rate of one right per share. For every 23 rights held, the bearer was entitled to buy one $100 convertible bond which was convertible into stock of the company at a price of $26 per share. The rights were good only until April 4. The common stock was then trading at $22 per share and the rights were freely available between 50¢ and 56¢.

HECTOR M. CHISHOLM & CO. LIMITED

MEMBERS
TORONTO STOCK EXCHANGE
MONTREAL STOCK EXCHANGE
CANADIAN STOCK EXCHANGE
82 RICHMOND ST. WEST
TORONTO 1, CANADA
TEL. 36Z—4731

TO ⌈

| | | | | X | THE TORONTO STOCK EXCHANGE | | | DATE | Mar. 18/63 |

WE HAVE THIS DAY **BOUGHT** FOR YOUR ACCOUNT ON — THE CANADIAN STOCK EXCHANGE — THE UNLISTED MARKET — VALUE Mar. 21/63

BROKER	SHARES	DESCRIPTION	PRICE	AMOUNT	COMMISSION	TAX	TOTAL
Waite	1000	Trans. Can. P. L. RTS.	.56	560.00	10.00		570.00

E. & O.E.

PURCHASES OR SALES ARE MADE WITH THE DISTINCT UNDERSTANDING THAT ACTUAL DELIVERY IS CONTEMPLATED, AND ARE SUBJECT IN ALL RESPECTS TO THE BY-LAWS, RULES AND CUSTOMS OF THE STOCK EXCHANGE WHERE THE ORDER IS EXECUTED AND TO THE CUSTOMS OF THE BROKERAGE BUSINESS. IT IS AGREED THAT ALL SECURITIES CARRIED FROM TIME TO TIME IN THE CUSTOMER'S MARGINAL ACCOUNT, OR DEPOSITED TO PROTECT THE SAME, MAY BE LOANED BY US OR MAY BE PLEDGED BY US ON OUR GENERAL LOANS, EITHER SEPARATELY OR TOGETHER WITH SECURITIES OF OTHERS, AND EITHER TO SECURE ADVANCES WITHIN OR IN EXCESS OF THE AMOUNT DUE US THEREON. IT IS ALSO AGREED THAT WE RESERVE THE RIGHT TO CLOSE TRANSACTIONS WITHOUT DEMAND FOR ADDITIONAL MARGIN OR ANY OTHER NOTICE WHATSOEVER ON A STOCK EXCHANGE OR SIMILAR INSTITUTION, OR AT ANY PUBLIC OR PRIVATE SALE, WHENEVER WE DEEM IT NECESSARY FOR OUR OWN PROTECTION BY REASON OF INSUFFICIENT MARGIN OR OTHERWISE.

HECTOR M. CHISHOLM & CO. LIMITED

Within a very few days the Trans Canada stock had moved up 10% to $24.50. This produced a much higher percentage move in the rights, for they jumped up to 77¢.

MEMBERS:
MONTREAL STOCK EXCHANGE
CANADIAN STOCK EXCHANGE
VANCOUVER STOCK EXCHANGE
CALGARY STOCK EXCHANGE

TELEX - LATIMER, TORONTO - 02-2565
W. D. LATIMER CO.
LIMITED
244 BAY STREET, TORONTO 1, CANADA
TELEPHONE 363-8591
MONTREAL OFFICE: 1185 DORCHESTER BLVD. W.
TELEPHONE 866-8763

TELEPHONES:
CONFIRMATIONS
363-8921
DELIVERIES
365-7187
363-8926

DATE

Mar 22-63

WE HAVE THIS DAY — BOUGHT FROM YOU ☒ / SOLD FOR YOUR ACCOUNT AND RISK ☐

PLEASE HAVE CHEQUES MADE PAYABLE AT PAR IN TORONTO

BROKER	QUANTITY	SECURITY	PRICE	GROSS AMOUNT	BROKERAGE	PROVINCIAL TAX		AMOUNT PAYABLE
						ONT.	QUE.	
	1000	Trans Canada Ppl. RTS. IF AS AND WHEN ISSUED.	.77	770.00				770.00

E. & O.E.   FOR EXPLANATION AND TERMS TO WHICH THIS TRANSACTION IS SUBJECT SEE REVERSE SIDE

This right illustrates how the liability of a short life can be an advantage in disguise, because it results in the right's trading at its true value with no premium, and thus with a very high leverage. If the stock is volatile, large, rapid profits may result. The danger, however, is equally large, and for that reason rights should only be purchased on stocks that are trading at a low price in relation to assets or earnings. If this precaution is taken and if the rights do not move up in price, there will be no great disadvantage in exercising them.

Incidentally, this Trans Canada Pipeline issue once again illustrates an underpriced situation in which everyone made money. Speculators in the rights made 50% on their money in two weeks; sellers of the rights received 50¢ per share for something which they had received free; those who exercised the rights saw the convertible bond go up by 75%; and finally the shareholders made huge profits as their stock boomed up over $40. Truly a dream issue!

Another great advantage of a right to the stockholder is that it allows an increase of holdings in the company at a very favourable price and without the necessity of paying any commission. Therefore, a shareholder receiving rights and who has free money available is well advised to exercise his rights rather than sell them.

In summary, rights are a form of dividend which should be exercised when received free. For the speculator they represent the opportunity for rapid capital gains, but the risk is high. The rules in purchasing a right are:

1. Do not pay any premium over the right's true value.
2. Make sure that the leverage factor is high and the stock potentially volatile.
3. Do not buy any right if you have no cash available to exercise the right if necessary.

One other subject which should be considered is the stock split. This is the practice of subdividing a company's shares so as to keep each share at a relatively low price. That is, rather than have 1 million shares worth $100 each, after a 5 for 1 split there will be 5 million shares worth $20 each. A shareholder who held one hundred shares before, worth $10,000, will now have 500 shares worth $10,000.

The worth of a share, however, does not always decide the price at which it will trade. Its price depends on supply and demand—on the number of persons wishing to buy a stock in comparison with those wishing to sell. This factor will often temporarily make a stock sell too low or too high in relation to its true value. One of the phenomena of recent years has been that announcement of a stock split almost always produces an immediate substantial increase in the price of that stock.

The theory behind this activity is that when a stock sells at a lower price more individuals are likely to buy it, and this in itself will give it a higher value. Also it is felt that owners of stock in a company are more likely to use that company's products, which will help sales and earnings. That this theory is just an explanation for stock market sentiment becomes clear when we look at some of the companies which have split their stock. For example, pipelines obviously will not have more customers regardless of how many shareholders they have, and many of these companies find that the number of their shareholders continues to increase at the same rate as before the split.

Anyway this is not too important. What does matter is that stock splits produce higher prices for the stock, even though there may be no commensurate increase in stock value. After all, one is purchasing a stock because of its earnings or its potential, not because of the number of shares outstanding or their unit price. It is therefore a good basic rule that if one owns a stock in which a split is announced, and the stock then moves up in price, *sell it immediately.* It is not wise to wait for the actual split to occur. All too many of these split stocks have subsequently lost all of their recent gains and more. One example was Pembina Pipeline. This company's stock moved from $55 all the way to $72 on news of a four-for-one split. The new stock briefly traded at $18, and then slid all the way back to $6.

Ultimately earnings and assets must determine the price of a stock. The number of shares outstanding is immaterial.

On occasion a speculator will see a stock selling at much higher prices than its earnings or assets warrant. In these circumstances there is a temptation to sell the stock "short" in the expectation that the price will decline and it will be possible to buy it back cheaply and make a profit. Short selling is the most dangerous type of speculation in the stock market and should be left strictly to the professional. This is because in the purchase of a stock, the total possible loss is the amount of money invested, but in a short sale there is no limit to the possible loss. Every few years a short "squeeze" develops, in which even the professionals are taken—the Chatco Steel swindle was a classic.

In 1955 Chatco was a small manufacturer of metal products with total assets of less than 5 million dollars, annual net profit of only $20,000, and with only 60,000 common shares authorized and outstanding. These were listed on the Toronto Stock Exchange and traded infrequently around the $4.00 level. By June 4, 1956, the company suffered from a shortage of working capital, and the stock had slipped to $3.30. At that time the shareholders approved an increase in the amount of authorized common stock to 600,000 shares. The somewhat naive directors of the company searched for a way to sell some of this stock, and when a Montreal lawyer offered to arrange an underwriting of 100,000 shares at $4.50 per share, they jumped at it. What the directors did not realize was that the group buying the stock consisted of a number of Americans associated with a master stock swindler, Alexander Guterma, who by 1961 was convicted and/or pleaded guilty to fraud involving five different companies. Four of these individuals now joined the board of Chatco, and one of them became the chairman, although the old president was allowed to continue as a figurehead.

In August, 1956, Chatco's shareholders were informed that this new underwriting had brought the company into association with "a group of financially strong, well informed and broadly connected director personnel through whom your company's scope of operations will undoubtedly broaden". Chatco stock now began to climb, reaching a level of $12.00 by September. This climb was accompanied by a huge increase in volume of stock traded and by a high-pressure sales campaign led by three U.S. investment brokers.

It was obvious to the brokers and professional traders at the Toronto Stock Exchange that Chatco stock was not worth anything near its $12.00 price level, and many of them began to sell the stock short. Very soon the short stock amounted to over 25,000 shares. The brokers felt that, when the underwriters had sold their 100,000 shares and the high pressure sales campaign ended, the stock would then collapse.

In September, 1956, the new chairman of Chatco issued a statement through a New York public relations firm in which he deplored the "distrust caused by stock swindlers" between

Canadians and Americans. "So many Canadians and Americans have been shabbily treated by the neighbour country's high pressure stock promoters in the past few years that there is a certain amount of tarnish on the mutual respect and confidence that has existed between the two nations' businessmen." The statement went on to advocate "a stepped-up flow of investment money in both directions across the border".

On November 2, 1956, Chatco stock reached 16⅝ on increasing volume. The Toronto brokers who had been selling the stock short in increasing amounts were disturbed. In all previous cases where they had sold stock short in volume sooner or later their adversary had run out of money or determination and the stock had collapsed, giving the brokers large profits. Now they found that they were short over 100,000 shares and showed a potential loss of a half a million dollars.

At a meeting of the Board of Governors of the Toronto Stock Exchange, the decision was made to suspend trading of Chatco stock on the exchange. This was done on Monday, November 5, and the president of the exchange made the following statement. It has been "found that a high pressure stock selling campaign, operated from New York City, was carried on over the long-distance telephone to American investors. The Board of Governors will not permit the facilities of the exchange to be used in stock selling campaigns of this nature. In this particular case the entire campaign originated in the U.S. and all recent sales were made to residents of the U.S. and not to Canadians. The suspension was, therefore, made to protect the interest of American investors."

In all previous cases in which a stock had been suspended, it would immediately collapse, and the brokers who had sold short now expected to make large profits. Sure enough, the next morning Chatco began trading over the counter at $10.00 with the only bids showing being those of the brokers who were short. They had not counted, however, on the determination of the U.S. wolves to skin these Canadian professionals, and within hours a flood of buying poured into Toronto brokerage offices from New York City. By noon the stock was $12.50 bid, and by the close of trading at 5 p.m. it had moved all the way back up to $16.00. The distraught Toronto brokers attempted to force it down by further heavy short selling the following morning, but the American buyers absorbed all offerings, and that night (November 7) Chatco closed at $17.00.

Suddenly the short sellers realized that they had been beaten. In the following few days they decided to take their loss and buy back their short sales—but now to their horror they found that there was no stock available for sale, because the U.S. swindlers were not willing to settle for a modest profit. Two weeks later the stock was quoted $22.00 bid with no offerings, and there was still a short position of over 100,000 shares.

On the morning of December 1 the Toronto brokers who had sold stock short received a registered letter demanding delivery. That afternoon they each received a phone call from the broker who represented the U.S. sharks, offering to sell them the amount of stock they were short at $25.00 per share cash. They bought it, as they really had no choice. The next day the stock opened at $1.00 and declined to 25¢ within a week. Ten months later Chatco Steel declared bankruptcy "due to lack of working capital", and the stock became absolutely worthless.

Here was a case where the short sellers were 100% right in believing that the stock was overpriced, but they lost over a million dollars in spite of being right. And these men were almost all brokers or professional traders. The moral is quite clear: Do not sell short. The possible gain is not commensurate with the dangers. Short selling is essential to the proper maintaining of regular markets but should be left strictly to professionals.

21

OTHER INVESTMENTS

The purpose of an investment should not be just to make more money, for accumulating dollars per se appears a barren labour. There are unfortunately a considerable number of individuals in our society for whom both work and investing are just for the purpose of having x more dollars. They are not satisfied to have surplus assets of $100,000 or 1 million dollars or 10 million dollars, or for that matter any amount. They will work out their lives scrambling for more and more money and will die dissatisfied because they can never have it all.

There are some others who invest and play the market for the fun and thrills involved. They are very like bridge players or poker players or some sportsmen to whom the game is the thing. A great deal of their satisfaction comes in correctly analyzing a situation. The profit that is made from the analysis is a secondary factor.

Many investors are seeking the illusion of security through their profits in investments. Unfortunately security is the one thing that a human being can never have, and no investment or huge sum of money will provide the security illusion for very long.

Fortunately most investors seek profits from securities for more fulfilling purposes. They want to make life a little easier for their children, they want the pleasures of travel, the pleasures of being able to surround themselves with beautiful things, the satisfaction of being able to help others.

For those in this latter group it is possible to arrive at many of the goals without waiting out the years of successful investing. For there is one investment field which gives continual and constant pleasure in the act of investment, which can have the security of the best bond, and yet which can rise in value like the most volatile warrant. That is investing in art and antiques. It is a field which should be carefully considered by more middle-income investors. Those who have done so have been repaid in dollars many times over and in pleasure and satisfaction have been given a daily dividend. This can truly be a case of eating your cake and having it still, for where else can one have continued pleasure and be paid for doing so. A single example of my own at once comes to mind. In 1954 my wife fell in love with a beautiful oil painting of a fountain in Nice by Raoul Dufy which we purchased for $6,000 from the Laing Galleries. This picture hung in our living room for seven years, giving us a repeated pleasure every time we entered that room. In 1961 we finally purchased a home, and in order to pay for it, sold the Dufy among other things. It reached $17,-500 at Parke Bernet Galleries in New York. Few stock or bond investments did better.

Investing in antiques has three disadvantages, however, which should be noted.

1. There are rarely any dividends from this type of investment, although occasionally an advertising firm or greeting card company will pay 10% of the value of an object for permission to reproduce its photograph on a card or in an advertisement.

2. There is an actual financial outlay necessary for purposes of insurance. This should amount to only ⅓ of one per cent per year or less.

3. Art investments are not so liquid as stocks or bonds in that they usually cannot be converted into cash as rapidly as other securities. However, with the rise in recent decades of the large international auction galleries, antiques can now be changed into money within two or three months at the outside, and these galleries are usually quite willing to give a large immediate cash advance.

The art field for purposes of investment can be subdivided into ten different groups, in one of which every person should be able to find something of personal appeal. These are:

Pictures and drawings
Jewellery
Silver
Objects of art and vertu
Antiquities
Porcelain
Books and manuscripts
Furniture
Arms and armour
Stamps and coins

Space available does not allow for detailed writeups in all of these groups, for this would take the entire book and more. But because in North America the vast majority of art investments fall in the fields of pictures, objects of art, antiquities, and stamps and coins, I shall describe only these four fields. However, it should be noted that those persons who invested ten years ago in the specialties of antique jewellery, silver, porcelain, or furniture have done very well financially, for prices in these fields have multiplied many times. Armour has not done so well, but even here prices have doubled.

Paintings and Drawings

Of paintings and drawings there is such a large variety that every taste can be satisfied. Most paintings have no commercial value as art but are purchased because they are appealing or in order to fill a specific spot on a wall. Paintings that can be considered as investments will fall into four categories.

1. The old masters
2. The more recently accepted schools e.g. the impressionists
3. Nineteenth century North American artists
4. Modern art, op art, pop art

The old masters are the convertible bonds of the painting world. These are paintings produced some hundreds of years ago by great masters like Rembrandt or minor masters like Hobbema. In recent years these works have tended to be gradually bought up by museums, but even today less important works of the old masters are available to the public at reasonable prices, and there is no question that their value will continue to rise at the same steady pace as in the past. Here are two examples from different price ranges. The etching in *Plate* 1 is by Rembrandt and is entitled *Death of the Virgin*. I purchased it in 1956 for $35.00. A similar etching sold in 1966 for $1,200.00.

The various owners of one painting by Meindert Hobbema have been recorded all the way back to 1752. In 1955 it sold for $19,000.00. Today it would bring at least five times that figure.

Much larger price moves have occurred in recent years amongst the impressionist and post-impressionist schools of art. Paintings by Renoir, Boudin, Matisse, Monet, Cézanne, Van Gogh and many others have gone from a few dollars to hundreds of thousands. This last decade has seen a further price multiplication of this type of art, until today a painting Renoir completed in 1914 may very easily sell at double the price of an old master of similar size completed 300 years ago by Van Goyen or Ruisdael. I think that at this point as an investment one should sell his impressionist art and buy old masters. Unfortunately sentiment often precludes such a sale. I purchased this little painting by Renoir (*See Plate* 2.) in 1956 for $15,000. Since then I have received huge purchase offers, and business sense says that it should be sold, but my family and I have become far too attached to it.

In any case impressionist art is now like blue chip stocks—at tip-top prices—and its purchase cannot be recommended.

American and Canadian primitive art is probably the best buy now available in the painting world. These paintings, by men like Remington or Krieghoff, show America as it was one hundred to two hundred years ago. There were no photographers about at that time, and so these paintings carry a double value—both as art and as history. Most of them are far better history than art, but this in a way enhances their value; a certain type of newly rich businessman who wants to collect American or Canadian art will automatically seek them out, for he is ill at ease with modern art and has a deep suspicion that today's artists are making a fool of him. This type of primitive art, although it has shown some price appreciation, has not gone up in value by nearly the same amount as other accepted art forms because it does not sell outside of this continent. The American buyer of old masters or impressionist paintings must compete with the industrialists of Berlin and the oil sheiks of Kuwait, whereas American primitive art presents no interest to these worthies. Despite this, in the past decade American primitive art has begun to move up in price as museums and the public have begun to compete more vigorously. As a result U.S. primitives have shown good price increases, but Canadian primitives like Paul Kane and Cornelius Krieghoff have lagged because of their more limited market. Today the finest and largest habitant scene Krieghoff ever painted would probably bring less than $25,000 at auction. In years to come these prices will undoubtedly appear as ridiculous as when the same situation applied to the impressionists twenty-five years ago.

Modern art presents quite a different problem. This is the warrant of the painting world—luckily chosen a painting from this group may zoom in value from $100 to $20,000 within two or three years, as did the paintings of Bernard Buffet. But unfortunately most modern work is trash that will have no value to succeeding generations.

The perfection of colour photography has made the work of today's artist immeasurably more difficult than that of preceding generations, because in earlier centuries a good artist merely attempted to duplicate nature. Today the best artist cannot do this as well as an average photographer and so the artist has reached further and further away from reality in an effort to produce something "different". From painting impressions he has moved to painting colour and form and space and finally to just smearing paint. The other great problem affecting modern art as an investment is the huge number of painters and galleries now turning out work. It has reached the point where a city of one million like Toronto has twenty-odd galleries, each supporting about a dozen artists. Obviously from the many thousands of artists now painting in North America today, only a very, very few will have their works live after them. This makes investing in modern art a very chancy affair, and only one piece of advice can be given—don't. If a modern painting appeals, buy it for its appeal and pay only what that appeal is worth to you. There will probably be no resale value.

There are two pitfalls which the investor in paintings must avoid. These are name collecting and forgery.

Name collecting is the practice of buying a painting only because it was painted by a specific artist and irrespective of its appeal. Thus we find foolish individuals spending thousands of dollars to buy a poor Cézanne just because Cézanne put his name on the canvas. It must be remembered that good artists can produce bad paintings; if a painting is being purchased partially or wholly as an investment, it should be one of the artists' better paintings. The good works will probably go up in price. The poor ones likely will not. There is nothing more pitiful than the collector with a dozen paintings by various artists, each of which represents that artist at his worst. This is not only bad investing, but it must inevitably produce feelings of embarrassment rather than pleasure.

Forgery is a far more serious problem. Right at this moment in New York there are a dozen artists busily turning out excellent pictures "by" Goya, "by" Picasso, "by" Gainsborough, and indeed by every selling artist. In today's seller's art market there is a ready sale for these forgeries, and there are galleries in every large city carefully feeding them out to the gullible. The extent to which this racket has grown is truly remarkable, and some of the largest private collections now contain more forgeries than originals. In order to avoid this trap, several rules should be followed:

1. Get an independent opinion before purchasing any expensive painting. Many public galleries will be glad to assist.
2. Never buy an expensive painting at a bargain price from a small gallery or private source. Ten to one it is a fake.
3. When buying a painting as an investment, insist on a complete pedigree. Newly discovered works of great artists of the past are usually only a few days old.
4. Buy your investment paintings either from one of the great established galleries like Knoedler; from a gallery that specializes in an artist as Laing does with Krieghoff; from one of the international auction houses—Sothebys or Christies; or in France, where the government stands behind all paintings sold at international auction.

By following these four rules the prospective investor in paintings will not only avoid buying forgeries, he will also find that he has succeeded in buying his paintings at the best possible prices.

In summary, buy paintings as an investment only when they

appeal as paintings, when they represent the artists' best work, and when the price is reasonable in relation to that of the old masters. This method must produce both pleasure and profit.

Objects of Art and Vertu

Objects of art and vertu comprise the interconnected fields of the goldsmith, the enameller, the engraver, the mechanic, and the painter. Here we find the beautiful works of Fabergé, the exciting enamelled automata watches of the French court, and the golden goblets and cups of the middle ages. Truly this is the one investment field which contains a maximum of beauty and value in a minimum of space.

Because objects in this field represent an international form of value and beauty and have the added virtue of easy portability, they are much sought after by uneasy wealthy men, by holders of shaky crowns, and by owners of hot money. If sudden flight is necessary, there may be no time to sell bonds or stocks or there may be no room for large paintings or bullion, but in this form of wealth a fortune can slip into a pocket. Because of this there has been a steady growth in the prices of these objects, and some have multiplied ten or twenty times since the late 'forties. It is an interesting sidelight of the portability factor that in direct contrast to paintings, the smaller the object, the higher the value. Thus the small automata watch bearing five moving figures, illustrated in *Plate 3*, sold for $6,000 in 1965, while simultaneously the clock illustrated in *Plate 4*, which is of equally fine workmanship with a much more complicated mechanism and a far more valuable case, sold for only $1,600. The watch would be of greater value not only to the monarch considering flight but also to the rich American apartment dweller with no room to place the clock.

As an example of how these objects have jumped in value in recent years, consider this pair of matched musical watches with moving musician figures which I purchased in Hong Kong in 1959 for $250 (*See Plate 5*.). Prices have jumped so rapidly that last year a dealer offered $5,000 for the pair.

It is interesting that the finest objets d'art of this type all were produced for the French and Russian courts in the last years preceding their collapse. The most valuable pieces from these periods were worked in precious stones and metals, particularly gold, pearls, and jade. In the French period there were dozens or perhaps hundreds of outstanding craftsmen and workshops, but in the Russian period there was only one who stood out—Carl Fabergé.

The workshops of Fabergé in St. Petersburg between the years 1870 and 1918 undoubtedly turned out the most beautiful works of art that human ingenuity has ever produced. They varied all the way from highly elaborate and complicated Easter eggs to simple jade figurines, from priceless presents for a Czar to inexpensive charms for a bracelet, from useful things like cigarette cases and watches to the extreme in pure ornament; but regardless of the object's price or size, Carl Fabergé insisted that it be the ultimate in beauty of its kind, and so one knows that to own anything by Fabergé is to own the best. Because of this, all Fabergé has shown a steady price rise since the workshops closed in 1918, accelerating in recent years and showing no sign of tapering off. Fabergé today represents excellent value. There can never be more produced and it is rapidly disappearing into museums. If you have the opportunity to acquire such a piece, do not let it pass by—you may not have a second chance. The little charm illustrated in *Plate 6* was purchased by my wife for $175 in 1960. It could easily bring $500 today. What better investment than to enjoy beauty and watch it increase in value simultaneously?

Where should these pieces of beauty be purchased, and how much should be paid for each object? There is one shop in North America that carries a consistently fine selection of both Fabergé and French bibelots. This is A La Vieille Russie on Fifth Avenue in New York and this shop, together with its Paris branch (now closed), represents a continuation of the original business in St. Petersburg. But, perhaps because A La

Vieille Russie sells only the finest and most beautiful objects, its prices tend to be somewhat high.

A visit to their store can be an experience reminiscent of how the old type of royalty must have shopped. The store itself is carefully laid out with cases of beautiful jewellery, silver, and jade but if Mr. Paul Sheaffer or his father, or their assistant, Mr. Charles Boutelle, believe that you are a prospective purchaser, he will seat you in a private showroom and from the huge safe will then individually bring rare watches or snuff boxes or musical toys or automata, which will be carefully unwrapped from boxes within boxes. After being displayed, each object disappears before the next comes out—the beauty of one must never be allowed to detract from that of another. Only if requested is the price mentioned, and then deprecatingly. "It's only $21,000, but how can you equate money with such exquisiteness." Thus little jewelled birds will sing and move as though alive, to be followed by an enamelled clock in the form of a harp, and then perhaps a tiny watch on which moving figures play and work, and then a little diamond-crusted caterpillar which will slowly creep across the table. I doubt if even in the great shops of Europe like Wartskis could A La Vieille Russie's variety and quality be surpassed.

Although I strongly recommend A La Vieille Russie to the rich collector, this is not where the investor should buy. He should make his purchases at auction, and there are only two auction houses he should consider; they are Sotheby & Co. and Christie Manson and Woods, both in London, England. When a fine collection of Fabergé, automata, or watches comes to the market, it is practically certain to be sold through these two firms, whose clientele includes every great dealer and almost every large collector in the world. Because of this the prices realized at their sales tend to run about midway between dealer wholesale prices and collector retail prices, although occasionally very high prices will result from two collectors wanting the same object; more rarely a very low price will eventuate.

Catalogues are prepared some months prior to each sale, and

the more valuable objects are illustrated and fully described. These catalogues are sent airmail to subscribers on payment of a small annual fee which works out to only pennies per catalogue. The catalogues themselves are a delight to the eye, and many are purchased for their own sake with no intention of bidding at the sale.

Those who do wish to bid, however, can do so without attending the sale in London and at no charge to themselves. After one determines the maximum price one is willing to pay for an object, this bid is sent to the auction house by registered airmail, and an employee of the auction house will bid on the collector's behalf just as though he were there himself. Unlike certain auction houses in North America, both Sotheby and Christies are scrupulously honest and will never pay a penny more for an art object than is absolutely necessary. (In some other firms a "shill" will bid up the price to just under the maximum price sent in by the mail bidders.) I have often found occasions where I made a purchase at a tiny fraction of my maximum bid. For example last year I authorized Sothebys to bid up to 2,000 pounds for the magician box illustrated in *Plate* 7. They purchased it for me for only 900 pounds.

If something is bought at such a sale, a bill will be forwarded for the net price with no added commission, and after payment is made the art object will be sent by insured air post.

How much should be the maximum bid for each object? After all, the private collector is bidding against dealers who are far more knowledgeable of value in their fields than the collector can be, and so he would appear to be at a serious disadvantage. In actuality the exact opposite holds true, for the collector is able to economically pay one-third or more higher than the dealer, who must resell at a profit. There are several ways to get a true valuation of art objects appearing at these auctions. The simplest, most reliable, and cheapest is just to write the auction house, who are glad to send out a free current valuation. I have found that these valuations are a very good guide to true value, and auction prices tend to run within

10% of these estimates. When bidding it is wise to bid about 15% to 20% above the auction house's estimate, for this will neatly cut out competition from the dealers. If the object should sell cheaper, nothing will have been lost by entering the higher bid.

As an example of how these auction purchases can increase in value, the watch shown in *Plate 8* sold for 50 pounds at auction in 1950. This year it was resold in the same auction house for 1,200 pounds.

This type of investment can easily give the highest profits as well as the greatest pleasures.

Antiquities

To purchase an elaborately decorated Greek pot made 2,400 years ago, or an irridescent glass made in Syria 3,000 years ago, or even a necklace made for an Egyptian princess 4,000 years ago, represents beauty, investment, and a link with the past all rolled into one. Yet the cost of such a purchase is less than that of the cheapest bond. This pot would cost $250.00 today, this glass $100.00 and this necklace $200.00 (*See Plates 9A, 9B, 9C.*).

There is no question that antiquities today represent the greatest value possible of any form of art investment. Although prices have moved up slightly in recent years, there has been nothing yet like the price movements seen in paintings and objets d'art. This is undoubtedly yet to come and can be easily participated in by the reader.

Antiquities include all remnants of ancient worlds, including Greek, Egyptian, Roman, Syrian, Pre-Columbian, and so forth, and here value depends on the three factors of rarity, beauty, and demand. Thus a very, very rare ancient Nepalese figure may bring only a few dollars because of the few collectors seeking such works, its large size, and its lack of twentieth-century beauty, whereas the Mesopotamian armilla illustrated in *Plate 10* will bring thousands of dollars because of its small size and the fact that Mrs. Collector can wear it to her next cocktail party.

There is one steady buyer for antiquities of all types, the local museum. Yet somehow museums are not given the large budgets to purchase antiquities that art galleries receive for paintings. Thus a leading public art gallery might spend $100,-000 or more on a single picture, a figure which would represent a ten-year budget for purchase of antiquities by most museums. A museum is far more likely to spend its budget in seeking out "new" antiquities through archaeological digs, rather than step into the market and buy. This fortunate factor has helped to maintain the current, relatively low prices for antiquities.

For a collector of antiquities there are two ways in which I would recommend purchases. For the new collector the best possible introduction is through the firm of Messrs. Spink & Son Ltd. in London. The five-storey building off Picadilly is worth a trip to England in itself, for on the various floors is an almost complete cross-section of the art world, all at very reasonable prices. To step down into the basement is to enter the ancient worlds of Caesar and Cyrus. Here are cases full of Egyptian amulets, dozens of beautiful Greek amphorae, jewellery from ancient China—truly something for everyone and to fit every pocketbook from the initial $25 purchaser of an amulet to the sophisticated museum director seeking a mummy. A visit to Spinks can be a day-long, or a week-long, exercise in self-control.

However, Spinks is not the cheapest place to buy antiquities, and after the prospective investor has increased his knowledge through one or two small purchases, he should then again look to the auction houses of Christie and Sotheby. Several times a year these firms run auctions of collections of antiquities from various cultures. All are well illustrated, and the prices received are invariably at the current low museum level. (Many dealers do a lot of buying here.) The arrangements for bidding and purchase are exactly the same as described under objets d'art, and I strongly recommend their consideration. This is truly the current bargain basement of the art world.

One word of caution. There are dozens of small stores in

the United States and Europe selling antiquities. Many forgeries are sold by them unknowingly. A pedigree means little to an antiquity, unlike a painting, for even if ownership can be traced back three hundred years, it proves nothing. Ancient Rome was plagued with forgeries of Greek amphorae. So restrict your purchases of antiquities to those bought from experts. You are then sure to make money.

Coins—*The South Sea Bubble Made in the U.S.A.*

As far back as history goes, men have collected things. Some of these things were collected for beauty, like paintings or statuary; some for utility, like livestock, and some because of their rarity, like gold or stamps. Whichever of these three categories a collection contained, it would give either pleasure or service to its owner. In recent centuries thieves have preyed on men's cupidity by persuading them to buy and collect things that are neither beautiful, nor utilitarian, nor rare in relation to their price, although they may contain minor provisions of all three. The great tulip swindle in Holland in 1636 has set the model for these boom-and-bust promotions. We are currently in the middle phase of just such an insane boom.

Coin collecting has been a hobby for centuries. In ancient times coins were collected because there was no paper money; coins represented real value which could be carried on one's person and could be easily hidden in times of danger. Then the important fact regarding value was the weight of the coin and the metal it was made of; the date and manufacturer were quite insignificant. The coin represented utility and security.

In more recent centuries people began to collect coins as a hobby and their value now began to develop from their attractiveness and rarity. Being relatively indestructible, coins will remain unchanged for centuries, and an ancient coin collection can bring joy, history, and a link with the past. Because there have been so many civilizations preceding ours, no individual or museum could hope to own every coin ever minted, and so collectors have tended to specialize in one area of this field—

perhaps in ancient Rome or Greece or the crowns of England. In any case the many different possibilities have tended to keep the price of old coins very moderate, and today it is still possible to buy an English silver dollar (called a crown) minted five hundred years ago for $10 and a coin struck by the Emperor Vespasian to celebrate his victory over Israel for even less. It is a thoroughly delightful hobby.

Unfortunately, as an offshoot from this hobby, in the past decade there has developed a strange speculation in modern coins, specifically the coins of the United States and Canada. This speculation has produced large profits for its originators and is certain to produce equally large losses for its current blinded devotees, because this gamble is based on constantly rising prices which allow waves of speculators to continually sell out to new speculators. Like pyramid clubs, somewhere along the line the whole edifice must collapse.

Today's hoarders do not seek individual examples of each coin as did the old-time collector. Rather they will collect rolls or even bags of the same coin. Thus a bag containing one thousand 1964 dollars was originally purchased from a bank by a well-connected dealer for $1,000. This bag was probably immediately sold to a speculator for $1,040, and he took it back to the bank for storage. Within a month he had probably sold his bag of dollars for $1,100, and in the ensuing two years it was quite possible for such a bag to be resold five or six times, currently reaching a price of $1,600 or more. Similarly, 50-cent pieces, quarters, dimes, nickels, and even pennies are now purchased in huge quantities in the hope of a quick price rise.

The whole basis of this speculation is an artificial scarcity. Because rarity requires that there be more collectors than objects being sought, true rarity is impossible when millions of copies of the collected object are available. Therefore, two stratagems are used to push prices artificially upwards. The most important is for dealers to hoard vast quantities of coins and to encourage their customers to do the same by forecasting increasing prices in coming years. The second is to search for variety in each coin, perhaps finding a dot or other inconsequential variation and to ballyhoo this as a different variety which should be individually collected.

The very interesting difference between this bubble and others that have preceded it is that practically all the participants in the coin craze are quite aware of the potential possible collapse, but each feels that the bubble will not burst for a year or two yet, and that they individually will get out before that day occurs. In the meanwhile these collectors have succeeded in making silver dollars completely disappear from circulation; 50-cent pieces are almost gone, and silver quarters are not far behind. The United States government has aggravated the situation by debasing the silver coinage, thus adding silver hoarders to the coin collectors in helping to make coins disappear. The hoarders realize that if silver reaches a price of $1.38 an ounce, it becomes profitable to melt down the coins and sell the silver.

This gives the coin bubble its one chance of not bursting, for silver has already jumped from 90 cents to $1.29 because of increasing consumption. The U.S. government will probably be unable to hold the price at this level even by selling its entire stockpile, and within a few years silver could easily move to $2.00 an ounce. In this case coin hoarders will of course make money, but it should be remembered that they would do best if they bought coins at face value, regardless of condition. Those who are paying a premium for common coins in uncirculated condition must ultimately show a loss on their investment.

Stamps

Stamp collecting, on the other hand, fortunately has not slipped from the hands of the collector to that of the speculator. It still remains the most popular hobby in the world and has brought pleasure to millions of children and adults throughout the years. As an investment U.S. and Canadian stamps have treated their purchasers very well, increasing in value yearly by a modest percentage. Although collectors have not tended to get rich from this hobby, its peculiar distracting and time-consuming pleasures have paid large dividends in fun and satisfaction, and in addition it has been a rarity to lose money in this investment.

IN CONCLUSION—
THE IDEAL INVESTMENT

Some years ago a member of the New York Stock Exchange ran a series of ads warning that there was no ideal investment, but that they could assist the investor to success after he had made up his mind whether he was seeking safety, yield, or capital gains. As we have shown, the broker was wrong. There are ideal investments, carrying little if any risk, giving a good yield, often producing large capital gains and being liquid.

Unfortunately, the vast majority of the investments in which the public participates are far from ideal. In fact, most of them offer high risk, low yield, and little chance of capital gains. If investors and speculators will follow the advice given herein, if they will concentrate on high-grade convertible securities, their market results must improve spectacularly.

For those who wish to gamble, but with the odds in their favour, small participations in the commodity markets or in warrant purchases or in the if, as and when market can satisfy their gambling instincts and probably produce big profits as well.

Finally, the true secret of success in the investment and speculative world is not so much which good securities to buy, but rather which investments to avoid. In this book I have tried to point out the dangers and pitfalls in several investment fields.

And now the most important factor of all. In your investments and other activities, let us hope that you find—good luck!

PLATE 1

PLATE 2

PLATE 3

PLATE 4

PLATE 5

PLATE 6